GIRLS
TO THE
FRONT

GIRLS TO THE FRONT

SARA MARCUS

The True Story of the
RIOT GRRRL
Revolution

HARPER ● PERENNIAL

NEW YORK ● LONDON ● TORONTO ● SYDNEY ● NEW DELHI ● AUCKLAND

GIRLS TO THE FRONT. Copyright © 2010 by Sara Marcus. All rights reserved. Printed in the United States of America. No part of this book may be used or reproduced in any manner whatsoever without written permission except in the case of brief quotations embodied in critical articles and reviews. For information, address HarperCollins Publishers, 10 East 53rd Street, New York, NY 10022.

HarperCollins books may be purchased for educational, business, or sales promotional use. For information, please write: Special Markets Department, HarperCollins Publishers, 10 East 53rd Street, New York, NY 10022.

Many thanks to the following people for permission to reproduce images: Pat Graham, pp. 14, 152, 164; Allison Wolfe, p. 81; Molly Neuman, p. 84; Lee Snider/Photo Images courtesy Fales Library, New York University, p. 146; Mary Margaret Fondriest, p. 174; Ananda La Vita, p. 184; May Summer Farnsworth and Billie Rain, p. 232; Susan Now, p. 239, Ann Carroll, p. 281.

FIRST EDITION

Designed by Aline C. Pace

Library of Congress Cataloging-in-Publication data is available upon request.

ISBN 978-0-06-180636-0

10 11 12 13 14   OV/RRD   10 9 8 7 6 5 4 3 2 1

*For my parents
and for all the rebels*

CONTENTS

GIRLS TO THE FRONT

I WAS GOING TO BE ONE OF THEM

(AN AUTHOR'S NOTE)

I missed out on the first few years of Riot Grrrl. In the summer of 1991, when girls not far from my suburban Maryland home were talking revolution, I was fourteen and going to theater camp. In our production of *The Wiz*, I played the good witch who comes in near the end and teaches Dorothy that she can find her way home if she just believes in herself. I wore a pink satin prom dress and I rode onto the stage enclosed in an eight-foot lotus made of plywood painted pinkish-lavender. The stagehands, all sixteen years old and crass, dubbed my floral conveyance the Vast Violet Vulva. Moments before my entrance every night, they shut me up inside the vulva and I stood there, awaiting my cue, encased in shadows tinted the same pink you see when your eyes are closed but there's a brightness just beyond your eyelids, waiting for you to open up and see.

That summer, a few weeks after the end of *The Wiz*, I went to a clothing store, a Ross Dress for Less. While my parents were out browsing the racks, I tried on shirts alone in the fitting room, and the attendant, a young man probably in his late teens, struck up a conversation. We chatted through my fitting room's curtain and I answered his questions nonchalantly, tossing aside a T-shirt, considering a plaid button-down, and then he said something clearly indicating—whether explicitly or implicitly, I'm not sure, but his meaning was evident—that he would like to fuck me.

I froze in the tiny cubicle, a rejected shirt encircling my forearms, my hands disappearing in the collar. I was certain that I would vomit, right there on the pin-strewn gray carpet.

"Your parents are gone," he said. "They can't hear us." Or was it "They can't hear *you*"?

The threat I heard in his voice may have been real. It may also have been a shadow cast by the threat I had been taught that all girls, particularly from age thirteen onward, faced from nearly any man at nearly any moment. Having ingested endless lessons of peril and caution, I was now living a worst-case scenario: trapped, topless, near a man who wanted to violate me, with only a canvas curtain separating me from the would-be attacker.

Perhaps I could vomit on *him*. I had heard that that sometimes worked.

"Sara, did you find anything?" My mother! Gratefully, I went out to meet her by the three-way mirror, hugging the shirts and their hangers to my body like clumsy armor.

I never came any closer to genuine sexual danger, but for years I braced myself for it, while marinating in shame over having somehow led the fitting-room attendant on—him, and also Peter, the tall drummer in marching band who shoved me against a locker in an empty hallway one morning and held me there for a horrifying minute, as if trying to decide what to do with me, before the footsteps of an approaching teacher set me free. I never told anybody about either incident. They both felt like they had been my fault.

I experienced female adolescence as a constant affront with calamity always loitering nearby, licking its lips, waiting for an opening. I spent the beginning of my teens miserable, alienated, and isolated. And I was sure I was the only one who felt this way.

It wasn't an unreasonable thing for me to believe. I had no social group, no pocket of belonging. I had quit the drama club after its vice president, a short jolly girl who wore patchouli and crushed velour, told me that our gentle kisses in the front seat of her mom's Chevy Suburban went against God's plan for her. Cut loose from the only tribe I'd known, I drifted, too weird for the smart kids' clique and too diligent for the purple-haired rebels who smoked cigarettes behind the school gym during lunch.

I began escaping to DC on weekends, boarding the Metro at its last stop in the suburbs. A brief eight-lane highway dead-ended at the Shady Grove station's treeless parking lot, and when my parents dropped me off, I loved finding the waiting trains, behemoths idling on their lethal-voltage rails. Their eventual lurch into motion felt exhilarating, like dropping off a cliff.

Back at school, I ate my lunch alone in an empty hallway, then retreated to the school library, where I napped in a corner between the books on feminism and the emergency exit. Just getting through each day was exhausting.

I was desperate for something that might save me, or help me save myself.

I first learned about Riot Grrrl in autumn 1992. I had just come home from another dispiriting day of tenth grade and I was standing at the kitchen table, sorting through the mail, when an article in the new issue of *Newsweek* grabbed both my arms and shook me. The piece, titled "Revolution, Girl Style," opened with a scene of a girl standing up to a sexual harasser at school: "Don't touch me *or* my friends!" It went on to describe a nationwide network of teen feminists who came together to support one another, fight back against harassing classmates, and talk about "everything from tuning guitar strings to coming out of the closet." The girls, according to this piece, were "sexy, assertive, and loud." Although I wasn't sexy and didn't particularly want to be, I remembered that for a while in elementary school, and intermittently since then, I *had* been assertive and loud, and I missed being that girl.

I read the whole piece twice, not even bothering to sit down. It said the riot grrrls had recently held a convention in Washington, DC. Could this be true? There were girls in my area who might understand me?

When my mother came home and read the article, she remarked that the movement didn't seem like anything I would want to be involved in.

I had never wanted anything more in my life.

The riot grrrls were so near to me that I sometimes imagined I could smell their magenta hair dye. What if one of them went to my school? In the pre-Internet age, though, my search turned up only dead ends. Throughout tenth and eleventh grade, I scoured the *Washington Post* Style section, studied the "Meetings" classified ads in the *City Paper*, looked under "Riot Grrrl" in the DC phone book, and checked the bulletin board of the feminist bookstore downtown where I had begun to camp out on weekends, reading Alison Bechdel and Luce Irigaray. I uncovered no leads.

Still, the article had given me an idea. If I couldn't reach the riot grrrls, I would figure out how to be a feminist some other way. For a class project, I interviewed the National Organization for Women's chapter coordinator, who encouraged me to form a group at my high school. I did so immediately. The club attracted a dozen members and at least an equal number of antagonists, who conveyed their disapproval by defacing our bulletin board displays (FEMINISM: THE RADICAL NOTION THAT WOMEN ARE PEOPLE! became FEMINISM: RADICAL MEN PE E) and shouting "Dykes!" through the door of our meeting room as they sprinted down the hall.

Most of the club's members were wary of conflict, so we played it safe, delivering a series of morning announcements for Women's History Month, organizing a self-defense workshop, and posting a conciliatory, pleading bulletin board message that read merely FEMINISM: IT'S ABOUT CHOICES. But these actions didn't come close to addressing what I had felt in the fitting room at the Ross Dress for Less, nor what I felt when I read in the newspaper about restrictions on abortion, grants rescinded from gay and female artists, the gauntlet of Navy officers at the Tailhook convention in Vegas who stripped a teenage girl. And then there was the day a popular tenor came to choir practice wearing a T-shirt that said THE PERSON WEARING THIS SHIRT IS A POLICE OFFICER. JUST LIE DOWN AND DO WHATEVER THE NICE POLICE OFFICER TELLS YOU TO.

When I saw his shirt, I thought I would cry. Then I thought I would punch him. Struggling to collect myself and confront him productively, I walked up to him and said, "Your shirt really offends me."

In a high, girlish voice, he retorted, "*Your* shirt really offends *me*," and walked away, laughing. I was wearing a plain green tee.

The more I tried to sublimate my fury into a palatable, diplomatic rhetoric of "choices," the angrier I became. Even within the NOW club, I felt alone. The *Newsweek* article had said that the riot grrrls "may be the first generation of feminists to identify their anger so early and to use it." I had identified mine, all right. But how could I use it all by myself?

In early 1993, I finally found an address for the DC chapter of Riot Grrrl. It was printed in *off our backs*, a long-running feminist journal I had discovered during my weekend sojourns at the feminist bookstore. The women of the *oob* collective were publishing like it was 1973, doing their layout by hand and printing on flimsy newsprint. But one of them interviewed a few riot grrrls—and listed the group's post office box address.

At long, long last, I had found them. I mailed off an effusive letter. I heard nothing back for months.

Eventually an envelope came back to me with three xeroxed flyers. One flyer read, in part:

> *Okay, so I propose that those girls who wanna change things start writing stuff on their/our hands. Magic marker works good. You can draw hearts or stars or write words on yr fingers, whatever, it will just be a way for pro-revolution girls to identify each other.*

I was a secret agent, receiving intermittent clues and instructions from an unknown headquarters. The communiqués were coming more quickly now. I would comply. I drew lopsided stars on the backs of my hands, pushing a marker over spindly ridges of bone. I wrote on the last, longest joints of my fingers, one letter per knuckle: R-I-O-T on the right and G-I-R-L on the left. I rode the county bus; I rode the Metro; I went to museums; I went to class. I waited to see another one. I waited to stumble into a whole pack of them. I waited for a gang to stop me and say, "You're coming with us."

My piano teacher told me to go wash my hands.

———

I read the flyers over and over. One contained this line:

Riot Grrrl D.C. meets every Sunday afternoon at 3 P.M. at the yellow Positive Force House in Arlington, 3510 8th Street N., right by the Virginia Square Metro.

But I was afraid to go, scared that the girls would be too cool for me and I would have nothing left to hope for.

A friend of a friend at school gave me a Bikini Kill tape—I knew that the band was somehow linked to Riot Grrrl—and for a while no other music mattered, just that breastbone-shaking bass line and Kathleen Hanna's voice singing with all the concentrated fury of a firehose, "Dare you to do what you want! Dare you to be who you will!"

The final, decisive push came from, of all things, a necklace: an oval pendant the size of a watch face, cut out of Shrinky Dink plastic, inscribed with the words RIOT GRRRL and a few hand-drawn stars. I saw it around a girl's neck at a concert in the choir room of a neighboring high school, and I realized with a start that I already knew this girl; we'd gone to the same elementary school. I asked her about the meetings. She said I should go. I picked out a Sunday and wrote it in my calendar.

Three days before the appointed Sunday in April 1994, Kurt Cobain's body was discovered in a greenhouse in Seattle. I remembered that *Newsweek* had referred to Courtney Love, now Cobain's widow, as the riot grrrls' "patron saint," but I'd never cared about Nirvana or about Love's band, Hole. Fearing that a grief-filled meeting would separate me from the other girls right off the bat, I nearly stayed home.

Still, I went, and when I finally stepped over the threshold of Positive Force House into its first-floor living room, I found that nobody else at the meeting cared about Nirvana or Hole either. We talked about sexual harassment from classmates and teachers, crushes on boys and girls, our favorite kinds of tampons and ice cream, and our outrage over the sexist stories and images we saw in the newspapers and on television. These girls weren't all punk, they didn't all have bands, and while they were the coolest girls I'd ever met, they were cool in a way that drew me closer instead of shutting me out. They were courageous, profane, and powerful. They would have socked that fitting-room attendant in the face. They would have redone the NOW club's bulletin board to read MAYBE I WOULDN'T HAVE TO BE A FEMINIST IF YOU WEREN'T SUCH AN ASSHOLE. I was going to be one of them.

Talking to these girls, I began to understand that I didn't have to be miserable. Maybe being a teenager was always going to be a bloodbath to some extent, but it did not have to be this particular bloodbath. Its severity and the specific tone of its miseries were political, which meant they were mutable. I felt powerless not because I was weak but because I lived in a society that drained girls of power. Boys harassed me not because I invited it but because they were taught it was acceptable and saw that no one intervened. These things weren't my fault, and we could fight them all together.

For the first time in years, I knew that I was going to be okay.

Riot Grrrl DC had held nearly all its meetings, starting with the first in 1991, at the same house in Arlington, a long-running punk activist commune of sorts. In the foyer, beneath the staircase, stood a shoulder-high metal filing cabinet that held relics of Riot Grrrl's history, and one Sunday afternoon, when I arrived early for a meeting, I slid open a drawer and wound up crouching under the stairs, poring over the archives, till my knees ached and my feet fell asleep. I found phone lists full of names of girls I'd never met. I found old meeting minutes, convention schedules, directories of chapters across the country, and cardboard stencils misted with spray paint. I found pasted-up originals of old zines, the typewritten articles' corners curling up, set free by weakening glue-stick bonds. I found drawers stuffed full of letters from girls like me who had happened upon the address and written in, seeking encouragement, hope, connection.

I also found a thick scrapbook of photographs showing girls at slumber parties, girls at shows, girls marching at the Capitol, girls playing croquet topless on the National Mall. I stared at their faces in the quiet minutes before the meetings began. Who were they? What had become of the people on the phone list? What had happened to the other chapters? These files haunted me. The newest items in the drawers were perhaps six months old; the others dated back a couple of years at most. Yet the past they hinted at felt long gone: half legend, half mirage.

Years went by. I wrote a dozen issues of a zine, joined a band, went to college, formed another band, went on tour, started writing about music and politics for magazines and newspapers. In the late '90s, someone told me that the Riot Grrrl DC post office box had closed and the weekly meetings had petered out. I began to hear people talking about Riot Grrrl in the past tense. Some spoke of it as having been a radical feminist movement of young women, but most people thought of it as a music scene, an expired trend: at best, a period of openness to strong female performers; at worst, an ideology of bad musicianship or a style of dress. Girls playing guitars sloppily were referred to as riot grrrls, as if it were a genre like rockabilly or grindcore. A "Riot Grrrl" Halloween costume for sale online (child sizes eight to ten) looked like a Goth cheerleader outfit with moon boots. Even feminist books on gender and rock music downplayed the movement's political aspects—because, I suspect, people didn't know how to treat the lives of teenage girls as if they mattered. The truth about the movement was getting buried. I longed for someone to set the record straight, or at least tilt the balance in the right direction. Then I realized that I could pull everyone's stories together, and I devoted myself once again to finding the riot grrrls.

I spent five years researching this book: traveling broadly to interview people I'd tracked down through friends of friends or on the Internet, combing people's personal collections of artifacts as well as institutional archives, scrolling through microfilms of British music magazines and old feminist newsletters. A decade had gone by since I'd made my last zine and attended my last Riot Grrrl convention, but I hadn't ever lost that curiosity I'd felt while squatting by the file cabinet in Arlington, my toes growing prickly and numb. What I *had* lost, a little bit, was the feeling I'd had in my teens that what my friends and pen pals and I were working on was beautiful and vital; the consciousness that many of our emotional challenges (self-doubt, confusion, sadness) resulted not from personal failings but from political and social forces, and that we could do battle with them *as such*; the belief that we could and would, as one of the movement's manifestos had put it, change the world for real. Through working on this book, I reconnected with these convictions, while also learning that many people's experiences with Riot Grrrl had been far more fraught than my own epiphanic bliss. The movement's flaws, and the personal(-as-political) beefs that the movement was ill equipped to avert, had been more ruinous than I had been able to see from my limited vantage point. Sometimes it's okay to have a little distance from the center of a cultural explosion—the impact may be reduced, but the burns are less severe. This book tells Riot Grrrl's story through the lives of a few central figures, musicians and nonmusicians alike, young women who were around at the movement's beginnings or whose involvement was particularly intense or long lasting. But there were thousands upon thousands of others whose stories are only hinted at here, and whose lives were indelibly shaped in the '90s by the ascendancy of Riot Grrrl.

Many of the movement's core values, I've come to realize, are as necessary now as they were then. The early '90s were a difficult time to be a woman, especially a young one, and too little has changed in the intervening decades. Yet nothing else has emerged since then to confront sexism with a fraction of Riot Grrrl's fire and prophetic drive. The self-righteous absolutism of adolescence eventually softens its edges, as it must. But we never stop needing that idealism and energy, that courage to name things as political if they are political and unacceptable if they are unacceptable, that dedication to crafting our lives and our communities on our own terms. Telling stories is just the beginning.

PROLOGUE: MASS MOVEMENT

This band is on fire. The lead singer is dancing with abandon, whipping her high teased-out ponytail around, doing aerobics moves, occasionally flipping up the back of her dress to moon her bandmates. The guitar switches to wails of feedback and Kathleen Hanna sings *Silence inside of me silence inside* four times in a child-like voice, never budging from a single note. She stands stock-still, looking plaintively at the audience and holding her left hand to her crotch, a gesture that twists the Madonna-esque virility pose into an act of pained protection. Then the guitarist tears into his chords again and, fed by the renewed clamor, Kathleen is instantly back in motion, leaning over as if she might vomit and roaring *I'll resist with every inch and every breath I'll resist this psychic death.*

She screws her eyes tight, pushing the words from her body with visible effort. Tendons pop out on both sides of her neck.

After the song screeches to a halt, she shifts unsteadily from foot to foot and turns away from the audience, pulling her dress down in back, perhaps suddenly wondering whether she has revealed too much.

The crew of girls up front cheer and yell. These are the riot grrrls—*some* of the riot grrrls, anyway. Their movement, if one could call it that yet, began less than a year ago, as a noisy message of female self-empowerment voiced by several punk musicians and a few of their friends, and already it has evolved into a whole mess of things, ranging from the half-formed to the full-blown. In DC it's primarily a group of girls who meet every weekend to have consciousness-raising discussions about their lives, create art and music, and plan political action. Erika Reinstein stands out: Her motions are more kinetic than anyone else's, her face more expressive. All her features are slightly oversize, which gives her the permanent look of living at an elevated decibel level. She always has her full lips open a bit, her head thrust up and forward, as if she's just thought of something new to say—which she probably has. She's known as a talker, a fearless girl who never shrinks from a spotlight. Recently graduated from high school in Virginia, she's built Riot Grrrl's numbers over the past few months by hopping onstage between bands at punk shows and inviting all the girls in the room to come to meetings. That's how Mary Fondriest, also up front at the Sanctuary, got involved. She's quieter than Erika, bad skin, bleached hair. She reads obsessively—before discovering feminism, her favorite book was *The Fountainhead*. She's been coming to meetings only a few months but in that time Riot Grrrl has become practically her entire life.

"Hey, riot grrrl!" Mary yells to Kathleen between songs.

"What?" Kathleen replies.

Mary throws a chocolate rose onstage. "I love you," she sings out.

Kathleen catches the rose in midair and grins broadly.

The girls are hawking wares tonight, silk-screened T-shirts and handmade zines—xeroxed pamphlets full of poems, photographs, and typewritten rants. One article begins by asking, "Why is 'feminist' a dirty word?" Near the end of a zine, there's a page with the words I WANT TO SCREAM written in block letters across the top. An unsigned monologue glitters with rage:

```
I'm so angry that I don't know what to write,
I just know that I want to write something,
that I want to say something, that I want
to scream something, something powerful and
strong to make up for the helplessness that
```

I feel now. . . . I want to scream at the
guy who told me that women should stop complaining because they already have all the
rights that they need. I want to scream at
my brothers who read the *Sports Illustrated*
swimsuit issue and who watch the Miss America pageant. . . . I want to scream because
I am just as much of a human being as any
man but I don't always get treated like one,
I want to scream because no matter how much
I scream, no one will listen.

The zines are a dollar, but if the girls—Erika and Mary, May
and Joanna, Ananda and Claudia—decide someone really needs a
copy, they'll let her have it for free.

The band onstage is Bikini Kill, a three-fourths-female group
that recently relocated to DC from the small college town of Olympia, Washington. Bikini Kill has spent much of the past year on the
road, building a fan base the way all independent bands cutting
their teeth do in the early '90s: piling into a van and crisscrossing
the country every few months, counting on a cassette-only demo
they sell, and on word of mouth, to feed enthusiasm.

So far, the strategy is working. Between the band's ecstatic feminist anthems, riveting live shows, varied publications (annotated
lyric sheets, xeroxed broadsides, zines dense with typescript), and
its charismatic lead singer's affiliation with this nascent feminist
force calling itself Riot Grrrl, Bikini Kill is quickly becoming one of
the most talked-about bands punk rock has seen in years.

The lead singer, jumping around in a white minidress and oversize
T-shirt with an off-center Riot Grrrl logo, is Kathleen Hanna. She's
twenty-three years old, passionate and poetic. She logged time as a
photographer, a writer, a domestic violence counselor, and a spoken-

word artist before she started writing punk songs. Now she's on a mission to make feminism cool for teenage girls. She introduces the next song by saying, "This is for Riot Grrrl," and the girls up front scream their pride and approval. Kathleen is one of theirs, and they are hers.

This concert isn't just another punk rock show; it isn't even just another benefit, though the proceeds are going to Rock for Choice and several women's organizations in DC. It's also a pep rally of sorts, coming on the eve of a major pro-choice march on the National Mall. The riot grrrls will be there tomorrow, as will the musicians and nearly everyone else that's crowded into this repurposed church, three miles due north of the march's kick-off point.

Before Bikini Kill's final song, Tobi Vail, the band's drummer and sometime singer, stands at the front of the stage in a red dress, fishnets, and sunglasses, and speaks into the mic. "I just wanted to say something about abortion becoming illegal," she begins. "To me, it says that not—not only do we live in a totally fucked-up patriarchal society run by white men who don't represent our interests at all, but we live in a—in a—country"—she's panting, trying to catch her breath or maybe not to cry—"where those people don't care whether we live or die. And that's pretty scary."

She turns around to face her bandmates: Kathi, the bassist, and Billy, the guitarist, tuning to each other; Kathleen, settling herself behind the drums. Tobi turns back to the audience but looks at her feet. "So we're gonna play a new song for you, and we don't know how it goes—"

"All *right*!" somebody shouts.

"—but it might work."

Excitement in the front row. Erika and Mary know what's coming. The laid-back bassist begins a three-note riff, over which a friend of the band, Molly, reads from a recent newspaper article attacking Bikini Kill: "What comes across onstage is *man hate*! A maniac rebellion against the world and themselves." Kathleen flails at the cymbals with exaggerated awkwardness, waving her arms like a three-year-old trying to break something. Billy taps his foot to keep track of the beat. Erika's moment is almost here. Tobi is singing about wanting rock heroes' approval: *If Sonic Youth thinks that you're cool, does that mean everything to you?* Then she raises her voice for the chorus, naming that band's iconic guitarist: *Thurston hearts the Who! Do you heart the Who too?* As if in reply, Billy swings his guitar toward his amp to make caterwauling wolf whistles of feedback and jagged bursts of Thurston Moore–style noise.

The chaos mounts. Billy throws his guitar up high, letting it flip over itself in the air, and then catches it. Kathleen walks to the edge of the stage and leans down to the girls in the front row so Erika can hurl bloodcurdling screams into the mic. The two of them share the mic for a second, Kathleen's *whoa-oh-oh* and Erika's virtuosic *EEEEEEE!*, and then Erika takes the microphone and climbs onstage: She belongs there, and she knows it. At the song's end, Erika is screaming nonstop at the top of her lungs; Molly is still reading that stupid article, almost screaming herself, rushing to get through the whole thing; and Kathleen faces the back of the stage and dances wildly, starting with a little-girl sashay and changing it into a stripper's move, presenting her ass in a slow pan across the audience. The girls go crazy as Bikini Kill leaves the stage.

Later that night, when Erika and Mary and the other riot grrrls are back home in bed, and the Sanctuary Theatre is silent, locked tight against the city, and most of the traffic lights have switched from solid signals to blinking reds and yellows perforated by darkness, the clocks in DC lurch forward an hour. They do this in unison, as if suddenly realizing, collectively, how far back they have fallen, how dreadfully behind the times they have become.

APRIL 5, 1992
NATIONAL MALL, WASHINGTON, DC

The largest women's rights demonstration in American history wasn't going to be big enough. No demonstration possibly *could* be. The organizers knew as much before the whole thing even kicked off, knew it as they surveyed the rally site on the bright, brisk April morning of the We Won't Go Back March for Women's Lives. A stage was set up at one end of the grassy Ellipse, with the White House as its backdrop; the sound system's powerful speakers sat heaped up in towers, their power supplies on standby. A call had gone out for people to come and save abortion rights, but nobody believed they would succeed.

The terrain was bleak. Clarence Thomas, who would cast the new swing vote on an important abortion case that spring, wasn't listening to them, these women and men who would soon fill up the streets between the White House and the Capitol building. Senator Jesse Helms didn't give a good goddamn what they said. President George H. W. Bush, at Camp David for the weekend, wasn't about to change *his* stance on the matter; he had an election to win that fall.

Feminist leaders were openly pessimistic: "I'm going to the Supreme Court and I'm going to lose," Elizabeth Kolbert, the ACLU attorney tasked with arguing *Planned Parenthood v. Casey*, told *USA Today*. Not "I might lose"; not "I fear I could lose." The right to an abortion, the most sweeping nationwide political victory the women's liberation movement had won since women had gained the right to vote, was on the ropes. The feminist movement, such as it was in 1992, was on the ropes too. What could one march do?

Still, it had to be done: plan a march, amplify a rally, bring the troops together. Eventually, maybe, it would count for something.

By daybreak the influx was in full effect. Marchers flooded the city, arriving on battalions of buses from all compass points, shouldering into the aisles of packed Amtrak trains that smoothed themselves heavily between pavilioned platforms. The feminist troops emerged, blinking at the sun, with their banners and windbreakers and bag lunches, some groggy and stiff, some energized. Many were already singing, and shaking small tambourines like afterthoughts. But the songs they sang were old. The young did not know them.

College students were streaming off their own chartered buses after riding all night. News media and commentators in the early 1990s voiced constant concern that the era's youth were alienated, disenfranchised, that they didn't believe in anything—their very moniker, Generation X, seemed to negate any possibility of meaning—but here they were, some of them anyway, roused from their supposed complacency by this new threat to rights they'd thought were safe.

High school students were arriving, too, in scattered groups. One knot of teenage girls scrambled from the subway into the sunlight that morning carrying a huge fabric banner, rolled up around sticks and crammed lumpily into a backpack. Whooping with laughter and anticipation, they walked arm in arm, almost knocking each other over at times, buzzing with the electricity of being in such a massive crowd. They had the sense of being these other women's kindred and at the same time being miles out ahead of them, seeing horizons unimagined by the older activists, who even now were adjusting microphone stands onstage or tuning the electric piano, its wired innards open to the morning, or trying to track down the TV reporter who had wandered away from the press coordinator and now was nowhere to be found. These girls with their hand-painted bedsheet banner weren't famous like Jane Fonda and Linda Carter and the other movie stars flying out from LA by the hundreds. They weren't icons like Gloria Steinem and Bella Abzug, who would be together at the head of the march. In some ways, they were regular girls: Joanna Burgess, Mary Fondriest, Erika Reinstein, May Summer, raised in the highway-laced suburbs of Northern Virginia and straining at the cuffs of high school life. In other ways, they were not regular at all. They were sixteen, seventeen, eighteen years old, and they were feminist revolutionaries.

Throughout the '80s, as articles came out year after year declaring feminism finished, and as the women's movement suffered national defeats on issues from the Equal Rights Amendment to abortion funding, the feminist movement had faltered, depopulated. Its radical wing, those activists who had always asked the biggest questions, fragmented amid bitter disagreements about sex and porn. In the late '80s and early '90s, artists whose work dealt with gender or sexuality were defunded and demonized, with innovators such as Karen Finley and Robert Mapplethorpe vilified on the Senate floor. As vanguard activist groups splintered and dissolved, the movement's major organizations occupied themselves instead with less controversial—and less exciting—issues, such as the corporate glass ceiling and Kiwanis club memberships.

It was hard to blame the movement's veterans for backing away from the struggle to fundamentally change what being female might mean. The front lines could be a punishing, thankless place; those who ventured there were rewarded most often with ridicule, or venom, or worse. And it hurts to keep losing. For critiquing domestic roles, feminists were labeled antifamily; for calling out male misbehavior, they were tarred as man haters; for agitating to expand the lexicon of acceptable female appearances, they were caricatured as "someone who is masculine and who doesn't shave her legs and is doing everything she can to deny that she is feminine," as one college senior had described a typical feminist in a 1989 *Time* magazine article on the subject. The piece's coverline was originally going to be "Is Feminism Dead?" but, because a recent cover had asked the same question about government, the editors instead went with "Women Face the '90s." Next to an image of a sculpture by the artist Marisol—a stunned-looking woman painted on a block of wood, holding a baby in one hand and a briefcase in the other— the cover asked, "Is there a future for feminism?" In the article, it was reported that 76 percent of American women paid "not very much" or "no" attention to the women's movement, and that only 33 percent of women considered themselves feminists. People felt either that feminism had completed its work or that its goals had been misguided in the first place, leading only to more unhappiness for women who had been duped into thinking they could "have it all" or brainwashed into wanting to be like men.

Feminism had taken a beating. To survive, it had by and large traded prophetic visions of whole-cloth cultural change for a reined-in, pragmatic focus on access and ratios: how many women in this or that state assembly, how many fewer all-male clubs. But in doing so, feminism had backed off, too, from constituents whose survival depended on the big questions—the artists, the radicals, the queers, the misfits, the young. And a movement that has stopped talking about cultural change is a movement that has had its heart cut out.

True, by that spring day in 1992, it seemed that the pendulum might be swinging back. Hadn't *Backlash*—Susan Faludi's impeccable exegesis on the past decade of antifeminism—just spent months as a national best seller? Wasn't this march shaping up to be double the size of a similar one three years ago? Weren't 16 women—an unprecedented number—running for open Senate seats, and 140 vying for spots in the House? Weren't pundits already predicting that the fall elections would make 1992 the Year of the Woman?

It was the Clarence Thomas hearings, in the fall of 1991, that had finally got folks riled up again. Even women who didn't believe Anita Hill—polls showed about half of them doubted her allegations of sexual harassment—still bristled at the sight of an African-American female law professor being grilled and dismissed by a panel of white male senators. *Washington Post* columnist Judy Mann put it this way: "At a profound level, the Thomas hearings demonstrated that women are not equal, that men still have the power to take away women's rights. They marked a national epiphany, much like the atrocities of the Vietnam War, which turned scattered protests against the war into a mass movement that changed the conscience of the nation."

Commentators such as Mann hoped the hearings, as infuriating as they were, would serve as a turning point. So did political groups like the Fund for a Feminist Majority—whose president told the *Washington Post*, "The Senate has done more in one week to underscore the critical need for more women in the Senate than feminists have been able to do in twenty-five years"—and Emily's List, a fundraising organization for female Democratic candidates, which more than tripled its roster of donors in the six months after the hearings.

The upcoming Supreme Court case on abortion, scheduled to be heard just weeks after the national march, stoked women's unease still further. Feminist organizations angled to capitalize on this mood. But a reinvigoration of twenty-five-year-old groups wasn't going to change the Court, let alone the whole country, anytime soon. And it definitely wasn't going to be enough to ignite a cultural shift among the younger generation, those Generation Xers who, depending on which newsweekly magazine one believed, were lazy slackers or nihilistic depressives or sought nothing except cheap thrills.

A movement that loses its young eventually dies out. The upswing prompted by the Thomas hearings might be enough to fuel a march and some media speculation on a "year of the woman," but it wasn't going to give feminism what it needed in order to thrive in the '90s and beyond.

Speeches were set to begin at 10. Premade signs, glossy and offset-printed posterboard stapled to splintery wooden pickets, lay in piles on the patchy grass, waiting for marchers to pick them up.

I AM THE FACE OF PRO-CHOICE AMERICA

CHOICE IS THE AMERICAN WAY

This emphasis on *America* was purposeful. The march's strategy was not to persuade the Court to spare *Roe*—few believed they had a chance on that front—but to galvanize women to elect women to

Congress and a Democrat to the White House. Then they'd have a shot at passing the Freedom of Choice Act that was currently marking time on Capitol Hill.

All the Democratic presidential candidates attended the march: Jerry Brown showed up, a contender once again after winning Connecticut and Vermont in recent weeks. Paul Tsongas, who had suspended his campaign after a string of defeats but told people to vote for him if they wished, marched with his teenage daughter. Bill Clinton, already widely seen as the most likely Democrat to challenge Bush in November, surrounded himself with supporters who chanted, "Pro-choice, pro-Clinton."

None of the candidates was given a turn at the microphone during the rally. Patricia Ireland, the president of NOW, addressed the crowd: "We are tired of begging for our rights from men in power," she intoned. "We are going to take power."

The details of this proposed power-taking, however, were not as bold as the applause line implied. No feminist revolution was planned—although, given the fact that the word "revolution" had most recently been seen following the word "Reagan," perhaps NOW's "Elect Women for a Change" campaign qualified as one too. In an interview that day, Ireland simply reiterated the well-known plan: "If the courts won't protect them, then Congress has got to enact laws to protect a woman's rights. And if Congress doesn't, then we're going to elect pro-choice women to Congress."

Although the right to choose an abortion was particularly endangered for girls under eighteen—thirty-six states had parental notification laws on the books in 1992—the march's strategy revolved around yet another choice that only people eighteen or older could exercise freely. The mass-produced picket sign from the National Abortion Rights Action League told the tale:

WE WILL DECIDE, NOV. 3

It was a fine message, as long as one didn't know, as nobody then could have confidently predicted, that on November 3, women would help elect as president a relatively weak Democrat—one with his own complicated relationship to women—who would immediately be stymied by opponents in most of his efforts to promote feminist issues. The Freedom of Choice Act would never make it to Bill Clinton's desk.

Still, electoral change might have been a fine message among many others—for people who were eligible to vote. But what was a seventeen-year-old girl going to get to decide on November 3? What place did a high school student have at a march that was billed as an abortion-rights demonstration but was really more of a get-out-the-vote rally?

More to the point: When you're a teenage girl who's trying with all your might not to hate yourself, trying not to get harassed or raped, trying not to let bikini blondes in beer ads crush your self-image, trying not to be discouraged from joining a sports team or math club or shop class or school newspaper, trying not to let your family's crippling dysfunction (and the confounding irony of enduring domestic cruelty in an age of Family Values) make you want to fucking *die*, a feminist movement that's mostly about electing new Senators might not be all that compelling to you.

But because you're looking for something, anything, to make you feel a little less crazy, you might go to such a march anyway. The fact remains, though, that if this movement, this feminism, is going to be relevant to your life in the long run—which is to say, if feminism is going to *survive*—you're going to have to do some tinkering, even some large-scale renovations. You're going to have to make this thing your own.

Despite abundant sunshine, temperatures remained in the low 50s throughout the morning rally, and a wicked breeze gusted around the demonstrators who were to march from the Ellipse to the Mall.

This would turn out to be the biggest protest Washington had seen since the Vietnam War—over a half million people would fill the National Mall before the day was over. The wind rippled the stage's bright-red backdrop, pocked with smile-shaped slices to let the air come through; it ruffled the yellow sashes reading "Honored Guest" draped over the chests of the female congressional candidates who stood in a cheery line onstage, grinning and waving vigorously like a row of pageant hopefuls.

Within the crowd, Erika and Mary and the other riot grrrls gathered their forces. A dozen or more young women beat on drums and plastic buckets, swarming and clamoring around their massive banner, which was covered in glitter and bore the words RIOT GRRRLS and CHOICE and a bunch of big Valentine's Day–worthy hearts, one of them dotting the "i" in CHOICE. The "s" in RIOT GRRRLS was half the size of the other letters; it tilted to the side, as if about to topple off a ledge.

Many of the riot grrrls made their bodies into signs that day, writing on their skin with markers. They wrote words and drew hearts and stars and woman symbols on their arms and on the strip of stomach that peeked out from beneath a knotted or rolled-up T-shirt. CHOICE was a popular message for the self-inscribers. GIRL LOVE was another one, deliberately ambiguous: Was said love romantic or not? When you're seventeen, do you ever really know for sure? It was an unfixed catchphrase, standing for the hope that girls could, against all odds, be everything to one another: that, amid the forces of adolescence that turned girls into enemies and rended friendships with envy, girls could simply, purely love each other. It was as much a plea as it was a slogan.

The march kicked off at noon, and demonstrators streamed down Pennsylvania Avenue for hours, a chaotic flux of clashing chants, errant drumbeats, and the odd giant puppet. They passed and jeered at the White House, which looked quiet and vacant, the only visible movement a fountain's insouciant splashing behind its wrought iron stockade. "Hey hey, ho ho, George Bush has got to go," they hollered, filing on down toward the Capitol building, where another rally awaited. The riot grrrls, bored by the standard-issue chants, raised up wordless screams of frustration as they marched.

Spring's grass hadn't taken hold of the Mall yet, and the wind kicked up a massive cloud of dust that filled the airspace over everybody's heads. It hung there, diffusing the light, and it was anyone's guess whether this dirty fog was lifting or growing darker. Onstage, Odetta sang "Amazing Grace," her voice warm and weathered; Cyndi Lauper sang a song she'd just written about a girl dying of a "back-alley job"; and Jesse Jackson roared, "Keep! Hope! Alive!" Fonda, looking in her white turtleneck and oversize shades like a glamorous revolutionary on the lam, announced, "We are here to say to the government: You got enough problems of your own; stay out of my womb." Steinem jokingly proclaimed that she would accept the crowd's nomination for president. She had just published the best-selling "book of self-esteem" *Revolution from Within*; another recent blockbuster feminist author—thirty-two-year-old Faludi—had spoken earlier, at the Ellipse.

The women and girls whose lives would constitute the next crucial chapter in feminist history were nowhere near the rally's stage on the Mall. They were mixed in among the record-breaking crowd, with their bedsheet banner and their bandmates. But they were closer to the spotlight than they ever could have imagined.

1989–92

ONE

DOUBLE DARE YA: THE BIRTH OF BIKINI KILL

In the beginning, someone told a girl to start a band.

The year was 1989. George Bush had just replaced Ronald Reagan in the White House; Madonna was getting pilloried for kissing a black saint in the "Like a Prayer" video; an obscure band called Nirvana was about to release its debut album, *Bleach*; and Kathleen Hanna boarded a bus in Olympia, Washington, bound for Seattle.

Kathleen was nineteen years old and finishing her junior year at Olympia's Evergreen State College. Her high school years, split between Oregon and Maryland, had been marked by beer and pot, sleazy guys, big hair, small-scale heavy metal and reggae concerts, and enough of a disregard for schoolwork that Evergreen accepted her only provisionally into its class of 1990. She took one women's studies class, which seemed to have nothing on the syllabus besides Simone de Beauvoir's *The Second Sex*, but she spent most of her time studying photography in the art department and working in the college darkroom developing film for the student newspaper.

She was going to Seattle to meet her hero, the writer Kathy Acker. Acker was forty-two, a star of the literary avant-garde, striking in her bleached crew cut and tattoos. Her work had been a revelation for Kathleen. "I was just writing all this crazy shit and I thought I was totally insane," Kathleen said. "And I got *Blood and Guts in High School* from one of my photo teachers, and I totally felt like, Oh, I'm not crazy! It was such a confidence builder for me. I wasn't even sure what kind of artist I was going to be, like if I was a writer or a photographer or what. But it made me feel like these other women had done this amazing shit and I could too."

Acker's insolent, demanding fictions tackled female sexuality head-on and took an ax to literary form. In *Blood and Guts in High School*, the 1978 novel that got Kathleen hooked, a young girl begs her father for sex, joins a gang, has two abortions, and goes to a Contortions concert—all in the first forty-three pages. The story is told in a fragmented, deadpan way, through shifting points of view and collage: fairy tales, scripts, poems, line drawings of men's and women's genitals, pages from a Persian-language workbook. *Blood and Guts* suggested that the realities of women's lives, especially with regard to sexuality and abuse, were too complicated to be told through typical narrative. Only contradictions, ruptures, and refusals stood a chance of conveying the truth.

We don't hate, understand, we have to get back. Fight the dullness of shit society. Alienated robotized images. Here's your cooky, ma'am. No to anything but madness.

Kathleen had begun declaiming some of her writings at the spoken-word nights her friend Slim Moon organized at the Capitol Theater in Olympia. After discovering Acker, she stapled some of these pieces into a xeroxed zine, *Fuck Me Blind*, which she published under the pseudonym Maggie Fingers. In late May, when Acker came to Seattle's Center on Contemporary Art for two days to teach a workshop and give public readings, Kathleen enrolled in the workshop, and she brought *Fuck Me Blind* to show the writer. At first it looked like Kathleen might realize her dream of being taken under Acker's wing and nurtured as a protégée: The writer had to choose one student from the workshop to be her opening act at the reading the following evening, and she chose Kathleen.

Emboldened but not satiated, Kathleen called Acker's press representative after the workshop's first day, claiming that she worked as journalist for the magazine *Zero Hour*, and scheduled an interview with Acker. "I was like, any way to hang out with her—I was so desperate, you know? I was there for the weekend and I wanted to pack it *in*." Kathleen wasn't a journalist, though. *Zero Hour* was the publication of the friend she was crashing with in Seattle, Alice Wheeler, a photographer and Evergreen graduate who lived in a sort of commune called the Subterranean Cooperative of Urban Dreamers. She hadn't asked Kathleen to write anything for the magazine yet.

Kathleen couldn't believe how easy it was to bluff her way into a one-on-one with Acker. It taught her, she said, that "you should lie to people to get things you want; you can make things happen for yourself just by acting confident." She interviewed her idol while sitting at the counter of a café in the Pike Place Market. A handful of yards away from steely Elliott Bay, they discussed feminism, sex, and art. But Acker took issue with some of the younger woman's ideas. The pair's main disagreement was over how sexism affected men: Kathleen felt they benefited from it, and Acker argued with force that it harmed them emotionally too; that Kathleen was making an intellectual and political mistake by viewing sexism as an us-versus-them game.

Kathleen wasn't convinced, just deflated. "I walked away from the interview with my tail between my legs," she said. "But I kept thinking about the shit that she said to me. You know how when your feelings are really hurt, or you feel really humiliated, you can't stop thinking about it? She actually did me the biggest favor anybody could have done me: She treated me like I was really a writer and that I had ideas of my own and that I was strong enough to be challenged. And I *wasn't* really strong enough to be challenged at the time, but it made me *want* to be that. I had a dream of becoming cool enough that I could become friends with her at some point."

Kathleen had a game plan for achieving this level of coolness, because Acker had told her straight out, on the second day of the workshop, what she should do. Everybody had gotten a brief one-on-one conference with the teacher, and Kathleen's meeting had taken a strange turn.

> **Acker**: Why are you writing? Why are you doing spoken word?
>
> **Kathleen** (*Tearing up a little. She feels it so deeply.*): I feel like my whole life no one's ever listened to me. I want people to listen.
>
> **Acker**: If you want people to hear what you're doing, don't do spoken word, because nobody likes spoken word, nobody goes to spoken word. There's more of a community for musicians than for writers. You should be in a band.

People never do anything life-changing for only one reason. Kathleen started a band because she wanted to impress Kathy Acker, but also because she had a strong singing voice, which had once landed her the lead in a school production of *Annie*; and because she had chosen to go to college in arty Olympia, where starting a band was simply what people did for fun; and because she and some friends ran an art gallery that had become a place for rock shows, making her a booker of concerts. If Acker hadn't been the proximate cause, something else would have been. But Acker's admonitions did the trick, giving Kathleen not just a push but a lineage, not just an idea but a creation myth.

Kathleen's first band was Amy Carter, named after the thirty-ninth president's once-gangly daughter. Kathleen sang and played keyboard, Tammy Rae Carland played bass, Heidi Arbogast played drums, and Greg Babior played guitar. Kathleen's friendship with Tammy Rae and Heidi, born in the college darkroom, had evolved into a collective in which they got together to discuss their own art and the work of trailblazing feminist artists such as Jenny Holzer, Barbara Kruger, Sherrie Levine, and Cindy Sherman. The collective evolved still further after Kathleen had a run-in with institutional censorship. Several months before the Acker weekend, Kathleen and her friend Aaron Bausch-Greene had set up an exhibition of their artwork on campus—not in any great space, just a hallway that led to a cafeteria. Kathleen's contribution included a photostat from a childhood picture of herself, dressed in a bikini and a tiara with a beauty-pageant sash across her chest, a scrawl of SLUTSLUTSLUT roiling the whole background. When school officials took down the exhibition without any warning, apparently in order not to offend some visiting Boy Scouts, Kathleen and Tammy Rae and Heidi decided to open a feminist gallery downtown. They scored a vacant garage on East State Street because Kathleen had heard that the guy who lived there was about to go to jail; she called the landlord and got dibs on the space. She and her friends called the space Reko Muse and mounted numerous exhibitions there, but they quickly realized that this was not the best way to cover the gallery's rent.

What Olympia really needed, and what people were willing to pay money for, was a place where touring bands could play shows. By the summer of 1989, Reko Muse had become one of Olympia's most dependable music venues, hosting shows by national acts like Babes in Toyland, regional powerhouses like the Melvins, local ramshackle pop groups like the Go Team, and a new band in town that played one show at Reko Muse under the name Industrial Nirvana but usually just called itself Nirvana.

Once Amy Carter had a few songs, getting a gig was as simple as the Reko Muse women adding their band to a bill. It didn't matter that Greg was the only band member who had ever played with people before. Olympia didn't require expertise of its musicians, only passion and originality. "A great thing about Olympia is that everybody will clap for *anything*," songwriter Lois Maffeo, who had a long-running all-girl radio show on the community radio station KAOS, said later. "You could get up and sing some godawful song and everybody would be like, 'Yeah! Good for you, that's so excellent!'"

The town embraced the dorky, the quirky, the strange-verging-on-mad. This was a tone set largely by Evergreen, an experimental state school founded in 1967, where grades and majors didn't exist and classes often assigned creative projects instead of term papers. The college's mascot was a geoduck, a mud-burrowing giant clam and rumored aphrodisiac that wore its thick trunklike siphon outside its shell; the school motto, accordingly, was *Omnia extares*—"Let it all hang out." Before Evergreen opened its gates to the tribes of dreamers and seekers and freaks, Olympia had been a sleepy hamlet at the southernmost extreme of Puget Sound's clan of salty inlets, a town held afloat by nearby logging operations, a modest shipping port, and the seasonal influx of state legislators who flooded the tawny capitol building before retreating to Aberdeen or Kennewick or Wenatchee. But the college changed the town for good. Since there was no dependable rock venue for touring bands until the mid-'80s, a self-sufficient and decidedly all-ages musical culture developed, with small house parties and informal performance nights welcoming to the stage anyone who had something to share.

By the end of the '80s, the town's punk scene was thriving, even magical. "Punk" here meant not mohawks and spikes but do-it-yourself, or DIY: creating something from nothing, fashion from garbage, music and art from whatever was nearest at hand, whether that be kazoos or ukuleles or strange garden implements on liquidation special down at the Yardbird's. DIY was a philosophy and a way of life, a touchstone that set its industrious adherents apart from the legions of Americans who passed their lives—as the punks saw it—trudging from TV set to first-run multiplex, from chain record store to commercial radio dial, treating art and culture as commodities to be consumed instead of vital forces to be struggled with and shaped, experimented with and created, breathed and lived.

One Olympia artist, Stella Marrs, threw parties where everybody who came *had* to contribute something—a performance or a song or something to eat. Another artist, Nikki McClure, used to take long walks in the woods around sunset, making up songs and singing them to herself at the top of her voice; when she hit on something that sounded good to her, she'd run back to whatever house was hosting a show and sing into the mic, knowing the audience would be receptive. The scene's flagship band for most of the '80s was the willfully unvirtuosic Beat Happening, a shambolic trio that played a messy, barely amplified, childish pop of folk chords on acoustic guitars, sparse rhythms beat out on just a few drums at a time, and snapped fingers; their songs were often affectingly tender (and even slyly randy) ditties about secret picnic spots or dancing with fish at the beach.

Kathleen had loved music her whole life, and she appreciated the permissiveness of the Oly scene. But the cutesiness of the Beat Happening "love rock" circle wasn't her aesthetic. She was more excited about hosting shows by Mecca Normal, a Canadian band whose singer, Jean Smith, fiercely held forth on gender politics over swirling guitar squalls: "Man thinks 'woman' when he talks to me / Something not quite right." Many of the out-of-town groups that played the Muse on tour, though, were offensively bad, with their canned moves, filched riffs, and rote performances. This was not art but routine, and it offended Kathleen, who worked her ass off so these guys could autopilot through their shows. "I did everything from painting the floor to cleaning the grease off the floor to wiping their stupid cock-rock graffiti off the wall after they left," she said, "and picking up their cigarette butts, and spending my own long-distance money to book their dumb bands into our club, and then having them yell at me because there's not enough orange juice backstage, et cetera. And they were just doing boring work."

Her internship was the realest thing in her life. She worked at Safeplace, a domestic violence shelter, doing crisis counseling and giving presentations at high schools on rape and sexual assault. She had started a discussion group there for teenage girls, and hearing those girls talk openly with one another about their past traumas, watching how supportive the girls were of one another, Kathleen felt she was witnessing one of the most beautiful things in the world. It was with these girls in mind that she formed a new band, Viva Knievel.

This hard-rock group had two women and two men, with Kathleen as the singer, and most of the songs she wrote were about sexual assault. In the summer of 1990, one year after the Kathy Acker workshop, Viva Knievel went on a low-budget national tour, playing in basements and sleeping on floors for two months. After shows, girls from the audience would come up to Kathleen, wanting to talk about their own abusive fathers, violent boyfriends, and incest flashbacks. Kathleen would switch gears from performer to counselor; she'd find a quiet place away from the crowd to listen to each girl in turn, tell her it wasn't her fault, help her identify supportive people in her life, and urge her to call a local crisis line. "Essentially," she said, "I was doing the same work that I did at the shelter." Some nights it felt like every girl at the show, the ones who came to talk to her and the ones who didn't, had some terrible story. Some days Kathleen felt like the only way for her to redeem the traumas of her own adolescence—traumas she referenced obliquely from time to time—would be to keep other girls from going through the same kinds of hell, or at least to help them find ways to emerge stronger. But the sheer scale of the girls' need was overwhelming. She couldn't save them fast enough.

Kathleen knew the facts from her work: A woman was battered every fifteen seconds. Half of all female murder victims were killed by their husbands or boyfriends. One in four girls was sexually abused before the age of eighteen. One in four women had experienced rape or attempted rape, and 78 percent of these involved someone the woman knew personally.

These things weren't abstractions to Kathleen. Her own childhood had been harrowing, and she didn't feel any safer when she got to college. Near the end of her junior year, an Evergreen student was assaulted at the campus beach. That summer, right after Olympia's daily newspaper ran an article about how dangerous the sprawling, forested campus could be, another assault took place at the same beach.

Kathleen lived off campus with her best friend, but they had to move out of one apartment after a guy came in one night and beat up Kathleen's roommate. "The guy woke her from a dead sleep and attempted to kill her," Kathleen said. They had to leave their next apartment too, she said, after they heard the woman next door trying to convince her screaming boyfriend to put down his gun; that guy was acting manager of the building, so he had keys to Kathleen's apartment. It felt like danger followed her wherever she went.

She was haunted, too, by the high-profile acts of violence against women that hit the headlines every few months. The so-called Green River Killer, who had murdered at least forty girls and young women near Seattle in the '80s, was still at large; three more victims' bodies would be discovered in the early '90s. In April 1989, a woman jogging in New York's Central Park was raped and savagely beaten. On December 6 of the same year, a man in Montreal walked into a roomful of engineering students, ordered the men to leave, and opened fire on the women who remained, saying, "You're all a bunch of feminists. I hate feminists." By the end of his rampage, he had killed fourteen women.

Two days before that attack, *Time* had published its article about how most women didn't consider themselves feminists. For Kathleen, that article, combined with the massacre's coming right on its heels, settled the matter: The world was officially insane. Women were continually under attack but weren't supposed to acknowledge it, weren't supposed to resist it. If feminism's work was finished, then what were all the women at Safeplace doing there? Kathleen knew, too, that feminism was alive and well—she saw this every time she looked at what she and her friends had built with Reko Muse—but the world at large thought it was dead: The term *post-feminist* was already making the rounds. Most important, Kathleen knew that feminism could save people's lives. How could the girls she met on tour possibly fight against what was being done to them if they lost the ability to name it, to analyze it, to see how it was part of a system?

When Kathleen was growing up, her mom told her about the volunteer work she did with survivors of domestic violence, and she took her daughter to a rally where Gloria Steinem spoke. Her mom also subscribed to *Ms.* magazine, which didn't always feel particularly relevant to a still-young girl—for every item like the cover that named Cyndi Lauper a 1985 woman of the year, there were many more articles about the glass ceiling in the corporate world. But by college, Kathleen was well aware that it was the feminist movement that had founded domestic violence shelters and rape crisis hotlines, and that without feminism, women who'd been abused would have no place that took them and their safety seriously.

Now, as Kathleen was conducting impromptu therapy sessions in rock clubs and dingy basements, Susan Faludi was rigorously researching a conservative backlash that tarred feminism as an outmoded idea that had hurt women more than it had helped. Internecine struggles within the movement were contributing to its woes as well. When Kathleen went looking for her activist peers at Evergreen, she found a feminist movement that had been riven for a decade by debates over porn, censorship, and sex work. She attended a talk by Andrea Dworkin on the evils of pornography, and she went to a meeting in Seattle of the Feminist Anti-Censorship Task Force (FACT), but she felt out of place at both events. Dworkin, the intellectual architect of an antiporn orthodoxy that was the most well-known strain of feminism at the time, took the view that all sex workers were victims of patriarchy. Kathleen worked as a stripper, and she considered it a choice she had made freely; she liked to tell people that it felt no more degrading than working as a waitress, and it paid a lot better. When she brought this up during the Q&A, Dworkin's response left Kathleen in tears. "To her, feminism and sex-trade work were diametrically opposed conceptions," Kathleen recalled. "She said, 'Oh! I appreciate you coming out and saying this in front of all these people. And I just want to tell you that if you think this experience has not affected you, I want you to know that it's going to affect the whole rest of your life. You'll be paying for it forever, blah blah blah.'"

The women of FACT went too far in the other direction. At the meeting in Seattle, Kathleen saw a woman who worked at a club she, too, had danced at briefly, a place that she knew mistreated its dancers and was a miserable place to work. But the woman kept talking at the meeting about how much she loved her job, which gave Kathleen the creeps. And when Kathleen and her friends asked questions about how the porn industry was run by men, the FACT women became defensive and called them Dworkinites.

Art and music were the only places Kathleen saw that had room for contradiction and ambiguity. But even within punk rock, her peers seemed to think feminism was no longer useful. When she met other female musicians on tour, she interviewed them, asking, "How does the fact that rape exists affect your life? How does being female affect your work?" With distressing frequency she got the same answer: "Oh, it doesn't matter that I'm a woman; I'm a musician first." One musician admitted that her male bandmates pressured her to wear a tight dress and lipstick at shows while the guys dressed more casually. Yet she insisted she had transcended gender.

So the punk world was just as oblivious as the world at large. How could gender be irrelevant when so many girls were coming up to Kathleen in tears; when an AC/DC cover band had the nerve to accuse Viva Knievel of being a novelty act because there were two women in the group; when Kathleen and her bandmate Louise were so often the only women onstage the whole night; when they had to open for a band in Ohio whose singer blurted, between songs, "Incest is best, put your sister to the test"; when Kathleen felt a terror in dark alleys behind rock clubs that the men in her band never experienced? What fantasyland were these other women living in?

Kathleen knew only one other girl rocker who saw how much gender mattered: Tobi Vail, an Oly punk who played in the Go Team and wrote a fanzine, the thick and hyperliterate *Jigsaw*. Tobi was a good drummer and a superb writer, her prose a long fuse sparked with little explosions of enthusiasm and celebration. "First of all, I would like to inform you that the Go-Go's don't suck so stop putting them down. YES that means you Mr./Ms. rock journalist," she wrote in *Jigsaw* #2.

```
Secondly that kind of thing is just so TYPI-
CAL. Of course if there was ever a good girl
band . . . and they were A BAND . . . in
the top 40 of course it would be likely to
get a bad name . . . because girls + gui-
tars is equal to sex + power . . . which is
something that is not supposed to be as-
sociated with women in our culture. It is
threatening to the power structures that
be. Of course we are told that there are
never any good girl bands and are deprived
of our heroines!
```

Tobi had a gift for taking the stuff of everyday life, snacks and walks and little one-off bands and art projects, and making them sound like the most exciting things in the world. She had read the Beats, learning from Kerouac and Ginsberg how a breathless tone and a stance of wild romanticism could transform ordinary goings-on into adventure, everyday life into myth, and a self-contained scene into a veritable pantheon of mutually reinforcing genius. Everything was accessible, everything was meaningful, everything was available to be discussed and assessed and incorporated into an exuberant and revolutionary worldview.

It was a five-page article on gender titled "Boxes" that convinced Kathleen to write Tobi a letter. "I've always been interested in playing music with other women," Tobi wrote in her article. "And it seems like I've always been misunderstood and gotten called sexist for it. I don't know, maybe I'm crazy, but to me it seems natural to notice the difference between men and women and I don't understand WHY I'm constantly told to ignore that in the context of rock and roll."

She went on to break down the history of feminism as she'd learned it from a recent reading of *The Feminine Mystique*, and then turned her attention to all-girl bands that didn't want to talk about their gender in interviews. "I think denying the all-girl label is destructive," she wrote. "And the thing that really gets me is 'We want to be taken seriously, not as all girl.' What does that mean? That girls aren't serious about their music?"

When Tobi was going to high school in Olympia in the mid-'80s, girls had hung around the town's teen punk scene and went to shows, but of the kids who participated in obvious ways, by playing music or skating the Lacey ramps, most were boys. Tobi herself had unusual encouragement; her dad, a musician, taught her to play drums when she was twelve, and three years later Calvin Johnson, a KAOS DJ who had just founded Beat Happening and a record label called K, asked her to form a band. This band, the Go Team, was great fun, but she didn't want to spend all her time with male musicians. While continuing to play with Calvin, Tobi also formed an all-girl group, Doris, with some of her high school friends.

Tobi had been aware of Kathleen for several years. "I thought she was very brave and I knew people talked shit about her, which made me want to get to know her better," Tobi said. People in town said Kathleen was too political, or too angry, or that she'd converted to punk suspiciously fast. Women in Olympia often referred to their home as a girls' town, and it was true that many female artists, especially those who'd been active since the early '80s, flourished there. But rules still remained for girls to follow, and punishment awaited anyone who stepped out of the lines. People in the scene talked trash about Tobi, too: that she was a slut, a bitch, too cool for school.

Hearing those things made Kathleen want to be Tobi's friend even more. There had already been a few little breakthrough moments between the two of them: During Kathleen's Acker weekend in Seattle, Tobi had reached her hand out to Kathleen from inside a sold-out Fugazi show and pulled Kathleen into the venue, although they hardly knew each other yet. A bit later, Kathleen booked one of her favorite Portland bands, the Obituaries, to play a show at Reko Muse, and almost nobody at the show liked it except for Kathleen and Tobi. The band was loud rock 'n' roll, and the musical orthodoxy in Olympia was sweeter, cuter, quieter, but Tobi got it. A similar thing happened at a Babes in Toyland concert, with Tobi and Kathleen and another girl, Kathi Wilcox, who worked with Tobi at a sandwich shop: "Everybody was debating," Kathleen said, "could they play their instruments, was it fucked up that they were pretty—what are they supposed to do, wear bags on their head?— was it fucked up that she was wearing a dress: All this kind of ridiculous questioning! And me and Tobi and Kathi were just like, that's the most amazing thing we've ever seen."

But none of these things coalesced into a friendship until Kathleen read *Jigsaw*, right around the time that she went on tour with Viva Knievel, and she realized that she and Tobi were meant for each other. Kathleen was doing her interviews with musicians she met on the road, "and I thought, I'll send them to that girl Tobi and try to get her to like me."

When the tour ended, Kathleen moved to Portland, into a house where Kathi also lived, for the few months before school started again. Kathleen was working two jobs, tired all the time. She'd been procrastinating, but she finally decided it was time to send the interviews to Tobi. A friend of Kathleen's had just brought her favorite typewriter down from Olympia, so she eased a sheet of paper behind its cylindrical platen, turned the knob and felt it give way. The paper advanced in measured spurts through the wheels of the machine.

She could hear a bunch of boys hanging out downstairs, listening to Cheap Trick and talking about the first records they'd ever owned. Kathleen couldn't take part in the conversation; she couldn't let the boys know that the first record she'd bought with her own money had probably been something by Donny and Marie Osmond—definitely nothing with underground cred. Punk was a society of misfits, yet it had its own set of standards, rigid markers of coolness that she knew she couldn't live up to.

But she could write. "I read Jigsaw and it made me so happy," she wrote in the letter she sent to Tobi along with the typed-up interviews. "I felt like we are/were trying to do some similar type things and I felt validated. I know what it's like to have a girl tell me that she doesn't think it really means anything that she's a girl. I could tell you were nice and wouldn't laugh at me, too much, for writing to you."

Her gambit worked. Reading that letter, Tobi said, "I knew we were going to start a band when she came home from tour." Kathleen moved back to Olympia that fall to finish up some final credits at Evergreen, and she and Tobi got started right away. Tobi even had a name all picked out. A few years earlier, her old band Doris had played an all-girl-bands show that Lois had booked at the Capitol Theater. Tobi ran into Lois backstage and said, "Hey, what's your new band going to be called?" Lois answered, "Either Bikini Kill or the Cradle Robbers."

"I was like, God, Bikini Kill is the coolest name for a band!" Tobi said. "I remembered it forever." When Lois settled on the Cradle Robbers, Tobi thought, *Good, now I get Bikini Kill.* She didn't know that several years earlier, Lois had done a one-night performance by that name, with her friend Margaret Doherty. Lois and Margaret had worn black wigs and "punk cave-girl costumes out of fake fur," Lois said, and they reenacted a 1967 B-movie they had become obsessed with, *The Million Eyes of Sumuru*, by singing, "Two bikini girls kill one bikini girl, glug glug glug she's dead . . . " In *The Million Eyes*, an evil woman controls an army of brainwashed sexpots (in bikinis, of course), with whose help she plans to achieve world domination; when one girl deviates from the plot, two others are sent to kill her.

Tobi liked how the word-pair encapsulated the nexus of sexiness and violence. It also reminded her of the bathing suit's namesake in the Pacific Ocean: the Bikini Atoll, where the United States had conducted nuclear tests in the 1940s and '50s. Gender politics, geopolitics—it was all connected. She sent Lois a letter informing her that *she* was claiming the name.

Tobi and Kathleen rented apartments across the hall from each other, and they would hang out for hours on end, visiting back and forth, trading reading lists, discussing politics and art and music. They found, as so many feminists had found, that two people could be opposed to sexism while disagreeing heartily over the details. Tobi had never given much thought to the sex trade; Kathleen's insistence that a feminist could also be a stripper was new to her. Tobi's politics were being shaped by black feminist writers such as Angela Davis and bell hooks, whose books got her thinking about how being white affected her own experience of being female; she was also influenced by poststructuralists such as Judith Butler, who wrote about the ways that gender was actively enacted and performed in relation to social power. But when Kathleen talked to women at Safeplace who'd been beaten by their boyfriends or raped by their uncles, they didn't care if "female" was an unstable category constantly called into existence through rhetoric and institutions. Kathleen saw women and girls who were being nearly destroyed by men; interrogating categories wasn't going to change that reality. Still, she read the books and articles Tobi lent her, and Tobi read the art theory and essays on white privilege that Kathleen gave to *her*, and gradually the two friends staked out common ground, arriving at a vision of a cool, accessible feminist movement that Tobi dubbed the Revolution Girl Style Now.

Tobi, who had an encyclopedic knowledge of punk history, turned Kathleen on to some of the genre's most famed gender rebels, Darby Crash of the Germs and Poly Styrene of X-Ray Spex. Crash was a queer man in the early LA scene who burned out fast; Poly Styrene was a woman who came to prominence during a moment in British punk, in the late '70s, when bands of women making sonically diverse, bluntly experimental music were all the rage: the Slits, Young Marble Giants, the Raincoats. Alongside these groups, X-Ray Spex landed several saxophone-embroidered punk hits that addressed gender, at times head-on: "Some people think little girls should be seen and not heard," Styrene pronounced in clipped, sarcastic tones at the outset of one such track, before she howled the song's titular retort: "But I say, Oh bondage, up yours!" Her vocal lines—though it's not accurate to call them *lines*, exactly; her voice was more like a tattooer's needle, jabbing repeatedly at a single spot—left lasting impressions:

> *Bind me tie me chain me to the wall!*
> *I wanna be a slave to you all!*
> *Oh bondage up yours!*
> *Oh bondage no more!*

One would never know it by looking at the punk bands that made up the genre's canon in 1990, when Bikini Kill got started—Black Flag, the Clash, the Sex Pistols, the Ramones—but the early history of punk rock was full of memorable women, in the United States as well as Britain. New York had Patti Smith, Sonic Youth's Kim Gordon, and post-punk dance bands Y Pants and ESG. The late-'70s LA scene had been even more gender-balanced: Exene Cervenka of X and Alice Bag of the Bags were magnetic performers, and the Bangles and the Go-Go's cut their teeth in that scene before cleaning up their sound to go mainstream. Even in Washington, DC, in the early '80s, where the teenage band Minor Threat was seeding the shouty, sinewy, overwhelmingly male hardcore sound, the all-female group Chalk Circle paid tribute to European bands like Kleenex and the Au Pairs.

So it wasn't as if punk had always been a male-dominated domain; far from it. But as the '80s drew on, hardcore became the dominant sound of punk. Its simple musical conventions were easy for untrained teens to imitate; its penchant for louder-faster-harder performances and frenetic slam dancing were catnip for boys anxious to blow off adolescent steam. The concerts' mosh pits, flurries of flying elbows and wandering hands, drove most girls to the sidelines or out of the scene altogether. Not that other options were any better. Turning on MTV in the mid-'80s meant being hit with video after video of male performers mugging amid cleavage shots, ass shots, phalanxes of inert robotic models.

By the fall of 1990, punk and mainstream rock were both on the cusp of enormous change, and Kathleen and Tobi were at the epicenter of that shift. Tobi was dating Kurt Cobain, who lived in Olympia and, having released one album on Seattle's still-small Sub Pop Records, was now plotting Nirvana's next steps. When Dave Grohl moved to town to be the band's new drummer, he and Kathleen hit it off, and for a while that fall, the four of them hung out frequently. One of the girls' friends remembers hearing them plan an evening by saying, "Let's go out with Nirvana." After one evening of spray-painting pro-choice slogans on the abortion-alternatives center in town, Kathleen graffitied "Kurt smells like Teen Spirit" on the guitarist's bedroom wall. "I was just super drunk and had seen the deodorant at the store and thought the name was hilarious," Kathleen explained. "There's no big story besides I was being a drunk idiot." Even though Cobain and Tobi were in love, he broke up with her later that fall. He then wrote a set of heartbroken songs (arguably about her) for the album they were working on—an album that would also include the song Kathleen helped name before it was composed.

The boys of Nirvana had their hearts set on fame and stardom, which made them unusual in Olympia, as did their polished, anthemic sound, all brawny power chords and cataclysmic drumming. Tobi was particularly critical of her friend's designs on success; she had nothing but scorn for "lame career-goal bands," which to her defeated the anticonsumerist raison d'etre of punk rock.

Whatever: Tobi and Kathleen had a band of their own to worry about. They knew from the beginning that Bikini Kill was going to be something special, not a feint at the Top Ten or at bourgeois stability. They had plotted it out carefully in strategy sessions: Their band was going to be a revolution. They would settle for nothing less.

Tobi thought Kathi would make a good third member of Bikini Kill. The cool, sophisticated film student, who had been Kathleen's housemate in Portland and Tobi's co-worker at the sandwich shop, had just moved back to Olympia. Though she'd never been in a band before, she had played clarinet, violin, and piano while growing up, and she was game to learn guitar and bass. The three of them gathered that fall in Tobi's practice space, a garage on the west side where she kept drums and amps and a PA for vocals, and they got started.

"I remember being nervous," Kathleen said, "but thinking I was on a total fucking mission, so I was just gonna fake my way through this 'being in a band' thing. I liked playing music with them from the start. I felt like I could write whatever I wanted, and they were really into the fact that I always showed up with a file folder full of poems and lyrics and stuff. I felt appreciated and also like the sky was the limit."

Tobi shared that sense of possibility. "So really, NOW, more than ever feels like something is happening bandwise here," Tobi wrote in *Jigsaw* #3. "Maybe it has a lot to do with being excited about my NEW band, BIKINI KILL. Not only is BK and Revolution Girl Style Now ready to indoctrinate the universe but there is one big time explosion of bands happening." She listed a few, and ended the list with "Bikini Kill Bikini Kill Bikini Kill!!! Yeah."

At the early practices, Kathi and Kathleen took turns playing bass. None of the girl guitarists they auditioned that winter felt right, but they started playing parties anyway, as a three-piece; before they had written enough songs to play all originals, they filled out their sets with covers of "Judy Is a Punk" by the Ramones and "The American in Me" by the Avengers.

By Valentine's Day, when the trio played a show at the North Shore Surf Club, they had already devised a tight and arresting set, including many songs that would stay in their repertoire for years: "Liar," "Feels Blind," "This Is Not a Test," and the statement of purpose "Double Dare Ya." Kathi had taken quickly to the bass, her slender violinist's fingers so long and agile there seemed to be an extra knuckle in there someplace. Tobi's playing had the casual heft that drummers who've played since childhood often have, giving the impression that each muscular fill and cymbal crash so naturally belongs right *there* that it scarcely takes any work to nail it. Her sticks floated like magic wands around her set, her upper body nearly motionless except for her arms.

Kathleen cut a fearsome figure onstage. With her pale skin, jet-black bob, and faded black T-shirt, she looked stark before she even opened her mouth. Singing, she became utterly magnetic. "Dare you to do what you want!" she roared, her entire torso rising with each breath before she bore down on the next line. "Dare you to be who you will!" Every muscle in her body drawn stick-taut, her eyes clenched shut, Kathleen danced like a convulsion, like she was trying to throw up or shake her skin from her bones. Her face blared rage, disgust, baleful accusation. A ferocious scowl erased the arch from her eyebrows. During a two-bar break in "Double Dare Ya," her gaze darted to the right and her mouth froze into a sneer as she marched in place, getting into repugnant character for the next verse—

> *Don't you talk out of line*
> *Don't go speaking out of your turn*
> *Got to listen to what the fuckin' man says*

—before turning again into the infuriated, manic playground provocateuse of the chorus—

> *Double dare ya!*
> *Double dare ya!*
> *Double triple fuckin' triple fuckin' dare ya!*

—casting feminist self-assertion as something one might do to avoid being shamed by a cooler, tougher girl. This was how girls spurred each other in youth to take dangerous risks; in adolescence, Kathleen wagered, it might move girls to save their own lives.

Despite its power, the three-piece lineup was limited. Again, Tobi had someone in mind: her sometime Go Team–mate Billy Karren had just moved back to Olympia from San Francisco. The lanky, good-natured boy was, Tobi said, "the best guitarist I knew"; most of his friends were girls, and he identified as a feminist and a revolutionary. Bikini Kill, tired of auditioning guitarists, was ready to compromise on the initial idea of having an all-girl group. As soon as Billy plugged in and started filling in the gaps of what the girls had written, the whole sound fell into place. They had their band.

Throughout the spring of '91, Bikini Kill played shows in Olympia and around the Northwest, but they were perplexed at how few people seemed to recognize their greatness. "Nobody in Olympia gives a shit about us," Kathleen lamented in an interview that year. "There's like five or six girls who go to all of our shows and stand in the front and support us. Other people are pretty apathetic to us."

Sometimes the reactions went beyond indifference. Nobody talked smack directly to Kathleen, but things would get back to her. "Why is she dancing like that?" her friend Allison Wolfe heard someone say about Kathleen at a Bikini Kill show. "Does she have to pee?" One time, a guy Kathleen was friends with asked Billy what it was like to be in a band with a bunch of "militant feminists." Kathleen was devastated when Billy relayed the anecdote; she'd thought this other guy was supportive, she'd even trusted him a little, and behind her back he was turning her passion into a punch line. She found it harder and harder to talk to anyone: Even if they were nice to her face, they might turn right around and shit-talk her. She holed up in her apartment, seldom leaving except to go to band practice. There were a lot of band practices, anyway; since she and Kathi were both new to playing rock instruments, the band logged long stints in the practice space, rehearsing several days a week for two to four hours at a time.

Bikini Kill's big chance to get out of town was coming up. Tobi had struck up a friendship with the DC punk band Nation of Ulysses, who invited Bikini Kill to tour across the country with them in June. To Tobi, Nation of Ulysses represented the future of punk rock. "They were political aesthetically, in an art-theory kind of way," she said, "and I was really drawn to that. They had an agenda, and they were deliberately creating a mythology." Against the classic punk stance of blanket opposition—the all-encompassing nihilism of the Sex Pistols' Antichrist—this gang of lean, stylish boys, who wore tight high-water pants and played a jazz-inflected chaospunk, counterpoised a gleeful energy of youthfulness and action. "Their intention," read the band's zine, *Ulysses Speaks*, skating a slender line between earnestness and parody, "is against dissipation, and for focus, transforming a simple space simultaneously into the fallow field universe of pregnant possibility, and the lush ripened mango of violence and petulant behavior."

Punks had long called for smashing the state, but in a city where advocating statehood was a radical act, Nation of Ulysses festooned its stages with a DC flag, the red stars and red bars against a white background acquiring the celebratory, propagandistic starkness of Russian Constructivist poster art. The face in profile gazing strongly into the future, as the stripes radiated from his head like rays of a blood-dawn sun, belonged to the band's singer, Ian Svenonius, a hyperactive art-school dropout in modish suit and tie who fervently spat aphorisms as if he'd swallowed a Little Red Book, chased it with a little blue pill, and was experiencing a euphoric bout of reflux. In performance, he yowled and twitched, testified and reeled, and fell to the floor in spasms: preacher, prophet, nut.

The boys of Ulysses liked to proclaim that their city was on the verge of becoming a youth mecca—"like San Francisco in the '60s," Svenonius had predicted the previous year in *Sassy*, when the cool girls' magazine had crowned him 1990's Sassiest Boy in America. And the members of Bikini Kill were open to persuasion. When they left on tour in June, they were actively seeking a new home base for the coast-to-coast revolution they planned to start: It would be as irresistible as Ulysses' quasi-Pentecostalist quasi Futurism, yet grounded, too, in feminist theory and the realities of girls' lives. DC seemed to have the strongest claim on Bikini Kill's future, but they couldn't make any decisions until they had seen the city for themselves.

TWO

COME OUT AND PLAY WITH ME: BRATMOBILE BEGINS

The girl down the hall was just about the most terrifying girl Allison Wolfe had ever encountered. The fall 1989 semester at the University of Oregon hadn't even properly begun yet; the students had all just moved into the dorms, and everyone was trying to make a good impression on the people who would be their neighbors for the next nine months. Everyone, that is, except the girl down the hall. Apparently she didn't give a fuck. She was on the pay phone at the end of the corridor, screaming and crying and yelling at somebody—a boyfriend, maybe? Perhaps she *wanted* people to hear her. Allison watched the raging girl as long as she dared. "I was like, 'Who is that crazy girl?'" Allison said. "She just seemed like a force to be reckoned with."

The girl on the phone, Molly Neuman, was noticing Allison, too. "I was like, 'Who the fuck is that? What is that?'" Allison stood out from the other first-year students: In the sea of batik dresses and dreadlocks that tided around the college town of Eugene, Allison wore loud-print thrift-store dresses and plastic-frame glasses that took up half her face; her bangs were a thick slab on her forehead. Molly's style was more low-key cool: cutoffs layered over leggings and a wide cloth headband holding her hair back from her face.

The two lived next door to each other; they fell into a friendship easily. Allison, who had grown up in Olympia, introduced Molly to the lo-fi pop music of her beloved hometown bands: Spook and the Zombies, Oklahoma Scramble, and her favorite band on earth, Beat Happening. Molly had never heard music that sounded so easy to make, music that seemed to announce with every note, *You can do this too.* Growing up in and around DC, she'd had glancing interactions with punk but listened mostly to hip-hop and R&B. Rap was in its golden age: Public Enemy had recently hurled *It Takes a Nation of Millions to Hold Us Back* like a Molotov cocktail into the commons, and female rappers Roxanne Shanté and Queen Latifah had just released their debut albums, which did double duty as feminist communiqués.

Until this point, Allison had held feminism at arm's length. Raised by a lesbian activist mother who brought Allison to anti-nuke rallies and founded the first women's health clinic in the Olympia area, Allison's version of adolescent rebellion was to roll her eyes and declare the women's movement a stodgy, mom-ish, uncool relic. But Molly made feminism sound cool, even revolutionary. She had come to it by way of her passion for racial justice—her father worked for the Democratic National Committee, and through him she had met leaders of the Congressional Black Caucus whom she admired deeply. She devoured the writings of

Eldridge Cleaver, had an "epiphany-style experience" watching *Do the Right Thing*, and attended Huey Newton's funeral in South Oakland in August 1989, just before starting college. Her political world had been all about race, and examining her role as a white person in society, until a former art teacher of hers, a black man, had written a letter encouraging her to think about how being female affected her life too.

Molly and Allison became inseparable. Together they enrolled in women's studies courses and checked out meetings of campus activist groups, dissecting ideas and tactics. In many ways, they were an unlikely pair: Molly was occasionally emotive but she was just as likely to project an icy smoothness, leaving folks wondering what she was thinking. Allison had no patience for coolness or phoniness or social conventions. She also had no filters. But the combination worked. "Our union was really fierce," Molly said, "because we both had this sense of fearlessness." They started to look more like each other; Molly, despite her perfect vision, started wearing glasses. ("Fake glasses," she said, "like a goober.") Their classmates got them mixed up, occasionally calling one by the other's name. Lying in their respective beds at night, they would reach up and knock on the wall between their two rooms if they wanted to talk to each other, or just to know the other was there.

They set out to explore Eugene's music scene, but the options were slim: To see good shows, they had to leave town. Neither girl had a car, so they'd post their travel wishes on the campus ride board and give a couple bucks for gas to whatever student or local offered them a lift heading north—preferably to Olympia, three and a half hours away. They liked the way everything in Oly felt ad hoc, with bands forming and unforming freely among friends. Tobi had summed it up in *Jigsaw*: "A band is any song you ever played with anybody even if only once." Most shows took place in people's basements, or even in an alley downtown; a band might run an extension cord out of a store or just play an all-acoustic set. And Molly and Allison liked the way music there wasn't a specialized activity for a cadre of skilled initiates; it was a simple thing that anybody could do if she just put some guts into it. The two friends traveled to Oly as many weekends as they could during that first year of college, spending their days hanging out downtown, seeing bands for cheap or free every night at Reko Muse or at people's houses. It was heaven for people like them: girls who hadn't spent years noodling around on guitars in their bedrooms, who would rather see a tiny show and talk to the drummer afterward than get crushed in a mosh pit at some four-hundred-person venue with fancy lighting.

The more Molly and Allison went to Olympia, the more enmeshed they became in the scene there. They met Kathleen, who was playing in Viva Knievel at the time. They were in awe of her—"I'd never seen a girl scream like that," Allison said. They got a copy of *Jigsaw* from Tobi in January 1990, midway through their first year of college, at a show at Olympia's Grange Hall where the lineup was Beat Happening, Nirvana, and the beloved Melvins. These musicians knew their rock history, and they engaged it with irony and overstatement: Cobain drew fake track marks on his arms with stage blood that night (he hadn't tried heroin yet, but many people already took the sensitive, emaciated boy for a junkie), and the Melvins closed their set by singing Neil Young's "Rockin' in the Free World." These knowing nods to rock conventions might have alienated Molly and Allison, but *Jigsaw* was the antidote. Reading that zine, "I realized that there were [other] people with these ideas" about feminism and music, Molly said, "that Allison and I weren't the only people. Because in Eugene we *were* the only people."

Instead of just accepting Molly and Allison's compliments on her writing, Tobi asked them: Why don't *you* start a fanzine? Or a band, for that matter? She was giving the girls something she had always felt from her hometown scene, a mix of cheerleading and gauntlet throwing. "One of the best things to me, about growing up in Olympia and the underground thing here," Tobi wrote in *Jigsaw*,

```
is this whole true punk thing of making
up songs and just singing them for your
friends and how that happens at parties and
stuff—just the way that I've always felt
encouraged in this one way, that people do
want to hear what other people are doing
and encourage each other to participate and
that whole support thing.
```

"It was as simple as someone going, 'You should do a fanzine' or 'You should start a band,'" Molly said. "At that point it was like, 'Oh, okay, that's what we should do.'"

Molly and Allison wrote articles for their zine and interviewed bands from the Northwest throughout 1990. In the process they became ever more integrated into the Olympia scene—Allison started dating the singer of Spook and the Zombies, and Molly grew close with Calvin Johnson, who, in addition to playing in Beat Happening and the Go Team, ran Olympia's main indie label, K Records, together with his business partner, Candice Pedersen. Through Calvin, Molly suddenly found herself in the company of scene big shots, including Bruce Pavitt, who ran Sub Pop, and Cobain. "I was nervous," Molly said. "I was really into these bands and all of a sudden we're, like, in their apartments. That wasn't my understanding of how things worked yet. And all of a sudden that was my life."

By winter break of their sophomore year, the first issue of their zine, *Girl Germs*, was ready to go to press. Home in DC for vacation, Molly, who had worked for Representative Morris K. Udall of Arizona in high school, used her Capitol Hill access to get into his office, and on the copy machine there she ran off several hundred copies of the zine. A winter storm hit the city, and Molly was snowed in alone overnight in the deserted building. Munching on candy bars and potato chips to keep herself awake, and taking brief naps on the couch, she copied and collated all night. When she flew back to Oregon at the beginning of 1991, she had the first print run of *Girl Germs* #1 in her suitcase, ready to be given to Tobi and all the other punks of Oly who seemed to be waiting for Molly and Allison to step up, to do something.

Molly and Allison were also determined to start a band, although neither of them played any instruments or had ever written a song. Molly had started taking guitar lessons, and Allison learned to finger a couple chords, and they came up with a killer band name: Bratmobile. Molly and Allison had both seen the new Tim Burton–directed Batman movie, and Prince's "Batdance" was playing everywhere. They would be just like that superhero pair, only younger and female. And without a car: They still had to rely on the ride board for their travels.

Months into their band-life, the dynamic girl duo had written no songs. "We were a fake band," Allison confessed. "We were all talk." They had worked up a few a cappella numbers, covers of Beat Happening and Go Team songs, and started grabbing the mic between the sets of reggae bands at frat parties in Eugene. Partygoers mostly ignored them, when they weren't laughing at them outright. Molly later described their guerrilla performances as "ridiculous—things that two years later I would never do, once you get some sort of self-consciousness, but we just didn't have any."

Bratmobile might have stayed in fake-band limbo for a long time if nobody had cared enough to call their bluff. But that winter, Calvin phoned Molly and Allison and invited them to play a Valentine's Day show in Olympia. The bill would be Bratmobile, scene mainstays Some Velvet Sidewalk, and Bikini Kill.

At first the girls tried to get out of it. "We're not really in a band," they said.

"But you always *say* you're in a band," Calvin pointed out. The girls, cornered, said yes.

Several weeks later, they realized it was almost Valentine's Day and they still hadn't written any songs. Desperate for guidance, they approached Robert Christie, one of the only musicians Molly and Allison liked in Eugene. Clean-cut and generous, he had been a founding member of Some Velvet Sidewalk and now played in the Eugene band Oswald 5-0. Christie loaned Molly and Allison the keys to his practice space and offered to let them borrow all his gear, but the girls wanted concrete songwriting advice.

"Listen to Ramones records," he said. "You'll come up with something."

Molly and Allison had never listened to the Ramones. "Something in me clicked," Allison said. "Like, okay, if most boy punk rock bands just listen to the Ramones and that's how they write their songs, then we'll do the opposite and I won't listen to *any* Ramones, and that way we'll sound different."

By the day of the show they'd managed to write five songs. War had just broken out in the Persian Gulf, and the flyers for the Valentine's Day show at the North Shore Surf Club announced its theme as "Make Love Rock Not War." The first song Bratmobile played was minimal in the extreme: two chords on Molly's guitar, two notes in Allison's sung melody, repeat repeat repeat. Molly methodically switched her distortion pedal on and off, paralleling Allison's vocal toggle between sweet singsong and nasal whine. We might be tempted to read something into that duality: a band's attempt, perhaps, to find its own way through a musical landscape marked out on one side by the tunefully twee Beat Happening and on the other side by fuzzed-out grunge? An abstracted etude on rock structure? A comment on girl rockers' historical dialectic between naughty and nice? All these themes were audible in the song. Fundamentally, though, this was just a band learning to write songs for the first time and airing that process in public. Even if the two-piece configuration of Bratmobile wasn't quite working yet, it was good enough for Olympia, because it was a heartfelt contribution to the community.

In contrast to Bikini Kill's haunted, unhinged vision of childhood, Bratmobile's earliest songs heralded a carefree, guileless one: "Come out and play with me / Come tell me who you are / Come tell me who I am," Allison sang plainly, like an eight-year-old in music class. Lest anyone forget that these girls were barely out of childhood themselves, they proclaimed in another song: "I'm not aged to perfection / I'm not stuffed up with your fears . . . / I'm a teenager." The kiddie trope made another appearance in "Girl Germs," which announced, in a melody like a playground chant:

> You're too cozy in your all-boy clubhouse
> To even consider having Kool-Aid at my house
> Girl germs, no returns
> Can't hide out they're everywhere

There wasn't much to the show, but that was part of what would make Bratmobile matter to so many girls over the coming years: This band made having a band look easy, because what it was doing *was* easy. "Bikini Kill were starting around the same time," Molly said, "and it was like, *'Kathleen and Tobi are playing music together!'*— like they were mysterious. We weren't that mysterious. They were *so* fierce, and we were *so* dorky. And I think that was helpful in some sort of accessibility."

This was already starting to inspire Corin Tucker, a moon-faced Evergreen first-year from Eugene who had met Allison at a YMCA weekend encampment during high school and had stayed in touch with her. Corin was making a documentary about the Olympia scene for a school project, and she interviewed Molly and Allison on the edge of the North Shore's stage before they played. When Corin asked a question about grunge, Allison stuck her tongue way out. "Aaahhh. Vomit! It's vomit!" she ranted, giggling. Molly allowed evenly that she liked most of the bands on Sub Pop, even though there were hardly any female musicians in the bunch. But Allison, not to be reined in by manners or circumspection, continued her castigation of Seattle, calling it the "Sub Pop boy grunge grab-your-dick scene" and griping that it was all about "Samson with his long hair, and his strength through long hair, and whipping it and lashing it around in front. Sub Pop's shows are really gross, because the girls always get pushed to the back and it's all this sweaty long hair beer belly thing in front. Girls need to reclaim the scene for themselves."

After Bratmobile's last song, as the sound system switched over to an old cut of "My Funny Valentine," Pat Maley, a gentle man (and onetime bandmate of Lois Maffeo's) who tried to record all Olympia's short-lived bands before they dissolved, ran up to the stage and offered to record the duo for free—how about tomorrow? "I thought they were fun," he said. "They were spirited and funny and charismatic, and I liked their stage presence." And Slim Moon, a slender, mustached guy who did spoken word and played in the art-rock band Witchy Poo, told Molly and Allison he wanted to include "Girl Germs" on a compilation he was putting together. He was going to call the record *Kill Rock Stars*, and if it did well enough, maybe he'd keep putting out people's music. They recorded the song with Pat the next day. A few months later, Slim would end up releasing it on the promised comp—and starting a record label of the same name.

The Bikini Kill girls, for all their fierceness and mystery, cheered the new duo on. Tobi put a photo of Bratmobile on the cover of the next issue of *Jigsaw*, namechecked the band repeatedly, and devoted a whole page to Molly and Allison's zine, "the most exciting thing that has happened in the pacific northwest in years":

```
Girl Germs is what they made happen in re-
action to the male-based-ness of 'the scene'
you know, and well its so fucking neato
because in their attempt at becoming more
actively involved in stuff they came up
against some pretty solid boy barriers and
they have since left them shattered . . .
this is a part of their process of creating
their own turf and reclaiming the domain
of punk rock.
```

It made them proud to think of themselves as reclaiming that domain—especially since it was hard to imagine they could have much effect on the world at large. The United States had begun bombing Iraq in January. Protests took place in both of Molly and Allison's stomping grounds: Eugene's rallies struck Molly as ineffectual and anachronistic throwbacks to the Woodstock era, just a lot of out-of-touch hippies singing "give peace a chance." In Olympia, some campus activists trained community members in civil disobedience, to prepare people for more militant actions. But even though the Olympia activists' energy and creativity excited Molly—this scene was younger, more daring, closer in spirit to the Black Power movement that was so meaningful to her—there was no chance that these antiwar protests would make a difference. This was America's most popular military action in decades, and President Bush was untouchable, with approval ratings pushing 80 percent—the highest of his presidency. Allison, incensed about the bombing and its positive news coverage, made xeroxed stickers that said PROPAGANDA, and posted them on newspaper boxes all over Eugene. But overall, trying to oppose Operation Desert Storm in the midst of the sea of pro-war yellow ribbons was a disempowering, alienating experience. Molly and Allison went back to the project they had some control over: Bratmobile.

When spring break of their sophomore year came around, Molly and Allison flew east to DC. Molly's stepmother had just had a baby, so there was a new brother to meet, and DC offered a packed social agenda. Molly was learning that her hometown's punk scene had many close ties with Olympia's. Several key Olympians had lived in the DC area—including Calvin and Kathleen, who both attended high school in Maryland—and K Records had an anticorporate soulmate in DC's Dischord Records, the label founded in 1980 by three punk kids, including Ian MacKaye, who was then the singer for Minor Threat. By 1991, when Molly and Allison made their first joint trip to DC, MacKaye was the frontman of the wildly popular hardcore crossover band Fugazi, whose code of ethics stipulated no alcohol, no drugs, no meat, no band T-shirts or other consumerist merchandise, and no ticket prices over five dollars. He also continued to run Dischord, which was now among the most influential independent record labels in the country. If Dischord's DIY philosophy—it refused for years even to print barcodes on its albums' packaging—was akin to K's denunciation of "the corporate ogre," Dischord's angular hardcore aesthetic was worlds away from K's melodious, defiantly de-skilled, coed music. Despite these differences, K and Dischord had just teamed up (as DisKord) to release a 7" single by Nation of Ulysses.

Heading to DC, Molly and Allison were most excited about spending time with Erin Smith, a dark-haired teenage girl from suburban Maryland who made a fanzine about old TV shows, *Teenage Gang Debs*, with her older brother. Calvin had introduced Erin and Molly during winter break, at a Ulysses show in DC, and they had become pen pals. A devoted record collector from age eleven on, Erin had been so obsessed with K Records and Beat Happening during high school that by the first time she went to Olympia—on a college visit to Evergreen in May 1989, when she was in eleventh grade—people there already knew who she was. "I was kind of infamous," she said. "I had to be the best fan possible; it never occurred to me to be anything else." Creating, too, was important to her. She took guitar lessons and was developing a distinctive surf-guitar style. She had a hard time finding collaborators, though. She didn't know any other girls who played music, and the boys at her high school didn't take her seriously. When she tried out for the talent show playing her Capa Minstrel teardrop guitar—a more affordable copy of the classic Vox Mark VI that the Rolling Stones' Brian Jones had once played on *The Ed Sullivan Show*—or even just walked through the halls carrying it, boys asked her whose guitar it was, as if it couldn't possibly be hers. Guys would walk past her guitar lessons, admiring the vintage gear she had picked out so carefully, and say, "Do you even know what you have there?"

She later described her pre-Bratmobile existence as being "in my room playing my electric guitar to my Beat Happening records all by myself." But there was something generative in that: "I think that was a really important thing that fueled all of us, was this kind of isolation," she said. "And then to have to work to find each other."

Erin could play but needed a band. Molly and Allison had a band but needed another member, preferably a girl who knew how to play. Shortly before spring break in 1991, Molly sent Erin a postcard that read: "My stepmother's having a baby. Let's jam."

At this point Molly and Allison were thinking of Bratmobile as a loose-bordered organization of sorts, perhaps even a teen-girl-power empire with overlapping regional branches. An Olympia syndicate of Bratmobile existed, with the girls' friend Michelle Noel on

guitar; the group with Erin would be Bratmobile DC. These fran-
chises invariably existed in concept form first: The acts of imagin-
ing, naming, and even hyping a project were necessary first steps in
its process of creation.

Molly and Allison flew to DC in March, picked up Erin at her
parents' place in Bethesda ("I open the door," Erin said, "and Allison has her backwards baseball cap and tights and shorts, and
I was like, 'Whoa, who's this girl?' She was kind of wild."), and
drove straight to the Embassy, a group house in DC's Mount Pleasant neighborhood that was the headquarters of Nation of Ulysses
and home to a revolving cast of local punks. There was a practice
space and rudimentary recording studio in the basement, where
Erin sometimes jammed with Christina Billotte, a meticulous musician, slender and blonde and serious. Christina also played bass
and sang in Autoclave, one of the only all-female punk bands DC
had produced in many years. (Mary Timony, who would most famously front the spooky-pop group Helium in the mid-'90s, was
Autoclave's guitarist and other singer.) The plan had been for Molly
and Allison to sit in on a practice of the Erin-and-Christina project,
but Erin and the newcomers clicked with one another instantly.
"The way we just came together, it was like nothing was ever wrong
that anyone did," Erin said. Christina favored the pristine pop of
Blondie, but the others were all devoted to the same ramshackle K
cassettes. Erin started playing a guitar part she had written, Allison
came in with some vocals, and suddenly, almost effortlessly, they
had finished a whole song.

The thrill! It could happen! It didn't even have to be hard! The
universe was full of songs, just waiting for you to get some friends
together and write them. And then you weren't just a fan anymore;
you were a member of the fellowship of people who made things.

Beat Happening and Nation of Ulysses were touring the East
Coast together at the time, doing a run of shows with Autoclave

that very week. The Bratmobile girls saw their friends play in DC and then, borrowing Molly's father's car on the pretense of taking a short trip to Baltimore, they drove five and a half hours to Bard College, north of New York City, to see the bands again. The concert began at midnight and didn't wrap up till well after 2 A.M.; Allison and Christina slept over at the college, but Molly and Erin drove back to DC in the wee hours so Molly could put in an appearance at her family's house.

The next evening, Molly and Erin turned right around and drove, on almost no sleep, back up to see Ulysses, Beat Happening, and Autoclave play at Maxwell's in Hoboken, New Jersey. In a fit of new-friend infatuation, DIY confidence, and a sleepless taste for adventure, the members of the newly minted Bratmobile DC decided they should perform their new song, "Stab," before Ulysses' set.

The other bands were completely supportive. "They were just like, 'Of *course* you're going to play our guitars,'" Erin said. So Molly, Allison, and Erin, along with Christina, grabbed their loaner instruments and got onstage to play their first show as a full band. Over a single furious chord and a relentless drumbeat, Allison sang, "You know where I've been, you want to stick it in, you want to tie me up." Then she screamed, "You fucked me up!" and launched into the chorus:

> *You want to stab me*
> *And fuck the wounds*
> *Stab me*
> *And fuck the wounds*

The band alternated the verses and choruses a few times, relishing the rush of being onstage in front of a real audience! Of strangers! Suddenly they looked at each other, realizing that they had never written an ending to their song. Having plunged into their performance without hesitation, they had no idea how to get out of it. Somehow they crash-landed "Stab" and left the stage. Some audience members must have been saying, as people so often said about Allison, with her funny clothes and fearless demeanor, "What *is* that?!" But the girls couldn't hear it. The cheers of their friends, their fellowship of people who made things, drowned it out completely.

The rest of the week in DC was a whirlwind. The girls practiced three more times and wrote five more songs; they played a show at a Salvadoran restaurant in the suburbs with MacKaye's sister Amanda's band, Desiderata; and they recorded their new compositions in the Embassy's basement studio with Tim Green, a recording engineer who was also the guitarist in Nation of Ulysses. One of Bratmobile's best new songs was "Cool Schmool," which opened with the singsong taunt: "We're so cool, yeah yeah / Fuck you, too! Cool schmool!" Over a bed of pure, sparse surf rock, Allison declaimed the verses in a cheerleader's *sprechtstimme*, snotty and withering. The chorus had almost no vocals at all, just a couple rich, open guitar chords that rang out warmly compared with the brittle staccato Erin played on the verses, and then the pithy takedown again—"Cool schmool!"— twice as terse as X-Ray Spex' "Oh bondage, up yours," and more carelessly dismissive.

The songs Bratmobile had unveiled at their first real show, back in Olympia on Valentine's Day, had protested against a general condition of phoniness and exclusion, and "Cool Schmool" continued this theme, but with more specificity. In addition to delivering another shot to the heart of social fakery ("I don't want you always telling me what's so cool about what I'm wearing / When you can't even tell me how you feel and you can't even be my friend for real"), the song also took aim at the Northwest punk orthodoxy in particular ("I don't wanna sit around and talk about the Wipers / Weren't those the good old days"), mocked the do-you-like-the-right-bands olympics ("I hate dogs so I love cats"), and skewered two traditional options for girls in punk:

> *I just wanna be one of the boys*
> *I just wanna be your little fashion toy*

Of course, this wasn't entirely fair. The poles Allison named, for all their magnetic force, had never been girls' only options in Oly or DC. But a more nuanced critique wouldn't fit into a two-minute song. With "Fuck you, too! Cool schmool!" the band had found its strategy: profane ridicule.

The end of spring break came too soon, but the girls were already thinking ahead. "We were like, wow, this is a really great time," Molly said a few months later. "What do you think could happen—this is what everybody was thinking—what do you think could happen if we had more than a week?" They decided to find out. Allison and Molly resolved to spend the summer in DC; back on the West Coast, Molly mentioned the plan to Bikini Kill and added, You all should come too. Bikini Kill had already booked a tour with Ulysses for most of June, which would end in DC, and they were considering moving there permanently. Sure, they could stick around for the summer.

And so it was set: The revolution girl style now, Northwest branch, was coming to take over the nation's capital.

The DC punk scene was way overdue for a girl revolution. Some of the city's punks were dimly aware of this, but Jen Smith, a scene denizen and University of Maryland student who lived at the Embassy, found it suddenly at the forefront of her mind. Jen wasn't related to Erin, despite their shared last name. But after spending a week with her and Allison and Molly, she felt like they were family. She had jammed with Bratmobile once during that week, and played a few songs with them at the show with Desiderata. Once Molly and Allison had left town, she was left to ponder how almost all the prominent people in the scene, nearly everyone who had a band or ran a label, were boys.

Here was the lineup: Ian MacKaye, who ran Dischord, and his all-male bandmates in Fugazi. Ian Svenonius and *his* all-male bandmates in Ulysses. Mark Andersen, who helmed the punk activist group Positive Force. Geoff Turner, who ran the WGNS cassette label. Mark Robinson, who had just started the Teenbeat Records label. Skip Goff, the owner of Silver Spring's famed record store Yesterday & Today. The list went on and on.

There *were* several legendary women in the city's punk history. People still talked about Fire Party, a beloved all-girl band from the late '80s. Most punks owned *Banned in DC*, a book of photos from the scene's early years, which had been compiled by female scene stalwarts Sharon Cheslow, Leslie Clague, and Cynthia Connolly. And even people who'd spent the age of New Wave in grade school had at least heard of Cheslow's band Chalk Circle, the scene's first all-girl group. "It was kinda hard being girls," Cheslow said in 1982. "But look, if men can do it, so can women, and we said, 'Who cares? We're gonna do it.'"

"We want to be taken seriously," her bandmate Mary Green pleaded in the same interview. "We want to be taken for people."

Yet throughout the '80s, any woman who played music was considered a curiosity. "People would be like, 'I'm going to see this band, and they have a *girl* bassist,'" MacKaye said. Women more often held support roles, taking photos or booking shows. When Bikini Kill and Bratmobile decided to spend their summer in DC, Connolly was booking shows at dc space, and Amy Pickering, formerly of Fire Party, was working at Dischord after having spent several years in the late '80s booking at the 9:30 Club. But very few women had places out front. Jawbox's bassist, Kim Coletta, and the drummer of the Holy Rollers, Maria Jones, were the exceptions, along with Autoclave, the city's one all-girl band at the time, which would soon break up without releasing a full-length album. And that was about it. Yes, there were women in the scene, but, as Jen put it, "The *personalities* were boys."

Through living at the Embassy, she was intimately acquainted with the scene's boyocracy. The boys jammed with one another in the house's basement, in rotating but usually all-boy lineups; they danced up front at shows. At one of the first parties Jen attended in DC, she walked into a room and saw a bunch of people standing in a circle, having a dance-off with each other. The dancers were boys, every one of them, all with the same long lanky limbs and short skinny pants and dyed-black hair ranging from military short to greasy bouffant, all dancing with the same twitchy moves. It wasn't hateful or mean; Jen could just tell she didn't belong. As she became closer friends with people in the scene, this sense of not belonging faded somewhat. "Connecting with the whole DIY aesthetic was a total revelation for me," she said. Still, Bratmobile's visit made her wonder: Why weren't girls more visible in DC? Would the summer change this for the better?

Her ideas about girl revolution got a jolt that spring from a real-life urban uprising. On May 5, 1991, four blocks from the Embassy, a Salvadoran immigrant was shot and critically injured by a police officer. He had been drinking with his buddies in a small park, and police said he had lunged at an officer with a knife. Rumors quickly spread through the neighborhood, though, that he had been shot while handcuffed; many believed he had died. People were already out in groups around the neighborhood, celebrating Cinco de Mayo, and they began to gather at the scene. A bystander threw a bottle at a cop, a crowd roared its approval, and by nightfall Mount Pleasant had hit flashover. As many as six hundred people took to the streets, throwing bricks and bottles at police, then racing in packs through alleys to outrun their pursuers. Sirens and angry shouts of "*Justicia!*" cut through the night. Squad cars burned out of control; the police threw tear gas canisters that hissed out their acrid clouds, sending plumes across Sixteenth Street. Officers in helmets and gas masks were beat back by the rioters.

An early morning rain finally quelled the crowds, but the following evening the unrest started up again. Stores were smashed and looted; a Dumpster was dragged into the middle of Kilbourne Place and set ablaze. Many Mount Pleasant punks, including several of Jen's housemates, went up to watch and even join in. One of her friends later boasted that he had cut his hand while throwing a rock at a cop car. But Jen stayed home, watching the melee on the news and listening to the helicopter that hung like a stuck clock pendulum over the neighborhood. It wasn't that the riots scared her; they just didn't feel like her fight. "I felt like, as a white person from a middle-class background, for me to go up there and participate was like me being a cultural interloper," she said. "I feel anger about the police state too, but it was another community's tension."

At the same time, all that anger and disaffection made an impact on her. The riots burrowed into Jen's unconscious and resurfaced a few days later, as she was walking along Park Road to her job at a health-food store across the street from the National Zoo. She used to make up little songs as she walked to work and home again. "Girl riot," she sang to herself one day in May. "Girl riot, not gonna be quiet." By the end of that month, the Supreme Court would uphold a regulation widely known as the gag rule, banning federally funded clinics from discussing abortion. Girl riot, not gonna be quiet.

Jen wrote a letter to Allison with a line like "This summer's gonna be a girl riot" or "We need a girl riot" or "I want a girl riot." Years later, she wouldn't remember the exact sentence, the letter would be long gone, and nobody's memories would quite line up. Like the first bottle thrown in Mount Pleasant, immediately lost among the thousands of projectiles that followed, Jen's utterance blurred into everything that would come next: its specificity dissolved, its power only magnified.

THREE

REVOLUTION
SUMMER GIRL
STYLE NOW

Kathleen turned toward the back of the stage at dc space and pulled off her T-shirt in a deliberate, prosaic motion. Bikini Kill had played its first few songs fully clothed, but now, wearing just a skirt and a scalloped black bra, Kathleen turned to face the audience so everyone could see what was written on her stomach: SLUT.

She'd begun doing this at shows in recent months, confronting audiences with what they might want to see (a topless woman) and what they might think of such a woman, all in one fell semiotic swoop. As if nothing had happened, Tobi started up the drumbeat for the next song, and then everything kicked in, a frantic, conflicted song about craving trashy pleasures whatever the cost:

I wanna go to the carnival
But I know that it costs fifteen dollars now . . .
I'll win that Mötley Crüe mirror
If it fucking kills me

June 27, 1991: This was the final show of Bikini Kill's cross-country tour with Nation of Ulysses, and the Olympia band's first show in Washington, DC. Buzz about Bikini Kill had preceded the band to the city, and the room was packed, the air jittery with excitement.

Nothing on tour had prepared them for the response they got in DC. The people in the audience, male and female alike, were dancing like mad for a band they had never seen before, cheering and whistling after every song. When Kathleen announced, "This is our last song," people cried out, "No!" and "More!" As soon as the set ended, people rushed the stage.

Kathleen was thrown off balance: "I thought they were just trying to pull me away from the crowd so they could kill me or something!" she said that summer. "People usually aren't that nice."

"I was totally awestruck," said Kristin Thomson, who had recently founded a record label, Simple Machines, with her friend Jenny Toomey. "I was completely enthralled by the band, especially Kathleen, who could deliver songs with such emotion, yet be concerned that the girls had room up front. It was really inspiring."

"They were *incredible*," Ian MacKaye said. "I was completely blown away by them." He offered to record them for free at Inner Ear studios; he just knew in his gut this band needed to be heard. The session they did at Inner Ear that week only confirmed his feeling. "Kathleen was really—she was dialing it in from somewhere else, like high up," he said. Some of the tracks, including "Feels Blind," would be released on a self-titled EP in late 1992.

Even people who weren't at the show heard about it nonstop

for weeks. "It was almost like an earthquake, the reverberations that went out through the scene," said Positive Force's Mark Andersen, who skipped the show and actually teared up years later at the thought of how much he regretted missing it.

Piggybacking on Ulysses' itinerary had let Bikini Kill play bigger shows at better venues than it would have been able to get for itself—with no releases other than an eight-song demo cassette titled *Revolution Girl Style Now*—on this, the band's first trip off the West Coast. But most of the audience members had been there to see Ulysses and hadn't known what to make of Bikini Kill. "People fucking *hated* us!" Kathleen said. "The total indie hipster people were like 'Fuck you' to us." In Olympia, too, people outside the band's inner circle had never seemed to *get* Bikini Kill. But the group had touched a power chord in the heart of DC. Maybe it was because their hard-edged roar of old-school punk went over better in Dischord's hometown than in Olympia's la-la land of love rock. Maybe it was because DC had always loved political bands, from Bad Brains to Fugazi. Maybe the scene was just starved for a band with some girls in it.

Despite their royal reception, the members of Bikini Kill weren't certain that the city could ever feel like home. For starters, the DC area was much richer than Olympia. While most Oly punks had gone to Evergreen—public, inexpensive, experimental—DC's punks had attended some of the country's best public and private high schools. In the place of Olympia's de-skilled musical collectives, DC grew polished bands from teens who had taken piano lessons in elementary school or received electric guitars as birthday presents before their small fingers could even press down a barre chord.

The city of DC itself was mostly black and mostly poor, with an overwhelmingly white professional class that commuted from the suburbs and a Congress that ran the company town, surveying its swampy demesne from a comfortable outpost on the Hill. Many punks hailed from suburban enclaves, but when they went to shows downtown, the discrepancies glowered unignorably, in the boarded-up storefronts and the blanket-wrapped bodies sleeping on sidewalks. In 1991, the city's murder rate hit its all-time high; fueled by a crack epidemic, killings had more than doubled in the past four years. With so many rebellious youth confused by their own privilege and seeking to expiate it, the DC scene wore a cape of scrappy altruism; many punk shows, for example, were benefits for organizations serving the city's needy. But the members of Bikini Kill couldn't afford to play benefits; they needed to earn money from their shows. Tobi was sharing a room with Ian Svenonius at Pirate House and snacking on crudités backstage at other people's gigs. In order to afford a room of her own in a group house near the Embassy, Kathleen picked up shifts dancing at the Royal Palace, a strip club just north of Dupont Circle.

Aside from the money issue, Bikini Kill and Bratmobile both appreciated the DC scene's activist orientation. In Olympia, activism often meant things like environmentalists teetering meters above the ground in the canopies of ancient redwoods. Punk politics there most commonly consisted of critiquing "the corporate ogre"—i.e., major record labels and other forms of mass culture—and tailoring one's consumption habits accordingly, but making overtly political music was frowned on. Despite the antiwar protests that winter, the main connection to national politics came through regional environmental issues, such as saving the spotted owl; aside from that, protesting about national matters felt futile so far away from Bush and Quayle. In DC, on the other hand, national marches regularly flooded the Mall, and the proximity of the White House provided an accessible emblem of power: Protest felt relevant.

The hardest thing to get used to about DC was the fact that girls didn't rule the town. But the newcomers weren't sure, at first, what they should do about it. With Kathi Wilcox leaving on a monthlong backpacking trip through Europe, Bikini Kill couldn't play any shows for a while. Bratmobile DC was temporarily stymied as well: Erin Smith had gone to New York to intern at *Sassy* for the month of June.

This summer was supposed to be historic. A girl riot had been prophesied. Sharon Cheslow, one of the grandes dames of DC punk, had just come back to town after several years in San Francisco; she'd met Kathleen at a Bikini Kill show out West and felt that something huge was about to happen in DC, that a group of women were stepping up and just might be taking over. The girls needed to prove her right. This window of time, free of obligations, was their chance to fashion—out of nearly nothing but friendship, noise, and restlessly majestic vision—a new era.

Summer already occupied a special place in DC punk mythology. The scene's previous golden age, in 1985, was what Fire Party's Amy Pickering had then dubbed Revolution Summer, a storied period of scene unity and creative ferment. Six years later, people could still be heard invoking the Revolution Summer spirit. Naming it, proclaming it to be something special, had *made* it special—a footnote, maybe, to Freedom Summer, the Summer of Love, and the many long hot summers of urban agitation. A single season could change the course of history. Even with the bands temporarily out of commission, this was going to have to be Revolution Summer Girl Style Now.

The summer was already fun; nobody had to work to make sure of that. Most of the West Coast visitors hung out nonstop with the Ulysses boys. It was like being on tour, only without the playing shows every night part or the getting in the van and driving several hundred miles part, which left just the getting pizza and making up jokes and talking about art and listening to records parts.

To Molly and Allison, being in DC with so many of their friends after two years of exile in Eugene—and the promise of finally having regular band practices with Erin, once she came back from New York at the end of June—was pure joy. Tobi, too, felt like she'd found heaven. The frustration she felt at the scene's lopsided gender ratio was outweighed by how fantastic so many of these boys were. "I felt like I had peers for the first time in my life," she said. "We were all really interested in culture, politics, and creating. I would just hang out in people's rooms for hours studying their record collections. It was a constantly rewarding, invigorating exchange of ideas and music." Svenonius turned her on to Dick Hebdige's *Subculture: The Politics of Style*, a foundational work of cultural studies that analyzed punk and mod fashions in late-'70s Britain as expressions of political disaffection. To Hebdige, mod style had been a form of protest for working-class youth, and Tobi saw potential parallels with the Revolution Girl Style Now. Madonna had gotten millions of girls to wear lacy gloves and crucifixes. What if Bikini Kill could launch a similar craze, but with an explicitly political message—a look that communicated not "I'm a fan of this musician" but "I'm a revolutionary feminist and I won't rest until sexism is obliterated"?

Kathleen kept thinking about how to spread the word through music. With Bikini Kill on its brief break, she started two new projects—the Wonder Twins, a duo with Ulysses' Tim Green; and Suture, a band with Cheslow and Dug Birdzell, who'd played in the '80s DC punk bands Beefeater and Fidelity Jones.

One night in early July, Allison, Molly, Kathleen, and Jen Smith went to Molly's dad's office on Capitol Hill and ran off copies of a new minizine they had just made. They had decided to put out one issue per week for the rest of the summer, so they'd have something to pass out at shows, a way to make connections with other girls who lived in DC. They named the zine *Riot Grrrl*: a blend of Jen's "girl riot" and the growling "grrrl" spelling that Tobi had recently made up as a jokey variation on all the tortured spellings of "womyn/womon/

wimmin" feminists liked to experiment with. ("Angry grrrl zine," she had written on the cover of *Jigsaw* #3.) A riot grrrl was a revolutionary update of a *Teen* or a *Young Miss* or a *Mademoiselle*: The new zine's title created its audience of girls by naming them, radicalized them by addressing them as already radical.

Riot Grrrl #1 was printed on a single sheet of paper folded into quarters, both sides crammed with the blowsy, uneven letters of a manual typewriter. The front cover image showed Madonna proudly punching the air above her head, surrounded by handwritten "XO"s; on the back cover, the logo of Utz potato chips—a mischievous-looking girl dipping her hand into a bag—had been altered to read "slutz."

The zine decried "the general lack of girl power in society as a whole, and in the punk rock underground specifically" and explained how to give a cop car a flat tire and how to rig postage stamps so they could be reused. One page announced Bratmobile's plans for the summer (concerts, an appearance on Erin's brother Don Smith's college radio show), another listed Bikini Kill's (recordings, an appearance on Don Smith's radio show), a third listed some angry grrrl zine addresses (*Girl Germs, Jigsaw, Chainsaw, Teenage Gang Debs*, and a couple others), and a half-panel piece proclaimed, "Clarence Thomas is not your friend." (President Bush had announced his Supreme Court choice on July 1; Anita Hill's allegations wouldn't come out for several months, but activists who knew of his opposition to affirmative action were already vowing to bring him down.)

The girls handed out the zine at a barbecue in Erin's parents' backyard on the Fourth of July. The Ulysses boys were there in force, throwing fireworks around, and Bratmobile DC played its first show of the summer, with Allison on vocals, Erin on guitar, and Molly and Christina Billotte switching off between guitar and drums. (Jen sang one song with them, almost frozen with stage fright, and decided she was done with music for a while.) The group had had almost no time to practice since Erin's return from New York, and they played a sloppy, seat-of-their-pants set. Allison liked it that way. "I think it's important to show people that these structures onstage can totally be broken down," she told Andersen in an interview that summer. "I'm not trying to play bad music, but who's saying it's bad?" Molly was committed to becoming a strong drummer, but she was comfortable with letting people see her learning process. "I think it's really good for bands to go out when they're not ready," she said during the same interview. "Because then, as you do get a grasp on your instruments, people see you in a continuum, as opposed to just you jumped out of nowhere, which is what I always thought: The boy comes out of the womb with a screaming Led Zeppelin guitar, and I feel like I'll never know how to do that." Christina was farther along on that continuum; she and her bandmates in Autoclave were all experienced musicians. She seemed annoyed after Bratmobile DC's set, left the barbecue early, and promptly went out of town, even though the band was already booked to play a free outdoor show at Fort Reno Park a week later.

Bratmobile DC began its next practice in the Embassy basement freaking out over what to do now that Christina was gone. The band needed to find another guitarist *and* another drummer, or maybe a guitarist-drummer, to play her parts. Bikini Kill's Billy Karren was upstairs, and the girls called him down to play with them. "I'm a terrible drummer," he protested, and proceeded to play so badly that Allison suspected he was screwing up on purpose. Then he announced he was going back upstairs to make a sandwich, leaving Bratmobile alone in the basement to spin straw into gold. Or at least into something interesting.

Christina got back into town the day before the show and didn't mention the band at all. Everybody understood, without having to say anything, that Bratmobile was now a trio. Over dinner at a friend's house the next evening, someone said, "Aren't you guys playing a show tonight?" Christina demurred: "I don't know . . ." And Allison echoed: "I don't know . . ." Just a few years earlier, DC's high standards had forced the all-girl Fire Party to incubate for six obsessive months before setting foot on a stage. Now, Bratmobile's insistence on their right to play a sloppy show, as long as they had something to say and their energy ran pure, was changing the game.

At the Fort Reno show, they handed out the second issue of *Riot Grrrl*, which had taken shape in a week. Its cover image showed a woman, apparently clipped out of a comic book, charging toward the viewer. Sashed with an ammo belt, she wore a short skirt and brandished an assault rifle.

The zine had doubled in length, to eight quarter-sheet pages. Half of these were taken up by Tobi's scene report, "riot grrrl dc/olympia news," which touted the fast-approaching International Pop Underground Convention, a K Records–sponsored music festival that would take place in Olympia in August; an upcoming show at "Molly's parents' house" (no address given); and a Friday night dance party to be held at a Mount Pleasant group house near the Embassy, identified here by both the address (1830 Irving Street) and the designation "way cool riot girlHQers0069."

The issue's centerfold, reprinted from that winter's *Bikini Kill* zine, was a two-page list of instructions written by Kathleen that

riot grrrl
a free weekly mini-zine.

please read and dis-tribute to your

could perhaps be read as her reminders to herself. Its exhortations
included:

> Recognize that you are not the center of
> the universe.
>
> Figure out how the idea of winning and
> losing fits into your relationships.
>
> Be as vulnerable as you possibly can.
>
> Recognize vulnerability and empathy as
> strengths.
>
> Don't allow the fact that other people
> have been assholes to you make you into a
> bitter and abusive person.
>
> Commit to the revolution as a method of
> psychological and physical survival.

By all accounts, she was taking the last of these imperatives
extremely seriously. She struck everyone around her as unusually
solemn and intense. She didn't seem to allow herself any time-outs;
even while watching television, she was likely to speak up with a
critical takedown of the television show's sexual politics. And she
hardly ever hung out on the living room couches at the Embassy
with her bandmates and friends. She was too busy strategizing
about how to launch a feminist revival that could save all the girls
she met on tour, along with all the girls who weren't plugged in
enough to even come to a show.

Kathleen thought a collectively produced magazine might be the
way to go: a younger, hipper remake of the *Ms.* magazines she had
read when she was growing up. But who would join such a collective,
other than the few women she already knew in town? Meeting other
girls wasn't easy: Most DC punks had known one another since high
school or earlier, and could be slow to embrace outsiders.

On the back cover of *Riot Grrrl* #2: "We don't know all that many angry grrrls, although we know you are out there." The angry grrrls were, in fact, out there. But many of them didn't feel much need for making common cause with temporary transplants. They had come to terms enough with the scene's gender dynamics to stick around, and though they knew there was room for improvement, many bristled at the interlopers' attitudes. "It was jolting to have a group of people move there and speak in directives," Melissa Klein, another resident of the Embassy, said.

Kathleen heard the complaints. "That's one of the critiques I've gotten since putting out *Riot Grrrl*," she said that summer. " 'Oh, that's easy for her to say, she's just going to pick up and leave.' " But she insisted, "I'm not gonna let something like not knowing where I'm gonna live next month make me someone who has to stay silent. Just because I'm visiting doesn't mean I'm going to stop being a revolutionary."

As a matter of fact, she was going to step it up. In the time-honored tradition of revolutionaries everywhere, Kathleen decided to call a meeting. "It was like, 'God, if we're thinking of actually moving here, I want to know if there'll be women to do things with—not just our band and Bratmobile,' " she explained. "We can't work in a vacuum."

She didn't want to hold the meeting at the Embassy or any of the other Mount Pleasant group houses of DC's hipster-punk demimonde. She had her sights set on the Positive Force House, a big, homely yellow wood-frame building—more evocative of a Midwestern grange hall than a suburban abode—in Arlington, Virginia, just across the Potomac River from DC. It was the headquarters of Positive Force, a six-year-old activist group that channeled young punks' idealism and anger into activism and community service. The Embassy denizens fused Situationism and Futurism into agitated manifestos, but during the antiapartheid struggles of the mid-'80s, it was Positive Force that had organized punks to protest outside the South African embassy by banging on drums and ten-gallon buckets. Ulysses had its DC flag and the hometown-pride anthem "You're My Miss Washington, D.C.," but it was Positive Force that set up benefit shows for local organizations such as the Washington Free Clinic and the Washington Peace Center, Positive Force that arranged for punk kids to work volunteer shifts at a homeless shelter and to deliver food to low-income senior citizens, Positive Force that held well-publicized weekly meetings that were open to all comers.

When Kathleen learned about the group, she was impressed and grateful. She felt like much of the groundwork for what she wanted to build was already in place. "In Olympia it felt a lot more politically isolated," she said that summer. "Music everywhere, but talking about politics and stuff, no. I felt like, oh, I have to set up my own thing. And it's already set up here." Plus, Positive Force, by being headquartered in middlebrow Arlington, was separate both from in-crowd Mount Pleasant and from the private-school geographies of Maryland's Montgomery County and DC's Upper Northwest. Neither too cool nor too rich, and easy to reach by Metro, Arlington was relatively neutral ground.

So one weekend, Kathleen went to a Positive Force meeting in the house's front yard to propose her idea. High school boys in wire-rimmed glasses and army shorts, teenage girls in Birkenstocks and band T-shirts, and politics majors on summer break from the city's universities were clustered on the patchy grass, taking turns talking and volunteering to make a flyer for a benefit show or to research area food banks. Andersen, one of the group's founders and practically its patriarch at age thirty-one, gently nudged things along when necessary, but stepped back as much as possible, to let the younger kids run things themselves.

One of the teenage girls at the meeting was seventeen-year-old Ananda La Vita, a passionate activist who had run the animal rights club at her high school and was living at Positive Force for the summer to escape the pitched battles between her mother and stepfather. Erika Reinstein was another teen habituée of the group; assertive and garrulous, she was often the one to go onstage at benefits and explain that there was to be no smoking, no drinking, and no fighting at the show, and that everybody should make sure to check out the literature table at the back.

"I'd like to hold a meeting here," Kathleen told the gathered idealists. "It would be for girls only, to talk about teaching each other how to play instruments."

Later, Ananda would wonder whether Kathleen had downplayed the meeting's agenda on purpose, to keep the boys of Positive Force, aspiring revolutionaries themselves, from clamoring to be allowed in. Kathleen actually wasn't sure what her agenda was. It would depend on who showed up and what they wanted to do. Maybe her magazine idea would materialize, maybe a music-lessons exchange or a show-booking collective, maybe something else. Girls would get together in one room to figure it out.

Permission granted, she printed a notice announcing the meeting in the third issue of *Riot Grrrl*. She got onstage at several rock shows to invite all the girls and women in the room; she and Allison walked around with a clipboard asking girls directly if

> An all girl meeting to discuss the status of punk rock and revolution will be held at 7pm on Wed. July 24th at "The Positive Force" house. We'll be talking about ways to encourage higher female scene input + ways to help each other learn to play instruments + get stuff done.
>
> Call 202-232-0776 for directions and ask for Kathleen, Jen OR Christina.♥

they were interested, and wrote down phone numbers so she could call to remind them to come.

The first Riot Grrrl meeting—as it would retroactively become known—began a little after 7:30 P.M. on Wednesday, July 24, 1991. The marigold evening air was finally cooling off a bit; it had been a blisteringly hot week, with the temperature topping one hundred for several days, but on Wednesday the mercury stopped at ninety-three. For someone looking for signs that girls needed a revolution, that day's *Washington Post* offered ample evidence: Three more women had come forward to talk about having been sexually attacked by William Kennedy Smith, who was already facing rape charges in Florida; New York City police had arrested a man for raping his three-year-old niece in a Manhattan park in broad daylight; and the federal government had canceled a nationwide study of teenagers' sexual activity, even as HIV rates among teens were rising.

Twenty or so people attended the meeting, which felt like "an overwhelming response," Kathleen said later, considering that the information had been passed around by flyers and word of mouth. Positive Force's small second-floor living room was jammed full. Ananda and Erika were there, along with other Positive Force members, a contingent of Mount Pleasant punks, and Molly, Allison, Tobi, and Kathleen representing for the Northwest carpetbagger crew.

They started off with a go-round. It took hours for each person to say what she had come for and what she wanted to get out of the meeting. Some were seeking community with other female musicians or artists, some wanted to organize shows, but the biggest appetite was simply for talking and listening—especially among the younger girls, girls who went to shows with a handful of friends from high school or Positive Force but might not have known anyone else there. These girls had never been invited to discuss and dissect the way they experienced the world as girls, and they were stunned at what came pouring out. "It wasn't until the option was in front of me that I realized how much I needed it," Ananda said.

A second meeting took place the following week, and it was mostly the teenagers who came back, suddenly aware that they were desperate to find a community of girls to help them make it through late adolescence unmaimed. They were stuck in that aggravating period of time when girls get hit from all sides, belittled as children *and* sexualized as women. They needed safety and support; they needed one another.

Right after that second meeting, Kathleen, Molly, and Allison sat down for an interview with Andersen. He was writing, very slowly, a comprehensive history of DC punk (to be published in 2001 as *Dance of Days*), and he wanted to hear more about this fledgling feminist movement that struck him as possibly being the epitome of everything he loved about punk: politics, community, marginalized people making noise.

The four of them talked for nearly two hours. Allison spoke about the word *girl* and how academic women's studies rhetoric "alienate[s] teenage and younger and prepubescent girls. And it alienates punkers, I think." Molly reflected on the place of activism in her life: "Revolution is kind of my spirituality," she said. "I've come to understand that this is what I rest my head on."

Kathleen was most eager to discuss what the meetings might grow into. "Even though we haven't had an official objective or any kind of real strategy or plans, just to hear them talk and see how kind of relieved they are to hear each other speak, it's so great. It makes me kind of like, God, I wish I could really start to DO—I wish I could stay with these girls. But I'm convinced that there's these girls everywhere, and these girls everywhere really need to have some kind of—" She broke off, realizing how grandiose she sounded. "And I'm not a crusader," she finished, convincing nobody.

Near the end of the conversation, Kathleen offered the closest she ever came to a vision statement. Despite having been a main instigator of Riot Grrrl, she was never technically its leader; she would dodge that designation many times over the coming years. And to whatever extent the thing that grew out of these meetings could be considered a movement, it was something a bit different from what she put forward that evening in July. Still, it's a window into what she was thinking.

"I've had so many people come to me with stories of sexual abuse and being battered by their parents," she said. "People talking about sexual abuse and getting beat up and emotional abuse in their houses is so important, and making bands around that issue is, to me, the new punk rock—can be the new punk rock. And I want to encourage people—"

"To break their silence?" Andersen suggested.

"Yeah, to break their silence," Kathleen allowed. She went on: "I'm really interested in a punk rock movement—an angry girl movement—of sexual abuse survivors. . . . I seriously believe it's the majority of people in this country have stories to tell that they aren't telling for some reason. I mean, with all of that energy and anger, if we could unify it in some way—"

She trailed off. Her voice had been the loudest voice on the tape during the whole interview, but now it diminished to a whisper. It's easy to imagine her looking down at her hands, overcome with the intensity of her vision.

The girls at the meetings *were* beginning to unify their energy and anger. Teenage girls from the suburbs like Ananda, whose stepfather screamed at her and her mother when he got drunk, and sometimes kicked them out of the house, and Erika, who was wrestling with memories of sexual abuse, knew right away that this group was exactly what they needed. Kathleen "didn't have to do much at all,"

Ananda said. "It was just a matter of calling this meeting, and then those of us who were into it, were *really* into it. I was, like, *so ready*. It was what I was waiting for."

Riot Grrrl would later be spoken of as girls challenging sexism within punk. The DC girls did have complaints about punk, but all boiling down to this: In a subculture that congratulated itself for presenting an alternative, in a realm that should have been a refuge, they found more of the same crap. Boys' efforts were lauded and girls' were unrecognized. Objectification and sexual assault went unaddressed. The mosh pit was a perfect figure for what was wrong with the scene: Boys about to dive into the surging sea of testosterone would strip off their black bomber jackets and hand them to female friends—*Here, hold this*—leaving a strip of girls-as-coatracks along the wall, literally sidelined. Punk wasn't really the point, though. The problems with the scene burned the girls up precisely because it echoed the way the world at large treated them.

The girls were furious about things like parental-consent abortion laws, bikini-clad women who hawked beer and cigarettes on billboards and TV, and the archaic gender roles that pervaded the cartoon section of the *Washington Post*. They were ready to revolt over things like hallway gropes and sidewalk heckles, leering teachers, homophobic threats, rape, incest, domestic violence, sexual double standards, ubiquitous warnings against walking certain places or dressing certain ways . . . The affronts were neverending. The girls couldn't block these things out and they didn't want to; they wanted to stay acutely aware of the war against them so they could fight back.

> *You've got to know what they are* (Kathleen sang)
> *Before you can stand up for your rights . . .*

They were mustering for battle against the idea that to be a girl was to be in grave danger that you could never fully escape, only manage by narrowing your life, your range, your wardrobe, your gaze. The end of the summer was near, but the girl revolution was just beginning.

Another opening salvo was heard in late August, at a concert in Olympia called Love Rock Revolution Girl Style Now, and Bikini Kill and Bratmobile drove back West to be part of it. Girl Night, as the Tuesday-evening show came to be known, kicked off the International Pop Underground Convention, a five-day event—part music festival, part summer camp, part family reunion—organized by Calvin Johnson and Candice Pedersen of K Records. They were calling it a convention to emphasize that this was not a typical music fest or industry hobnob; it was an ingathering of tribes and exiles, a drawing together of secret agents and underground reps who'd been living in the wilderness, tenuously connected to one another by vinyl-only mail order and once-a-year tour dates and third-generation dubbed cassettes passed reverently from hand to hand.

Fifteen acts were on the Girl Night bill, including Bratmobile, Tobi playing solo, and Kathleen's two summer bands. The show had originally been planned as a female-performer-only event, but the parameters were loosened so Margaret Doherty, an original "Two bikini girls kill one bikini girl, glug glug glug" performer and one of the show's organizers, could invite a new coed duo, the Spinanes. The planners wanted to encourage experimentation and inexperience. "It was really about getting the young women in the audience who were sitting on the edge of, 'Maybe I'm gonna play in a band, maybe I'm gonna pick up a guitar, maybe I'm gonna write a song about how I feel,'" Doherty explained. "It was mostly about putting a fire under them to get themselves out there, and to know that you can jump off a cliff and your community will catch you." This Olympia-style creative risk-taking, combined with the political consciousness-raising that had just begun in DC, was what made the summer of 1991 so catalytic. Without either one of these components, there would have been no Riot Grrrl.

One of the first-time bands to play Girl Night was a pair of teenage girls, Corin Tucker and Tracy Sawyer, calling themselves Heavens to Betsy. Until now, the group had existed only theoretically—a cool name and a trumped-up mythology wrapped around a few basement jam sessions. But once again, Olympia threw down the gauntlet, and Heavens to Betsy more than rose to the occasion; within a year, the band would be touring the country with Bratmobile, the third group in the canonical trinity of Riot Grrrl–associated bands.

Corin and Tracy had grown up in Eugene and become best friends during high school. Corin was fearless and outgoing; Tracy was cautious and shy. But they both liked music. A lot. In the late '80s, when the newly titled genre of alternative rock was the most accessible option for high-school malcontents, Corin and Tracy programmed their family VCRs to record MTV's *120 Minutes*, which played videos by the Cure and the Cocteau Twins, and they watched the documentary *Athens Georgia Inside/Out* over and over. The documentary painted a dreamy picture of the Southern college town that had given rise to R.E.M., the B–52s, and countless smaller groups—kids who met at parties or art school and got together to jam and went from there.

Corin finished high school in 1990, and she and Tracy—who had one year left before graduation—made a summer pilgrimage to Athens, taking a cross-country train from Oregon to Georgia. Pylon, a much-beloved Athens band from the '80s, had recently reunited to do some tour dates with R.E.M., and the group was playing a club gig during Corin and Tracy's visit. Too young to get in to the show, they stood out on the sidewalk and listened through the venue's open windows. Corin was captivated by the singer, Vanessa Briscoe, a live-wire dervish of a woman whose voice ricocheted between monster howl, gutteral growl, and smooth monotone. When

Briscoe sang "Hey, kids" in the song "Stop It," the "hey" slid down from a falsetto peak to the midrange, languid come-on of "kids," which gave way, at last, to the song's hoarse, urgent refrain: "Now! Rock and roll now! Now, now, now, now!"

Corin and Tracy heard the message. "We were sick of just watching it; we wanted to be a part of it," Tracy said. They bought a few pieces of a drum kit in Athens and took them home on the train. For the rest of the summer in Eugene, Corin practiced on her father's rehabbed old Les Paul guitar, and Tracy started learning her way around the drum kit. Corin played these drums, too, and Tracy taught herself bass. But before these explorations had time to condense into a band, Corin went up to Olympia for college, while Tracy stayed in Eugene to finish high school.

That Olympia was the West Coast equivalent of freewheeling Athens didn't surprise Corin one bit; she'd chosen Evergreen largely for that reason. And just as she had first become acquainted with Athens through a video, she set out to make sense of Olympia the same way. During her first winter in town, she and a classmate started making a documentary about local music scenes. The two soon parted ways, because the other girl wanted to cover the Seattle scene and all the Sub Pop bands, and Corin was enamored with Olympia. She loved the scene's small size, with the same twenty or thirty people at each basement or gallery show. A continuum of musicianship was regularly on display, from groups on the brink of national fame to bands whose songs still lacked bridges, titles, second verses.

Some bands were plainly bound for wider arenas, and Bikini Kill was one of them. The first time Corin saw them play, she said to herself, "This is the most amazing band I've ever seen." It was Bratmobile, though, that really yanked Heavens to Betsy into existence. "In the same spirit that Bratmobile had started," Corin said, "where they had just picked up the instruments and started writing, I thought Heavens to Betsy could be that kind of band. I felt like, 'I could do that.'" Corin had known Allison Wolfe for years: After meeting each other at the YMCA retreat, they had seen each other again at a Pixies show in Eugene. Corin watched it all happen, watched Allison go from a dorky-strange girl to the lead singer of a real band: still dorky, but with a microphone and an audience. Corin saw that you could do your growing in public and people would appreciate you anyway, that they might even appreciate you *for* being so honest.

Visiting Athens had made playing music feel necessary. Living in Olympia made it feel possible. And watching Bratmobile emerge made it feel proximate, less like a needed leap than a simple but still audacious step. That spring, Corin started informing people in Olympia that she had a band, with her best friend from Eugene, and that they were called Heavens to Betsy.

It wasn't exactly a lie. She and Tracy played together a little bit that year, in Tracy's basement, whenever Corin was home from school. But they were nowhere near ready to perform when Corin's friend Michelle Noel called and invited them to play Girl Night. "I said, 'Okay. *Crap!*'" Corin recalled. "I don't think it would have actually happened had I not been prompted—like, put your money where your mouth is."

During the summer of 1991, Heavens to Betsy practiced regularly in Eugene, working up a three-song set: "Seek and Hide," "My Secret," and "My Red Self." For most of Corin's life, she had wanted to be a writer, but getting poems or stories down on paper had always been a struggle. It turned out that the stories she'd been trying to tell had wanted to be songs all along. Metaphors and images appeared in her mind, bright fruits hanging low in an arbor; she could smell their juice even before she pulled them off the vine.

The subject matter for the songs came easily to her too. She had hit puberty at eleven, before anyone else in her grade, and boys were always grabbing at her body. "It was just like, 'That's the way boys are,'" she said. "There wasn't the education that that kind of harassment can really damage your self-esteem and make you feel really ashamed." Her mother had gone on domestic strike the following year, to protest the family's lopsided division of household labor (pressed into service, her dad bravely concocted a failed jambalaya while young Corin applied herself to the family's laundry). By high school Corin was writing a feminist critique of Shaw's *Pygmalion* for English class. When she arrived at Evergreen, her classes gave her a basic literacy in key feminist texts by Betty Friedan and Audre Lorde; and the bands she interviewed for her video—Bikini Kill, Bratmobile, Calamity Jane—got her noticing the sexism that riddled the world like a network of fine cracks in china. She poured these observations into her songs. She had had only the barest musical training—a few years of piano lessons in high school, a couple guitar tutorials from her dad—but she had listened to hundreds, maybe even thousands, of records, and she knew when something sounded good.

When Girl Night arrived, Corin and Tracy realized they had underestimated how big the show was going to be. Even though the bill was mostly a roster of complete unknowns, a hundred people had come to the Capitol Theater, including some of the girls' favorite musicians—not only Bratmobile and Bikini Kill, whom they had met before, but the members of Fugazi, who were bona fide stars to them. Tracy froze up. "The thought of going up in front of people and playing was absolutely terrifying," she said. "I didn't think I was going to be able to make it through." Corin managed to convince her quaking bandmate to get onstage and do their three songs. The strongest of these three, the uncompromising "My Secret," put a sexual abuser on notice. Into the gaps of her distorted stop-start guitar part, Corin sung-shouted quick barrages of rage:

A knife
In you:
I'd stick it in
Listen
Listen
I'm about revenge

She sang the bridge's repeated line, "I am getting through this," in a strained voice of wild determination. She promised to name the secret crime—"I'll tell again and again"—but by the end of the song, any straightforward telling of abuse was made impossible by the murderous furor it provoked, as Corin's terse lines exploded into an arresting yowl:

My
Secret
Is
I WANT YOU DEAD I WANT YOU DEAD
I WANT YOU DEAD I WANT YOU DEAD

Listening to Heavens to Betsy, Allison cried. "Their performance was mind-blowing," MacKaye recalled. He ran up to Corin and Tracy at a picnic the next day so he could shake their hands and tell them how much he had loved their songs, and his bandmate Guy Picciotto chimed in that their set had really moved him.

"It was amazing to have that kind of support," Corin said.

"My heart dropped. My knees were all jello," Tracy said. "It all seemed really unreal."

The International Pop Underground Convention went on for four more days, musicians and fans from around the world cramming the compact downtown for what amounted to a giant homecoming weekend for nerds and weirdos. As if the nightly shows and post-show dance parties weren't enough, there was also a *Planet of the Apes* marathon, a pet parade, and a cakewalk, with elaborately crenellated confections laid out around the gazebo in Sylvester Park. Bratmobile played at Girl Night, with nearly everybody who had ever jammed with them getting onstage for a few songs, and then played again the next morning, a sleepless 10 A.M. set. Bikini Kill played at the North Shore, the front row packed with girls who knew all the words by now.

The IPU "was sort of an audacious idea," Calvin Johnson said. "We had hardly sold any records ever, and no one had ever cared much about anything that we did. It just seemed like if just the people who made the music showed up, that would be a success." In the end, nearly a thousand people came to Olympia to hear such bands as Fugazi, the Pastels, and the Melvins. The convention had been more of a success than anyone had dared to hope, and it changed Olympians' image of themselves; it changed what they thought they could accomplish. Slim Moon had pressed his first-ever record in time for the convention, the *Kill Rock Stars* compilation, and he ran around town hawking the discs while his mononymous friend Tinúviel frantically silk-screened the record sleeves by hand and hung them to dry on clotheslines in her basement. Moon sold three hundred copies over the week, a good enough number that he decided to keep putting out records under the name Kill Rock Stars, with Tinúviel's help. "There was a sense of power," he said of that period in Olympia, "a feeling that our little town could affect the world."

"It was the first time you got to be king—the freaks got to be king," K's Candice Pedersen said.

Having power, affecting the world, being king—such things felt positive in the late summer of 1991. Unlike the Sub Pop–ites up the road in Seattle, who spoke of "world domination," the Olympians didn't really want to rule anything; they just wanted to build a community strong enough to keep them from feeling terribly alone, and now they had done it. Few people realized how precarious this moment was. Nirvana's major-label debut, *Nevermind*, would be released the following month and go gold almost immediately, signaling the sudden marketability of punk rock culture. This development would violently breach the bulwarks that had protected Oly's small scene from the wilds of corporate rock and, by extension, from mainstream America as a whole. It would change everything.

But in August, with *Nevermind* the twelve-ton boulder rolling unseen down the valley, the Olympia scene basked in its coup. The IPU "showed that the ideas of how things could be aren't so utopian," Calvin said later. "It's not 'could be'; it *was*."

The convention also marked the return of Olympia's most vocal feminist musicians. "The coolest girls in my town had all packed up and moved across the country," Moon lamented. Now they were back. Molly and Allison, yielding to the inevitable, had transferred to Evergreen. And Bikini Kill was back in town, but only temporarily, a two-month stopover before going back East to make DC their home base.

One night, Kathleen and Kathi and Billy all slept over at Tobi's parents' house and watched *Ladies and Gentlemen, the Fabulous Stains*, a cult movie from 1981 that had gotten late-night airplay in the '80s after bombing badly at a few art houses. In the film, a teenage girl (played by a young Diane Lane) starts a punk band with her sister and cousin, and the group amasses a huge following of girls who turn up at shows dressed like the singer, with their hair done in her distinctive coiffure, a bleached skunklike stripe going up the side. Tobi and Kathi both had seen the movie on TV—it had been a main influence for Tobi in pulling together her all-girl band in high school—and Tobi had gotten her hands on a rare laserdisc copy, but this was Kathleen's first exposure to it. "I remember lying on the floor, watching *The Fabulous Stains*," she said, "and feeling like this was exactly the most perfect moment, watching that movie, being in a band with them, the whole thing."

Bikini Kill played up and down the West Coast that fall, culminating with a Halloween show at the Paramount Theatre in Seattle, where they were to open for Mudhoney and Nirvana. This concert was a big deal. Only two years before, Bikini Kill and Nirvana had been two underground bands living in Olympia, trying to solidify lineups and set lists. Now Nirvana was blowing up. The group's in-store appearance at Seattle's Beehive Records the previous month had been mobbed, two hundred kids lining up in the early afternoon for a 7 P.M. performance, begging for autographs. (According to one account, Cobain tried to tell the kids they should be listening to Bikini Kill.) By Halloween, it was blaringly obvious that Nirvana was going to be—was *already*—enormous, on a scale no punk band could even conceptualize. "Smells Like Teen Spirit" was dominating the airwaves, at least of those discerning radio stations that weren't afraid to broadcast such a ferocious song during daytime hours; MTV seemed to have the song's pep-rally-from-hell video on repeat. The unfathomable news of *Nevermind*'s going gold—selling half a million copies—came just two days before the Halloween show. The record would be platinum two weeks later.

Nirvana's success didn't shock Kathleen or Tobi or anyone in Olympia who'd known those boys. The band's chart-topping potential had always been obvious. Nikki McClure, an Olympia artist who was friends with Cobain, said that the first time she heard a tape of the group, she had a prophetic vision: "people with lighters in the Kingdome." But to many people close to Nirvana, the Halloween show felt, at least in retrospect, like the beginning of the end, the point when it stopped being fun. Cobain often spoke about feeling torn between Olympia's anti-fame values and the rock-star dreams he'd harbored since his troubled childhood. Calvin told a friend that Cobain had called him when the band was in LA recording *Nevermind* and Calvin was solidifying the IPU lineup. Cobain was wondering whether he might duck out on a planned European tour with Sonic Youth in order to play the convention in Olympia. The IPU's tagline was "No lackeys to the corporate ogre allowed," but this wasn't an ironclad policy, as L7's inclusion attested: The don't-ask-us-about-being-all-women LA band had signed to Slash/Warner Brothers but not yet put out anything on the label. Still, Calvin and Cobain "agreed it wouldn't be appropriate for [Nirvana] to play," Sub Pop's Rich Jensen reported; Cobain told Everett True, a British rock journalist, that he felt he'd been cast out of Olympia.

Nirvana had chosen the corporate route, the multi-page riders and tour buses with drivers, the gentlemen escorting them to the halls, the fancy rooms to trash and the guitars to smash and the junk to cook up that nobody would get mad about as long as they made it to the stage at the appointed time. And so the world of the spectacle, which Olympians held so meticulously at bay, was now right up in their faces.

Within the next few months, major-label representatives would begin sniffing around at shows in Olympia, looking for the next big thing. Someone from Nirvana's label would call K Records to see whether they could discuss buying the indie label. (Candice Pedersen would reject the idea out of hand. "You don't get it; we're talking a lot of money," the caller said. But the Olympia scene had never been about money, and it didn't intend to start now.)

The Halloween show was at the three thousand–capacity Paramount Theatre, making it easily Bikini Kill's largest audience to date. By having Bikini Kill open, Nirvana seemed to be attempting to bridge the gap between its Olympia past and its excess-laden rockstar present. Cobain also invited his old neighbors Nikki McClure and Ian Dickson to dance onstage during Nirvana's set while wearing T-shirts that read GIRL and BOY. This infuriated the label, which had hired six cameramen to film the concert: The Oly dancers' twee abandon kept ruining the videographers' shots of tortured anomie.

But even these gestures did little to erase the widening chasm between Nirvana and Olympia. Kathleen, hanging out backstage, didn't like what she saw. In a zine interview the following month, she talked about the show with contempt, saying that the people there "were totally into money and getting fucked up. Kurt, Dave, and Kris [Novoselic] are really nice guys . . . and I'm not dissing on them, but they're getting led around by their fucking balls. They don't know what's going on; they're not in control." The whole mindless display only made the members of Bikini Kill happier to be leaving the madness behind. The next day, Olympia's coolest girl band with a boy guitarist set out on the road again, the nose of its van pointed once more toward Washington, DC.

FOUR

WHEN SHE TALKS, I HEAR THE REVOLUTION

As the Revolution Summer Girl Style Now cooled off into fall, DC's new Riot Grrrl group continued to meet, drawing a dozen or more people to weekly gatherings at Positive Force House. A bunch of the girls went to the DC Rape Crisis Center's annual Take Back the Night march, filling the streets around Dupont Circle with chants of "Women, unite!" When Operation Rescue came to town, threatening to block abortion clinic entrances, the girls woke up at dawn to stand outside the clinics and keep them open. And after Bikini Kill got back to DC from the West Coast, Riot Grrrl collaborated with Positive Force to organize a Bikini Kill show to benefit local battered women's shelters.

Many of the girls had also been part of Positive Force, and Riot Grrrl was adopting that group's familiar template of stitching young punks into the city's activist fabric through meetings, concerts, and political action. This process had an especially well-suited facilitator in twenty-five-year-old Kristin Thomson, a regular at meetings who spent her days working as an organizer at the National Organization for Women. A longtime Positive Forcenik, she loved the brass-knuckles politicking that went on at her job almost as much as she loved running the Simple Machines label and playing bass in her new band, Tsunami; she found all NOW's jockeying for relevance and influence invigorating. One of her main duties was organizing outreach to colleges, and she saw how Riot Grrrl could energize younger women whom NOW wasn't quite reaching.

DC punk was in transition. The venerable dc space announced plans to close for good in December, making Positive Force the main organizer of all-ages shows. Simple Machines, the first DIY label in DC that had ever been run by women, was gaining more of a profile. Kristin and her bandmate and labelmate Jenny Toomey began by releasing a series of four-song 7" records, each including at least one coed or all-girl band, and soon they were putting out a proper roster of indie bands. They also published "An Introductory Mechanics Guide to Putting Out Records, Cassettes and CDs," a booklet that was available through mail order and featured in *Sassy*. Jenny and Kristin knew that a single label, like a Dischord or a K, could set the tone for an entire scene. People couldn't lobby a label owner to get him (and it was almost always a *him*, with Bettina Richards, the founding head of Thrill Jockey Records, and Lisa Fancher of the LA punk label Frontier, standing out as notable exceptions) to change what kind of music he liked. Better to put the tools in as many hands as possible. The manual explained how to contact a record-pressing plant, where to buy blank twenty-minute cassettes in bulk, and how to choose among the different options for CD cases. Jenny and Kristin hoped that by demystifying the process of giving music physical form, they might encourage other people to put out records and put their own stamp on their scenes.

A few more girls were stepping up in the DC scene that fall: teen quartet Choptank, whose members sometimes came to Riot Grrrl meetings, played good-natured shows around town, and Tsunami was starting to get well-deserved attention for its tunefully dissonant indie rock. Some bands started to invite girls to move toward the stage at shows, breaking up the mosh bloc. And among the people who took the mic between bands to announce meetings or protests, there was a new regular: Erika Reinstein talking up Riot Grrrl.

Erika was eighteen, and she already knew how to take up space in a room and on a page. Anybody who listened to her talk or who read the zine she had begun publishing, *Fantastic Fanzine*, could easily become hypnotized by her words' raw force:

> This world teaches women to hate themselves,
> but I refuse to listen to its message. I'm not
> going to let boys come between me and my girl-
> friends. I'm not going to try and be your idea
> of sexy if sexy means being thin and help-
> less, tottering around on high heeled shoes.
> I'm not going to stay home at night hating my
> sex because if I go out then I'm asking for
> trouble.

She'd spent the past few years bouncing between her mother's town-home in Reston, Virginia, and her dad's place in DC. Now, taking a year off between high school and whatever would come next, she lived in an apartment of activists in Arlington, a few blocks from Positive Force, and devoted herself to building Riot Grrrl.

By winter, the group was in a tenuous position. Several of the most enthusiastic founding members had left on tour or gone away to college; the girls who were still in high school had stuck around through the early fall, but gradually dropped off; and the few older punks who'd become regulars had drifted back to their previous lives, content to bring their conversations about sexism and gender back to the community they'd had before.

But Riot Grrrl *was* Erika's community. It was the best thing she'd ever been part of. And as the group's initial flare-up ebbed, Erika saw an aspirating glow that still might reignite. At times that winter of 1991–92, Riot Grrrl in DC was not much more than Erika talking about it at shows, inviting girls to come to a meeting and air out whatever was on their minds. Many such meetings consisted of Erika sitting in the Positive Force living room by herself, waiting for people to show up, or talking with her two good friends from high school, May Summer and Joanna Burgess. These three from Reston, a planned community deep in the suburbs, remained at the group's core. They had been the misfits of South Lakes High—dorky, demonstrative, smart but not at the top of their class, politically aware but not the student-government type—and they reveled in their not-fitting-in, their refusal to conform. Open about their bisexuality, they didn't really date other girls but were notorious for holding hands with each other in the halls and grinding up against one another at pep rallies and in the cafeteria, deliberately making a scene.

"It wasn't fun to be made a spectacle *of*, which I think happened to me a lot in high school," May said. "But when we did it ourselves, and we chose to do it, and the fact that we were doing it together—it was our joke on *them* to be dancing and freaking them out."

At Riot Grrrl meetings, Joanna would talk about her body; she had never felt pretty enough or thin enough. May would discuss her parents' recent divorce, and sometimes she talked about an abusive boyfriend she'd had a few years ago. That had been a horrific situation, but her older sisters had helped her get away and resolve never to let anyone mistreat her like that again. May wanted her experience to be helpful to other girls in similar situations, and the meetings made her feel that her story wasn't just something that had shaped *her*; it was part of a larger pattern, and seeing it that way was the key to unraveling it.

Erika had the most to talk about. Memories of incest were surfacing after what felt like a long, corrosive interment. Hearing Kathleen Hanna sing songs about sexual abuse had helped Erika realize she could open up to other people about the vivid nightmares she'd been having, dreams that seemed more like past events doubling back on her. The more she talked about them, the better she felt.

Sometimes new girls came to the meetings; sometimes they kept coming back. Other would-be, might-be girl revolutionaries who saw Erika announce the group at a show that winter were intrigued, but then did nothing about it for a while. The idea had to nudge its way down into the gut first, waiting for the perfect moment to shoot back up.

The spotlight twitters on. A low rumble drives its tentative glare. Singly or in pairs or threes, they appear.

This girl was raped by her boyfriend; this girl felt fat; this girl watched her father beat her mother; this girl had four friends who had been raped, and she knew it could happen to her; this girl was tortured at night by dreams of incest she only dimly recalled; this girl wished to touch other girls; this girl felt powerless, full of rage, for reasons she couldn't even specify.

It's okay to feel uncomfortable about this. We can go ahead and feel uneasy at the voyeurism that attends these girl revolutionaries parading down the runway of narrative, in their frayed cutoffs and oversize T-shirts.

If I tell only one or two, it won't be true. The point is that there were many.

The point is that no one encapsulated it.

The point is that they were various.

The point is that the pain of all girls is not alike.

Mary Fondriest didn't go to any meetings in the summer and fall of 1991. What was she doing then? It's hard for her to remember. Things that happen at seventeen have a habit of turning blurry and bleeding together when looked back on a dozen years later. Mary had grown up in Detroit with her mother, younger sister, and volatile father, then moved—minus the father—to Alexandria, Virginia. Mary started over at a new junior high school, unlucky enough to be the new girl in class at the age when fitting in is most important. She spent a lot of time at home by herself or looking after her sister. Belonging anywhere felt impossible. She became depressed. She finished junior high and moved on to high school. She made a few friends, all boys. She was smoking a lot of pot, drinking beer. She missed having a best girlfriend. Her mother worked three jobs. Mary felt unseen. A mass of instinctual, unfocused anger was assembling inside of her, with no place to go but out.

Then one night this girl got up on stage.

That's how so many of these stories go. A girl onstage, a girl at a show: She seemed so cool, so tough, so together. Dozens of these moments, scores of them, are lodged here. It's the high school friend-crush mobilized to political ends. Then I saw this girl, and she gave me a tape, sold me a zine, told me about a meeting. Then I saw this girl—and the jolt of recognition and reflex-sharp longing: I wanted to get to know her, to learn how to be like her, to . . .

"Hey girlfriend," Kathleen was singing. "I got a proposition."

The proposition wasn't that you would go back to her room, alone; it was that you would come out into the common space with her and all the rest of the girls. There was a deliberate, fuzzy-edged erotics to this, for sure: "In her kiss, I taste the revolution!"

screeched the pinnacle of the song "Rebel Girl," which had come out that summer on Bikini Kill's *Revolution Girl Style Now* cassette and was well on its way to becoming a movement's fight song. But in that revolutionary kiss, there may not have been any tongue. As for third base—well, there is that line about hips, but we have to look at it in context.

It's the song's second verse. We've just had a chorus that went "Rebel girl rebel girl rebel girl you are the queen of my world," sung-chanted to a beat that could govern a drill line of revolutionaries in vulva-shaped berets. Dust is still settling from that seismic event, the distorted guitar slides into a low, ominous grumble, and we are held in place by a ceaseless bass line, steady report of snare drum flams, and Kathleen's voice:

When she talks, I hear the revolution
In her hips, there's revolution

These hips are made not for fucking, though, but for walking. And that's just what they do—

When she walks the revolution's coming

—walk over to the speaker in the song, so the hips' owner can—here it comes, mounting to an unbridled scream—

In her kiss I TASTE THE REVOLUTION

On the word "I," Kathleen sounds like her mouth turning itself inside out, every consonant of the alphabet dissolving into that vowel. She's gone over the edge; she's become something else. Listening, being one with her "I," we go inside out too.

The rebel girl is the queen of "my," not "our," world—the '70s collectivism ("We are a gentle angry people") has morphed into the self-centered language of alienated adolescence and been adapted for the political primacy, especially potent in the early '90s, of the personal story. Yet this chorus is written to be sung along to, first alone but then in a group: moving from the lonely bedroom or bathroom mirror to the front row of a show.

With this incantation, the girls raise the shade of the role model, the someone they've been longing to see. The intensity of their desire, the power of that projection, conjures her into the room. The invoked apparition sharpens, focuses. They make of each other that girl. They make her themselves.

I think I wanna be her best friend, yeah.

Honey, if you want it that bad, it's yours.

And so Mary Fondriest, depressed high school senior, was at a show in early 1992. What matters is not who played—she can't remember—but that between bands she saw this girl get up onstage: Erika announcing the time and location of the weekly Riot Grrrl meetings.

Mary already knew what Riot Grrrl was: a bunch of lame girls creating divisiveness in the scene, being sexist against boys, fighting sexism the wrong way or making up the problem altogether. Bitches; man-haters. That's what her male friends said, anyway. But something about seeing Erika onstage converged with something about that moment in Mary's life and made her decide to do the thing that was guaranteed to make her uncool in the eyes of all her friends.

She describes it as courage: "I just got up the courage to go one day." And rebellion: "It felt like something I wasn't supposed to be doing. It wasn't cool at all. It was really scary."

She made it to the meeting. She knew almost as soon as she walked in the door that these girls would understand her; she could just feel it. Talking with them, listening to them, made her knotted-up anger start to make sense. The roots of her rage: "Having been raised with an angry father. Having a mother that wasn't around. Feeling disenfranchised at high school. Typical things—just your average disconnection." At the meetings these problems changed from individual trials—from disconnection—into a system of unfairness, a room that could be torn down from inside. The girls just had to wrap their arms around the columns and tug.

By springtime, Riot Grrrl DC was growing. A core of about a dozen girls attended meetings faithfully, and a few new faces appeared each week. Some people came only once and decided it wasn't for them: A woman in her thirties felt too old for the group; a lesbian found the group not gay enough for her (most of the girls identified as bisexual, but by and large they dated boys if they dated anybody at all). Others showed up to find, like Mary, that they felt entirely at home.

Weekly meetings weren't rigidly planned. Occasionally there would be a project to work on, like silk-screening Riot Grrrl T-shirts or making stencil cutouts and then spray-painting woman symbols on sidewalks. Some days were zine days, when everybody filled a half-sheet of paper with writing or drawing or collage, then rubber-cemented the pages together into a plump compilation to be xeroxed by whichever of the girls had a good copy scam running at a local copy shop or a parent's office.

Mostly, the girls just talked. Their stories ranged from extremes of rape, incest, and child sexual abuse to those widespread indignities of female adolescence, so common that girls seemed to be expected to take them in stride: the makeup and hair-mousse ads warning girls they would never get a date unless they looked like models; the supposedly cool boy who forced a kiss at a party and acted like nothing had happened; the English teacher who everybody knew gave better grades to girls in short skirts; the man on the bus who said "What's your number, sweetheart?" and wouldn't back off.

In 1992, feminism was in the news again—Faludi's *Backlash* spent thirty-five weeks on the *New York Times* best-seller list—and the adult world was even beginning to pay belated attention to *girls'* problems. A new national study on rape grabbed headlines that spring, coming on the heels of high-profile acquaintance-rape trials against William Kennedy Smith and professional boxer Mike Tyson, and arriving smack in the middle of debates over the prevalence of rape on college campuses (Katie Roiphe's *New York Times* op-ed "Date Rape Hysteria" was published in late 1991, a precursor to her 1993 best seller *The Morning After*). The new report, "Rape in America," revealed that its titular offense skewed even younger than people had suspected: "The true shocker," *Time* magazine wrote of the study, "is that 61 percent of rape victims were younger than eighteen at the time of their attack." "A tragedy of youth," newspapers blared, quoting one of the study's authors. That same year, the American Association of University Women published a report, *How Schools Shortchange Girls*, about the gender gap in academic performance, especially in math and science; and feminist psychologists Lyn Mikel Brown and Carol Gilligan came out with a study documenting girls' higher rates of depression and anxiety, and tracking the nosedive girls' self-esteem took during adolescence. Gilligan and Brown described seeing in teenage girls "evidence of a loss of voice, a struggle to authorize or take seriously their own experience." Plus, now that the Anita Hill hearings had turned *sexual harassment* into a catchphrase, it was suddenly dawning on people that such harassment was epidemic in high schools and even middle schools; and that behavior which school personnel had long accepted as boys being boys was feeding girls' depression, anxiety, and self-criticism.

Not that any of this was *new*. God, no. Teenage girls were simply living some of the thick residuals of sexism the feminist movement hadn't managed to destroy. Rigid gender roles were alive and well and forced on girls as they hit puberty, which was especially difficult for children of the '70s to swallow. Many of the riot grrrls had been taught by at least somebody—if not a parent, then a supportive teacher or coach—that they could do anything they wanted, and that there were no barriers. Then they found out it wasn't true. *Hello!* Confusing! They could do anything *except* walk down the hall by the shop classroom, anything *except* stop shaving their legs, anything *except* wear that skirt to the party, anything *except* play drums without being exclaimed over like some sort of circus seal, anything *except* choose sex and not get whispered about as a slut. Why on earth wouldn't a teenage girl be confused, depressed, anxious, angry? How the hell could she not be?

And how could a new, energetic movement that finally acknowledged all this stuff, that invited girls to sound off about it, that promised—in an era of apathy—to make it cool for girls to give a shit, talk about how politics affected their lives, and take action—how could such a movement possibly stay underground for long?

That April, the night before the huge pro-choice march on the Mall, Bikini Kill opened for Fugazi and L7 at the benefit show-slash–pep rally that Kristin Thomson had organized, with help from members of Riot Grrrl and Positive Force. MTV had wanted to film the show: The network was launching a pro-voting campaign, Rock the Vote, and adding more political content to its celebrity-heavy news show. But it was still the organ of commodified youth culture, and true punks would have nothing to do with it. Plus, the channel wanted to install tracks for its cameras in front of the stage, cutting off the audience from the musicians. There could be no better metaphor for the sinister reach of the spectacle, trying to butt its way into the middle of a human interaction, to turn an authentic exchange of energy into debased image-production. Forget it. Bikini Kill and Fugazi both refused to be taped, and MTV backed off.

Bikini Kill was in top form that night. The band had spent the winter of 1991–92 touring and recording, honing its set to a poison-tipped point. Tobi was laid back and cool as ever behind her drum kit, not even seeming to break a sweat. Kathi planted herself in front of her bass amp, chewing gum and barely moving as she played. Billy, wearing a black sleeveless dress and sporting the word RIOT in block letters down both his arms, got a moment in the spotlight near the end of the set, when for two minutes he took the mic and shrieked "GEORGE BUSH IS NO HERO" over and over while prowling the stage like a rangy, loose-jointed jungle cat, then rolling on the ground and kicking his legs in the air.

Kathleen's voice was undeniable, her stage moves provocative. In "Lil Red Riding Bitch," she tore the old fairy tale a new asshole: "These are my long red nails / The better to scratch out your eyes." On the line "This is my ass," she whirled around, bent over, and flipped up her dress to reveal the pale globe of it, cleanly bisected by a thong bikini's thin black line. Later, while Billy handled some guitar troubles, Kathleen sang a snip of Hall & Oates—"Oh, here she comes; watch out, boys, she'll chew you up"—and segued into a Patti Smith–style spoken word piece:

I'm a man-eater
I'm a real bitch walking down your street
Cause you know there's two kinds of girls: good ones and bad ones.
And if you wear that dress tonight
and if you wear those high heels
and if you expose your bare ass to two hundred people
you KNOW what kind of girl you are, honey.

It was a night for the riot grrrls to be proud, dancing and whooping at the front of the theater. When Erika got onstage and Kathleen gave her the mic so she could scream her head off, that made it official: In less than a year, these teenage girls had gone from beleaguered outcasts of suburbia to creators of culture, makers of zines and shirts and necklaces, queens of their own scene, and anointed entourage of a badass band.

L7 played second. The LA band—whose breakout album, *Bricks Are Heavy*, would drop the following week—had recently founded Rock for Choice, an organization that sponsored benefit concerts to support abortion rights. L7 was also the only group that hadn't objected to MTV's designs on the night.

Fugazi closed the night with "Suggestion," a song about street harassment and rape. For the past five years, the song's first-person female viewpoint—"Why can't I walk down the street free of suggestion?" MacKaye would sing; "Is my body my only trait in the eyes of men?"—had raised no eyebrows. The band had long invited female singers onstage for the song; at the IPU that past summer, a girl who many in the audience knew to be a rape survivor had gotten through a few lines before breaking into tears. In DC the guest vocalist was often Amy Pickering, formerly of Fire Party, and she sang it at the Sanctuary that night, lifting up her shirt while shouting the lines "I've got some skin / You want to look in," and talking to the crowd about an abortion she had had. "Suggestion" was still Fugazi's song, though, and in recent months it had begun to sound to some riot grrrls like a self-righteous white boy appropriating girls' issues so he could appear more virtuous.

MacKaye resented the criticism. "It's a *human* issue!" he said. "And it was a deeply important issue to me." He had written the song after a female friend came home inconsolable after an attempted assault; it was his attempt to explore the emotional terrain of harassment and gender roles. The end of the song, when the speaker shifted from the female "I" to a gender-neutral "we," went, "We play the roles that they've assigned us," and the audience usually shouted the final line along with MacKaye: "We are all guilty." No other all-male group of such stature was playing a song that dramatized sexual assault and blasted its audience for being complicit. But the riot grrrls didn't want any favors from Fugazi. To find their own voices, they felt, they couldn't accept anyone else's attempts to do it for them.

Less than three weeks after the March for Women's Lives, the Supreme Court heard arguments in *Planned Parenthood of Southeastern Pennsylania v. Casey*, the case so many feminists feared would spell an end to *Roe v. Wade*. The Pennsylvania law at issue required married women to notify their husbands before obtaining an abortion, mandated a twenty-four-hour waiting period, and obliged girls under eighteen to obtain a parent's consent. By 1992, thirty-six states had such parental notification or parental consent laws on the books, though half these restrictions remained tied up in legal battles. Virginia's state legislature had passed one such law just that March. The Democratic governor eventually vetoed it, bowing to the outcry from his base—as the Democratic Leadership Council pushed the party toward the right on many issues, abortion was one of the biggest remaining differences between the two parties—but parental notification laws were extraordinarily popular nationwide, with as many as 75 percent of voters favoring them.

After arguments in *Casey* had wrapped up in May 1992, the justices took a preliminary vote on the case, showing that a five-justice majority was prepared to overrule *Roe*. Chief Justice William Rehnquist, who had penned that case's antiabortion dissent in 1973, triumphantly went off to draft a new opinion. Only a last-minute change of heart by Justice Anthony Kennedy saved *Roe v. Wade*. On the court's final day in session, June 29, the justices issued a ringing reaffirmation of a woman's fundamental right to have an abortion.

Among the contested clauses in the Pennsylvania law, though, only the part making women notify their husbands was struck down. In one curt sentence, the court allowed the parental consent provision to go into effect.

That spring, Riot Grrrl DC held a slumber party and went out painting graffiti on concrete walls. GEORGE STAY OUT OF MY BUSH, they wrote, and FUCK PATRIOTISM, and REAL BOYZ WEAR PINK. Another night, they stenciled Riot Grrrl logos on the sidewalks around Positive Force House.

"We were playful," Mary Fondriest said. "I remember sitting on the couch together was really significant because we were next to each other, we were touching—shared physical space."

They were teenagers, which meant that sometimes they were still kids. In many cases they hadn't been able to enjoy their childhoods, whether due to abuse, divorce, or just knowing that they were somehow different from their classmates. So now they embraced the word *girl*, they filled their zines with childish clip-art drawings, they had sleepovers, they held back their bangs with brightly colored plastic barrettes, they nestled next to each other on the couch. They would have another childhood for as long as they wanted, and they would be the ones to art-direct it this time.

Irene Chien came into the group in June 1992, while living at home in Maryland after her first year at college in Ohio. Irene wasn't desperate to find girls she could relate to: She had her best friends from high school, a tight crew of Chinese-American girls who understood her strict family and her anxieties about boys. She didn't need an introduction to feminist theory, either. She'd gotten that from her first year of classes at Oberlin, so effectively that at Riot Grrrl meetings she would sometimes catch herself thinking,

"Oh, this appears to be a third wave of feminism that is modeled off of consciousness-raising groups in the '70s but is also related to a different kind of feminism that's not radically separatist . . . "

Irene was drawn to the meetings because she wanted to link the theory she was learning with the visceral realities of her life. In short, she was there to get politicized, and to develop for herself an identity as "a defiant young woman, which was never the way that I thought of myself or that anybody thought of me." She became so passionate about the group that she baked up her own batch of Riot Grrrl Shrinky Dink necklaces and sold them, along with her zine, *Fake*, at punk shows. She enthusiastically applied her new tools of feminist analysis to everything she saw, including the meetings themselves. Frequently a girl would just complain in a time-honored female way about a boy not calling her back, and people might not take the extra step to discuss why she was putting so much energy into that relationship or what else she might want to focus on. Irene felt like these conversations reiterated boys as central to girls' lives, and they also made her feel less cool or worldly than the girls who had this complaining to do. Irene and her friends didn't ever talk to boys, not for any feminist reason but because they didn't know how.

When Kathleen was around, everything made sense, transcendently. In retrospect, Irene realized, "I wasn't looking for peers; I was looking for leaders." Kathleen came to meetings whenever she was in town that summer. At twenty-three, she had several years on just about everybody else there, and the girls felt the age difference. But Kathleen didn't lord it over people. She didn't play up her fame, either; any friction with bandmates or reporters—in recent months Bikini Kill had been written about in publications including the *New York Times*, the *New Yorker*, *Sassy*, and music magazines *Option* and *Melody Maker*—became just one more thing to discuss and analyze with the group.

The girls were grateful for Kathleen's consciousness, a telephoto lens effortlessly zooming out from specific experiences to the big picture. Ananda La Vita, who had just finished her first year at Eugene Lang College in New York City and was back in town, said Kathleen was so insightful and inspiring that just a few words out of her mouth could change the whole feeling in a room. At one meeting, after Ananda finished talking about her family troubles, Kathleen looked her in the eye and said something incredibly simple like "Of course your feelings are totally valid," and the way she said it was so compassionate and affirming that Ananda nearly started bawling. Kathleen had a way of talking that made all the present obstacles seem temporary; she brought the future victory into focus. When she talked about the revolution, it wasn't just rhetoric; she meant it. She never seemed to doubt that all these young women working together had the power to end sexism, rape, harassment, and abuse. Who could resist being part of that?

Once Irene heard Kathleen tell a story about a female relative, an aunt or grandmother, who had suffered from chronic pain and was always apologizing for not being able to take good enough care of the people around her: I'm so sorry that I can't do the dishes tonight, but my back is just hurting me too much.

Women of our generation don't feel like that exactly, Kathleen said. We don't expect ourselves to be tireless housekeepers and cooks for our husbands. The world has changed for the better that way.

But she went on to talk about subtler ways women and girls might put pressure on themselves to be heroes, to be loyal, to nurture friends or family, to heal people in pain. What is our programming as females making us feel obligated to do? she asked the group and herself. What do we let ourselves feel guilty for failing at?

By the time Kathleen told the parable about her relative, she had spent a year touring extensively, writing and recording two EPs, keeping her band together while starting two new projects, and finessing her role with Riot Grrrl DC. She didn't want to be considered the movement's leader, and while the girls themselves didn't see her as being in charge, exactly, she was set apart. "She was way older than us," May explained. "She seemed a little bit like—'Oh, it'd be so cool to be like you when we're grown up.'" Mary was blunter: "There was a hierarchy, even though nobody really wanted one."

Kathleen saw a younger version of herself reflected in these girls. "I knew they had their own specific shit going on as well," she said, yet her identification with them, and her empathy for them, ran deep. She told them that if they ever needed a ride anyplace, if they were stuck at home and wanted to get out, they should call her and she'd come pick them up. She went to Joanna's sleepover birthday party in Reston. She read the girls' zines and gave specific, encouraging feedback. In June, after Vice President Dan Quayle attacked the TV character Murphy Brown for having a baby out of wedlock, Mary made a zine about the incident; Kathleen told Mary that she loved the zine and had put it on her coffee table. Later, she would send Ananda a postcard that read, "You make me not wanna give up." She attended meetings whenever she could manage it, and when she had to miss any she felt compelled to apologize.

She had chosen to save herself by saving others, and she had a real gift for it. But her generosity was already beginning to take its toll on her.

Some of the riot grrrls knew their group wasn't perfect. They were good at talking about what they had in common, but they weren't sure how to approach their differences. For instance, while a majority of the people involved were white and middle-class, quite a few were Latina or black or Asian, and some had grown up in struggling families. These things were rarely discussed.

Academic feminism at that time was talking a lot about how being a woman meant something different for women who were black or poor or disabled or queer, and how the '70s feminist language of "sisterhood" and "women's issues" had concealed an assumption of whiteness, class privilege, and so forth as default traits. Some of the girls in Riot Grrrl looked around the room each week and, seeing the danger, wanted to learn from and avoid the pitfalls of the past. So far, nobody was issuing position papers or—well, it would happen in zines this time, and it hadn't happened yet; there were no angry writings pointed inward at the group or specific members, no furious denunciations or bitter trashings. They still had a chance, they hoped, to get it right this time.

The discussions at meetings were studded with intense stories of trauma, which made some girls uncomfortable. One member, a women's studies major at the University of Maryland, worried that people were trying to help each other with issues that nobody actually knew how to deal with. But what could she do? The girls talking about incest and rape were relieved to finally have a place to spill their guts, and if some of the others felt like they were in over their heads, they were glad to feel that by listening and being supportive they were helping, at least a little. It was like punk: If somebody gave you drumsticks and said, "Play a show," you'd just hit the drums. You'd learn that way. It might not ultimately be enough; for the girls staggering under the heaviest memories, simple support from peers could never complete the hard work of healing. But it could start a process.

If the girls had known how to get therapy, or even just that they needed it, they might have done that instead. But therapy might not have been the right thing for them then. From a teenage point of view, going to a shrink can imply that there is something wrong with you that needs to be in some way fixed. If you're angry or confused or depressed about things that are totally unfair, is it really your *reaction* that's the problem?

"When you get right down to the heart of the matter," Kathleen sings in the song "This Is Not a Test." Billy's guitar comes in at the beginning of the song playing in a different key from the one Kathleen is singing in. She holds her ground at first, but slides around and ultimately comes into phase by the time the verse starts. It's a breakneck song without any delicacy to it, the melody barrelling through atop three punk chords. Kathleen sings a litany of woes, as if running through a diagnostic checklist for a psychologist: "I'm sad. I can't sleep. There's somebody following me."

In the lead-in to the first chorus—"When you get right down to the bottom! of! it! all!"—the guitar seizes up for a moment, a quick breath, and Kathleen's voice muscles through the caesura. "You're dumb! I'm not!" she shouts: I may be feeling bad, but you are the one with the problem; you're the one who is the problem.

"You're FUCKED!" The guitar returns with a three-chord rebuttal, twice. "I'm not!" Kathleen sings into the next silence, and keeps singing over the guitar's subsequent re-entry, tracing a descending punk melisma with bluesy tone-bend at the bottom: "I'm nah-ah-ah-ah-aht." This is the nut of the song: It's here, in this fluid redirecting, this redefinition of pathology. And that "not," when it comes back, is what closes out the song, ends the battle of wills between fretted guitar and supple voice. Cymbals and chords cut out abruptly, at the push of a Mute button, leaving a full two seconds of the final "not," a single tone this time, boring its way through space, steadfast.

You're fucked; I'm not.

FIVE

GIRL GANGS MUST RULE

The riot grrrls of Olympia weren't holding any meetings in the fall of 1991. They didn't have to; they already knew one another. They numbered ten or so: Corin Tucker and Tracy Sawyer from Heavens to Betsy (Tracy had moved to Olympia after graduating from high school); Allison Wolfe from Bratmobile, and sometimes Molly too; Michelle Noel, a twenty-year-old Oly punk who had helped organize Girl Night; and a few of their friends. This girl gang would charge to the stage at shows, hollering "Girls up front!" and pushing people (sometimes even other girls) out of their way en route. There they'd stand, planting their legs in broad Vs and linking arms with each other or balling their fists at their waists, daring anybody to challenge their right to the space where moshing usually held sway. "It was like civil disobedience," Michelle said. "We would all hold on to each other and we would push up to the front and we would stop the pit." Michelle had a distinctive way of dancing—everybody remembered it for years—in which her feet stayed rooted to the ground, wide-set, while she swung her head and torso wildly from side to side, tossing her hair and flinging her fists to keep slamdancers at bay. She had grown up in nearby Tacoma, going to punk shows where the mosh pits were terrifying; she'd go home with cigarette burns on her back. She never danced at a show until she moved to Olympia at eighteen. "It was really spiritual for me," she said. "It made me feel like who I was really supposed to be: my essential self. I belonged there, dancing."

The other girls picked up Michelle's dance too, and they'd all do it together, facing the stage, rapt, performing complete absorption in the band that was playing—both as a retort to the slammers, who didn't ever seem to care what was happening onstage, and as a defiant embrace of fandom, so long a disempowering stance for girls but now rehabilitated. Because their fandom could draw art into the world, pull it into the open like heat bringing blood to the surface of skin. By going wild when Bikini Kill or Bratmobile played, the girls were making a promise to one another that as soon as any of *them* got a project going, there would be an adoring passel of girls up front, dancing like crazy. "Writing to that audience that I knew was immediately going to be there—it was an opportunity for me, for sure," Corin said.

Some of the girls developed a coordinated style, as groups of friends so often do: Many of them cut their bangs short and wore cotton vintage dresses with thrift-store cardigans, librarian-style. Everybody in Olympia's tight-knit punk scene knew who these girls were. And in the political isolation of the Pacific Northwest, it was easy to be satisfied with that instead of immediately trying to push a broader political agenda. "There was a possibility that I could change punk, 'cause I belonged there," Michelle said. "It didn't feel possible to change the rest of the world—because I didn't feel *part* of the rest of the world." If your scene was your whole existence, then the politics of that scene became supercharged with significance; changing the world could be as simple or as elusive as changing the scene. Similarly, if the revolution was a group of friends, then living the revolution could be as simple or as elusive as making friends with the most intimidating girls you'd ever seen.

"Girl Gangs Must Rule All Towns," read a headline on a flyer that would make the rounds at Bikini Kill shows. It went on:

```
What if we decided that we HAVE to have places
where we feel safe and can talk? What if we
decided that 'scenes' can no longer be ruled by
issues of coolness and hierarchy and instead
are here to help us feel good enough about
our identities as resisters that we can openly
challenge   racist/sexist/classist/homophobic/
speciesist/ageist standards? . . . We need to
start talking strategy, NOW.
```

The first formal meeting of the Olympia girl gang took place in January 1992. Allison Wolfe called it; she and Molly had just gotten back from DC, where they'd spent winter break practicing with Erin, recording some tracks at the Embassy, and hanging out with Bikini Kill. Seventeen girls showed up to the Sunday evening gathering in the white-walled laundry room of Michelle's apartment building. Ideas flew fast and furious. They could make zines, throw parties, set up monthly shows! A young woman from Seattle in her mid-twenties sat quietly in the circle, jotting things down in her notebook: She was working on an article about Riot Grrrl for the *LA Weekly*. It seemed a little strange that somebody wanted to write about them for something larger than a fanzine, but nobody saw it as a problem.

A week after the meeting, the group put on its first public event, billed as a Riot Girl Extravaganza, with Heavens to Betsy and the Spinanes playing. The cost at the door was three dollars for boys, two dollars for girls and for boys who showed up wearing dresses or bras. Some boys got into it, carefully selecting a frock for the night from a thrift store or a friend's closet. But other boys, Allison said, "were like, 'That's not fair! What about class and all this, and what if the guy is really poor?' And it's like, we're trying to make this night special for girls, and if you have such a hard time between the difference of one dollar, you've got a problem. The show's already less than five dollars. And if you dressed in drag, you could get in for the same price as girls. So it's not like they didn't have an option. I think it was just people who were whining to be whiners."

The group discussed putting on a show that only girls were allowed to attend. Tobi Vail had started floating the idea a year earlier, and Kathi Wilcox had been into it; talking to Corin for her documentary, Kathi had said, "You *know* that it would feel different as a performer to be on a stage when you knew that there weren't any boys totally evaluating what you looked like." But it never happened. Part of the fun of sisters doing it themselves, it turned out, came from showing the boys what girls could do. The only girl-only events were the meetings themselves, and the girls spent some of that time discussing how to coexist with the boys of the scene. One result of these discussions was a flyer, titled "Dance Floor Justice," that included contributions from several girls.

```
Keep yer boots off my head. If you wanna
mosh go back where you won't slam into me.
I don't like it, and I'll let you know with
a yell and a good hard penis punch. Stay
off my body.
```

> There's a new dance going on and it's the
> Revvvolution: RIOT GRRRLS twist go stand
> jump be anywhere i want NOW.

Meetings were held biweekly, rotating among the members'
houses and apartments: The first flyer the group made to invite
people to meetings didn't announce where the next one would be,
only gave a phone number to call. That flyer also included a handwritten assurance that perhaps protested too much:

> OK, Riot Grrls have met a couple times already
> but don't feel like we would treat you like an
> outsider or have inside jokes or secret codes
> if you came to join us. If you come to a meet-
> ing and do feel like this is happening just
> say so and I promise you will be filled in. I
> want you to feel safe girlfriend.

The crew could sometimes be a tough nut to crack. Tracy
Sawyer noticed that a lot of girls came to one meeting and never
showed up again. She saw "how noninclusive it could be. We were
a pretty tight group of friends, and that's really what a lot of it was
about." But it wasn't entirely closed to newcomers: Becca Albee, an
Evergreen student from Maine, dropped in on a meeting after she'd
seen a zine, and she felt instantly welcomed in. Meetings consisted
of "a lot of sitting around and talking," Tracy said. Sometimes the
conversations were consciousness raising–style feminist object lessons, but, Corin admitted, "it was also twenty-year-old girls sitting
around being like, 'Oh, my god. That is *so lame!*'"

The group didn't put on many more events that spring after
the first spate had passed. The girls were all busy enough with their
own bands and radio shows and schoolwork. Riot Grrrl for them

functioned essentially as a networking circle, a way to systematize their support of one another so they wouldn't need to seek boys' approval. To boys, girls were cool if they were cute and nice and funny and accommodating, but the riot grrrls were creating an alternate system in which what was really desirable was making things and being loud and bossy and taking up space—and not even calling it *cool*. Both sets of standards could breed hierarchies, but at least the girls' priorities empowered them to make art and feel better about themselves.

Corin and Tracy were concentrating most of their energy on Heavens to Betsy. They wanted to write enough songs to make a record, and to get good enough that they could tour with confidence that summer. They rehearsed in a communal practice room in the CAB building, Evergreen's version of a student union; because multiple bands shared the room, nobody could store gear in there, so Corin and Tracy kept their drums and amp in a locker nearby. Before every practice, they would load the gear onto a skateboard and wheel it to the practice space.

Molly Neuman, who was taking recording classes at school, helped Heavens to Betsy lay down a four-track version of "My Secret" in the Evergreen studios; K Records would release it that summer as a split 7" with Bratmobile's "Cool Schmool." Molly also recorded an eight-song cassette for Heavens to Betsy, including the songs from Girl Night—"My Red Self," "My Secret," "Seek and Hide"—and a bunch of new ones. The songs all spoke from a first-person perspective while throwing up roadblocks for any listener who might have wanted to assume that the songs' "I" equaled Corin. "My Secret" and the new, incendiary "Stay Dead" (in which somebody who'd done something unspeakably terrible was warned to "stay in the cemetery or I will set your tomb on fire") hinted movingly at childhood sexual abuse and a survivor's struggles to move on. And in "Baby's Gone Away," a girl who'd tried to end her pregnancy in secret, rather than tell her parents about it, said: "I did what you told me to do—now I'm dead. Goodbye." Corin's songs, which applied tactics of confessional songwriting to political issues, often yielded indelible results.

These songs uniformly gave the lie to the idea, which would become widespread within a year, that "Riot Grrrl bands" were a particular type of band with a particular sound. Even though Heavens to Betsy had formed in direct reaction to seeing Bratmobile play, the two bands' sounds had almost nothing in common. While Bratmobile was playing primitive surf rock as if interpreted by teenage Martians, Heavens to Betsy was creating stripped-down songs with a tuneful alt-rock sensibility. The cassette's first track, "Good Food," opens with a jangly, dissonant low chord strummed on a guitar, an intro that wouldn't be out of place on an early R.E.M. record. The song's structure is practically baroque coming from such novice musicians: Amid the three verses and chorus lurk not one but two different bridges, which intensify in volume and rhythm as they go along, toppling headfirst into the choruses that follow them. After a couple verses depicting self-doubt and self-hatred as a "bitter pill" that society force-feeds girls ("This is the sign of poison / It makes me say, 'I can't'"), and a few repetitions of a chorus in which the pill is held uncomfortably between ingestion and expectoration ("I have learned to close my mouth / But I will not swallow you"), the song's first bridge then floats along, spacious and nearly gravity-free, swirling in a wonderland whose girl wanderer, shrinking and swelling, proclaims, "I eat cake I made myself / I eat the cake that says I CAN." The second bridge, just one chorus later, follows up some seeming romanticism, "In my arms for so long," with a realization of toxicity—"In my veins for so long"—then hurtles toward the chorus, through Corin singing heatedly, "What you're doing to me is wrong / And there's no pity for you in my song."

But who is this "you"? The song doesn't say. Bikini Kill had counseled its listeners, "You've got to know what they are"—"they" being patriarchy, presumably—but knowing doesn't matter in "Good Food"; all that matters is for girls to decide that their crippling self-doubt is not an individual weakness but rather the work of some adversary, one that's external and can therefore be fought. Yet even this isn't a guarantee of victory: The song's speaker closes her mouth around the poison four times and expels it only once ("My body is mine, so I spit you out"), and that doesn't do the trick, because in the song's final lines she's back in her awkward limbo, the pill stuck between her cheek and jaw, softening a little at its edges, putting the girl on constant guard. How easy it would be, at any moment, to let the poison in.

Early in 1992, Dana Younkins, who'd been one of Allison Wolfe's best friends in high school and was now an Evergreen student, produced four episodes of a television show, *The Riot Grrrl Variety Show*, for her spring-quarter independent project. Aired on public access in April and May, the show was only loosely scripted. It was also only loosely linked to the actual group: Dana hardly ever went to meetings, and socially she was more ingrained in Evergreen's lesbian scene. (While most of the riot grrrls considered themselves bisexual, and some did occasionally date girls, the campus lesbians considered the Riot Grrrl thing too straight for them.)

"Variety," not "Riot Grrrl," was the key component of the show's title. Like an alternate-universe Smothers Brothers, Dana threw together separately produced segments and in-studio musical performances, and she would appear at the beginning and end of each episode wearing enormous sunglasses, flashy earrings, some outlandish off-the-shoulder tent of a dress, and a zany wig. "We've got a great lineup for you tonight," she'd tell her audience, absently, while weaving in space to the groovy background music. Segments included a self-defense training, a tutorial about safe sex between women, a lesbian dating show, and a women's-history game show called "You're a Riot," which Dana emceed along with a male cohost, "Manna White." (Molly Neuman, one of the competititors on the show, gave her occupation as "beauty school dropout.") Heavens to Betsy played a song on the show, as did Lil' Missy, a duo of Dana and Allison. Cuntz with Attitude, a lesbian party band that Dana was just joining, appeared several times.

Tracy and her friend Danni Sharkey shot two vegan cooking-show segments; in one, they made *The Farm Cookbook*'s chocolate cake while wearing just bras and shorts, with slogans written on their bellies: VEGANS TASTE BETTER and KISS THE COOK. The day after the first episode aired, Danni's male friends kept coming up to her and saying nervously, "I saw your show . . ."

"Oh, did you?" Danni replied, tickled that the boys didn't know what else they were allowed to say. If they said they'd liked the show, it might mean they had enjoyed seeing her and Tracy shirtless—a dangerous admission. So the boys just shifted from foot to foot and smiled sheepishly.

The first two episodes practically made themselves. Dana's whole community, it seemed, was willing to spend long hours in the windowless TV studio in the CAB building basement. But by the third episode, having called in all her favors and used up all her good ideas, Dana was desperate to fill the time. In one last-ditch segment, she played a solo song that had never been intended for public performance: "Nobody likes me, everybody hates me!" she screamed while playing bass. "I'm gonna eat some worms!"

By that summer, several of the riot grrrls, including Michelle and Becca, were living in the storied Martin Apartments, Olympia punk's royal compound. Situated downtown, just around the corner from the Capitol Theater and across the street from the Washington Center for the Performing Arts, the Martin looms large in any history of the Olympia scene. It was a small place, just a single layer of second-story apartments upstairs from a lingerie shop, arranged in a boxy U around a central rooftop courtyard. Across the courtyard, people could easily see into one another's homes. Most of the Martin's twenty-some units were occupied by scene stalwarts, who helped their friends bypass the building's waiting list by passing down leases hand to hand. Calvin Johnson and Candice Pedersen of K each had an apartment there, as did Nikki McClure, Molly Neuman, and Tobi's friend from high school Donna Dresch, now working for K as the label's first full-time employee and continuing to put out her *Chainsaw* zine. The Martin's laundry room had hosted Olympia's first Riot Grrrl meeting and countless band practices. Michelle handed off her apartment to Becca, only it wasn't technically Michelle's apartment; she was subletting from Tobi while Bikini Kill did its East Coast residency. A bigger unit had become available down the hall, and Michelle was taking it, but Tobi's place had to stay in the family so she could move back in when she got home. This, not meetings or formal affiliations, was the town's way: an in-crowd that perpetuated itself by hand-picking its next generation. It was stable, comfortable, and fertile. It created unique art and lifelong friendships. For the people it worked for, it really worked.

"People would be like, 'Oh, you live in the Martin?'—like that means you're a scenester and you're stuck up," Michelle said. "That kind of attitude always baffled me. I never felt like I belonged anywhere, and then I got here and felt like I belonged here. So to have somebody tell me that that's fucked up, and that I'm too cool, it was like, are you kidding me?"

When Becca moved in, she found the walls between apartments were so thin that she had to whisper the songs she was writing in her room if she didn't want her neighbors to hear the works in progress. Everyone who lived there was friendly with one another, it seemed, save the few longtime elderly tenants who sometimes stood alone in the downstairs doorway at night, smoking a cigarette before retiring. Doors were always open. People hung notebooks in the hall so friends could leave messages if nobody was home. Becca started playing music, casually, with her neighbors: Donna Dresch; Corin Tucker, who formed a band with Becca called Heartless Martin that played one show and recorded a five-song cassette; and Carrie Brownstein, a guitarist who had just moved to town from Bellingham. (The following year, Becca and Carrie would form a band, Excuse 17, that would tour widely and release two albums in the mid-'90s. And in 1994 Corin and Carrie would record their first album as Sleater-Kinney.)

Riot Grrrl's in-crowd got a little bigger that summer with the arrival of some new girls from Bremerton, Washington, a working-class navy town of about forty thousand people, an hour from Olympia. Angie Hart skipped the last week of twelfth grade there in order to hang out in Oly and go to shows; after her two best girl friends graduated from high school later that month, the three of them rented a house together on Olympia's hilly west side. She doesn't remember when she first heard about Riot Grrrl as a *thing*. "It was more just like, Oh, there's girls here! And girls who were making a particular—like, we have presence as women here. All eight of us are going to stand in the front next to each other and hold hands at a show."

The girl gang made the punk scene feel safer. In Bremerton, at the first punk show that Angie ever went to, there was a fight, and a guy was hit with a two-by-four and killed. Another time while she was in high school, kids riding the ferry back from a show in Seattle rioted violently. Angie wasn't on that boat, but many of her friends were. "The violence didn't register to me as something I should be afraid of," she said. "It was just the way it was." And not going to shows was not an option: "At the time, it was like, 'Well, we have to be punks, so . . .'" Where else could they belong? Not in their high school, with the arcane codes and social norms that struck Angie and her friends as fake and pointless. And not with their families, where drugs, abuse, and domestic dysfunction often made home feel like one more thing that had to be escaped. After surveying all the possibilities available to them—God, sports, drugs and booze, conforming to the culture around them—they had chosen punk. Punk made sense to these girls; it was one of the only things that did.

Angie's memories of that summer in Oly are ringed with the idyllic halo that adheres to one's first time living independently. The days were sunny and dry, filled with bike rides and get-togethers and long afternoons spent picking the blackberries that grew wild in spiny, bee-filled bushes along fences and meadows. Seabirds called out constantly over the boat-studded inlet that divided the west side from downtown, and the salty smell of cold seawater and marine life blew inland from time to time, filling the town with the feeling of being on the very edge of something vast.

The girl revolution was a gold thread running through the fabric of the time, inseparable from everything else. "Just living in Olympia was like, 'Oh, okay, Riot Grrrl,'" Angie said. "It didn't feel like, 'You've got to go to this meeting if you want to be a riot grrrl.' It just was like, 'Oh yeah, I was talking to so-and-so on the street on Tuesday, and then I ran into . . .' It just was in the air, I guess." When meetings started up again in the fall, Angie and her friends would go to some of them, and would participate in the soul-baring conversations that occasionally took place there. But these conversations were also happening at shows and at parties and on the sidewalks of Fourth Avenue downtown. Angie and her friends were bursting to talk with each other, to examine what it meant to be female in a patriarchal culture, and to figure out how not to let it all make you want to die. The same crew of people saw each other night after night, so the discussions of girl revolution overflowed and flooded the whole scene. That was what it meant for them to be riot grrrls. It felt like such a personal, specific experience that they often forgot there was an outside world that might want to take notice.

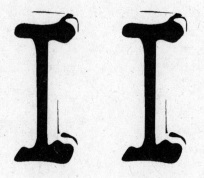

1992-93

SIX

CONVENTIONS

Back in DC, the summer days were growing heavy and slow. Tree branches sagged under the weight of the moisture in the air; heat hung like cobwebs between the dusky-green leaves. Most afternoons the sky would suddenly become dense and bruised, an overripe plum, then explode into hasty thunderstorms that vanished as fast as they'd come, leaving wet pavement to steam itself dry in the sun.

A few of DC's riot grrrls had become curious about fighting—actual physical brawls. What was up with this essentialist idea that girls needed to be protected from the scary, violent mosh pit? Maybe girls should think about fighting back instead. A couple of them approached Ian MacKaye about it. They knew the Fugazi frontman had been quite a bruiser in his teenage years, when DC punk was in its infancy and squares used to hang around in Georgetown, lying in wait for young rebels. Punks were fighters then, and MacKaye had loved the empowering feeling of not backing down from a threat. It wasn't until a few years later, in the mid-'80s, when he saw punks beating up other punks at a concert, that he swore off violence, going so far in the other direction that he'd stop Fugazi shows midsong if he saw people getting hurt. By the early '90s, violent conflict was anathema in DC's punk scene, perpetrated only by outsiders like skinheads or jocks. MacKaye told the riot grrrls that if they wanted advice on head busting, it wasn't going to come from him.

The would-be combatants were only a small subset of Riot Grrrl DC, anyhow. The group was expanding, as girls from the previous summer came back into town from college and new girls got drawn in by a friend or an announcement at a show. Many of the original core members were still deeply involved—Kathleen, Erika, Mary, May, Joanna, Ananda—but in just a few months, the group's phone list had nearly doubled in size, to fifty names, and had to be typed instead of handwritten for everybody to fit on a single sheet. All these extra hands were welcome, because the girls were busier than they had ever been. They had decided over the winter of 1991–92 to hold a convention in July, and planning that event was now taking over their lives. They needed to book bands, find a PA system, line up space for workshops and a dance party, figure out where all the out-of-town girls would sleep, and raise money to pay for the space rental and equipment, which they did by selling tickets for a raffle, with prizes donated by the Biograph art-house movie theater, the record store Vinyl Ink, and the punk café Food for Thought.

Who would come to the convention? There were still only the two main Riot Grrrl chapters, in Olympia and DC, plus a tiny group of college students in Western Massachusetts and an even tinier one in New York City, both started by girls from the DC group who'd gone away to school. But Bikini Kill had spent a good portion of the past year on the road, spreading the word, seeding a nationwide network that could be summoned into action. Many of the girls who'd seen these shows were already making plans to come to DC for the convention.

This mission had imparted an extra layer of significance to the unrelenting, often dulling rhythm of tour. Bikini Kill wasn't *just* a band; this wasn't *just* a tour. Some things about touring were inevitable: the endless procession of cities, the night drives when everybody but the driver was asleep and the only sounds were the road beneath the wheels and the occasional clatter of cymbal stands in back. Inescapable, the small-town rest stops where men in canvas overalls stared their curiosity or hatred at the freaks from away; the mega–truck stops where humble trailers in a corner of the lot offered free coffee to entice tired drivers to the Lord; the naked foul smell of clubs in daytime, without darkness or bodies to mask the old beer sticky on linoleum floors, smoke fossilized in vinyl couches; the numbing monotony of load in, wait around, sound check, bored sound guy snaking cables around the drums *Let me hear your snare please Let me hear your ride.*

That was all a given. But Bikini Kill had flared across the country that year, leaving burned-over districts in its wake, swaths of towns that had seen its light. Conflict dogged the band everywhere they went; guys called them sexists for inviting the girls to the front, man-haters for singing about rape and abuse. Tobi was shocked that a simple pro-girl message was enough to provoke such venom. It seemed to underscore how vital their project was. So the band, undeterred, went on spreading the girl revolution gospel, turning rock clubs into tent revivals, stages into pulpits, girl punks into devotees of girl power. Kathleen wrote her homilies in the van between cities, talking with her bandmates to pace out the show, deciding together when they would switch instruments and when Kathleen would face the audience and speak plainly to the people. At each show, the band would pass out copies of the

Bikini Kill zine and the lyric sheets they had printed up to make sure their message wouldn't get lost amid cruddy PAs or audience inattention.

They collected addresses for their mailing list—they would send postcards announcing future tour dates—and when girls

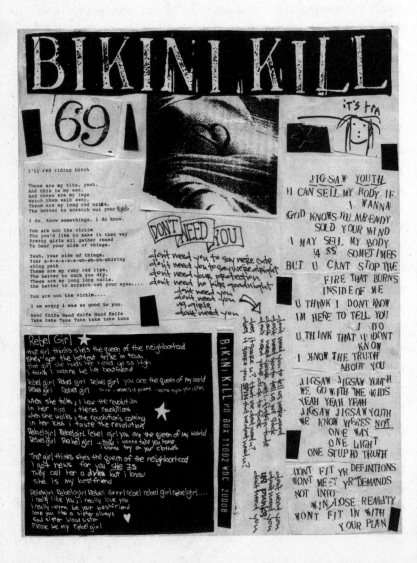

came to the shows Kathleen made them promise to bring all their girl friends with them next time.

In the spring, everybody on the mailing list received a flyer in the mail. "This is a newsletter for women/girls interested in female revolution," the flyer announced. One of the girls who got this flyer was eighteen-year-old Christina Woolner. Christina had seen Bikini Kill play that winter, in Western Massachusetts, where she was a senior at a progressive boarding school. Nobody at school gave her grief for dressing like a goth or declaring herself bisexual or being chubby, but she gave *herself* plenty of grief. She'd always been praised for being smart; she'd even been chosen as a fashion assistant for *Sassy's* reader-produced issue in the summer of 1991. But nobody had ever told her that she was *pretty*, and in her last year of high school she still had never been kissed, never been asked out. Even though she was bright and talented, and went to a school where misfits were the norm and cheerleaders didn't exist, she still felt like a loser because she wasn't a skinny girl going out on lots of dates.

When Christina saw Bikini Kill play in late 1991, she was instantly converted. She bought the band's zine for a dollar, a tremendous issue of fifty-six text-dense pages. Just the twelve-page taxonomy that classified and refuted ten types of male objections to feminism could provide many weeks' worth of ideas. "You take things too seriously" (#1). "You are exclusionary and alienating to men" (#2). "Complain, complain, complain . . . . . at least you don't have it as bad as a) women used to, b) people of color, c) women in other countries" (#10).

Back in her dorm room that night, Christina read the zine and latched on to one page that had the words DORK and COOL running all around the border. Having never seen coolness as an option for herself, Christina was comforted by this dork manifesto that started out, "Being cool in our culture means being cold, standoffish, uncaring (you're too cool to notice a lot of things) and self-absorbed," and continued:

> By claiming 'dork' as cool we can confuse
> and disrupt this whole process. The idea is
> that not only have we decided that being a
> dork (not repressing our supposedly femi-
> nine qualities like niceness and telling
> people how we feel) is cool and thus, valu-
> able to us BUT also that we are not willing
> to accept claims that how we are is wrong,
> undeveloped, bad or . . . . . uncool.

Christina was excited to transform her uncoolness into an asset through the alchemical power of some jerry-rigged feminist theory. But something wasn't lining up. The girls in Bikini Kill *weren't* dorks, not the way Christina was. They were self-assured, beautiful, thin: They looked like models, practically, so what were they doing preaching the merits of dorkiness?

Under different circumstances, the matter might have ended there. But the zine included two letters from readers, so Christina knew that if she wrote a letter it would be read. She wrote back that same night, saying that she loved the zine but also felt alienated from it because (she wrote), you see, I really *am* a dork, not like you; I'm chubby and dorky and a total nerd. What she meant but didn't write explicitly: I would love to claim my oddness as cool, but if beautiful girls take over the "dork" label, where does that leave me?

Kathleen was getting a lot of letters that year, from boys who felt excluded or attacked by her band, and from girls who felt galvanized or intimidated or both. She replied to as many as she could. In Kathleen's letter back to Christina, she wrote that lots of people feel uncool on the inside even if you can't tell by looking at them.

She also wrote that she was trying to use attractiveness as a tool for getting her message out. (The introduction of the first *Bikini Kill* zine had proclaimed bluntly: "Being a sexy and powerful female is one of the most subversive projects of all.")

Most important, Kathleen wrote to Christina, "You've got to do a zine, cool dork girl!"

The seed had been planted. It waited for her, winter long. While the girls in Olympia hosted their Riot Girl Extravaganza and the girls in DC marched on the Mall, Christina did her schoolwork, and her zine waited to emerge.

After school let out for the summer, Christina moved back in with her parents, just north of New York City. There she received the "female revolution" flyer, a collaged mix of Riot Grrrl propaganda, cultural recommendations, and coming attractions. It announced the convention that the DC chapter was planning and the June tour dates for Heavens to Betsy and Bratmobile:

```
Girl love is in for '92 in a big fuckin'
way as will be evidenced by the RIOT GRRRL
tour featuring HEAVENS TO BETSY and BRAT-
MOBILE. If you don't live in any of these
places please call yr friends and tell them
to come out and support, dialogue with and
feed these grrrls. This is their first tour
and they are forging new aesthetics and
ways of being.
```

The flyer also included the "Girl Gangs Must Rule All Towns" piece, followed by one called "Let's Write On Our Hands":

```
Okay, so I propose that those girls who
wanna change things start writing stuff on
```

their/our hands. Magic marker works good.
You can draw hearts or stars or write words
on yr fingers, whatever, it will just be
a way for pro-revolution girls to identify
each other . . . . If only two girls do it,
and they start to talk cuz of it, then I
guess it's been worth it.

So much comes together in this seemingly casual suggestion: not just the Madonna glove and the skunk hairdo from *Ladies and Gentlemen, the Fabulous Stains*, but also feminist art history, which Kathleen had studied carefully. Throughout the '60s and '70s, women had been making their bodies into sites of art, bringing attention to the roles women's bodies had played throughout the history of art, and using their own bodies to look at how culture uses women. By the '80s, some feminist artists, such as Barbara Kruger and Jenny Holzer, were bringing language into their images, while members of the AIDS activist group ACT UP—influenced, as was Kruger, by day jobs in commercial media and graphic design—created eye-catching visuals that placed their protests' message centrally and uncroppably in the frame.

Kathleen, by writing words on her body (SLUT on her stomach was the most common message, but she sometimes inscribed shout-outs to friends on her arms as well), was consciously merging these streams of feminist art and activist visuals. And now she was enlisting a whole generation of girls in that project. Soon the audiences at almost every Bikini Kill show included girls sporting words and shapes on their hands, arms, and stomachs.

Writing on hands caught on: It was free and infinitely accessible, and (unlike tattooing, its most obvious analogue) it could change from day to day, essential for this movement based on contradiction and fluidity. The gesture built off a punk predecessor, the straight-edger's X inked on the back of the hand, substituting for that abstinent negation a whole riot of messages. A girl's body was contested territory; this was a way to rewrite its meaning.

Proposing an underground identifying mark also seemed to promise comfort to any girl who felt like nobody understood her. It suggested that one-girl sleeper cells surrounded her at every moment, waiting to be roused. The revolution would proceed not through persuading or recruiting but simply through connecting together the girls who had already, in their hearts, enlisted in the cause. Girls were already fully aware of the forces that hemmed in their lives; they were only, perhaps, held back from open rebellion by a feeling of isolation. The problem of female adolescence was so enormous that knowing and naming wasn't always enough to counter it; you needed allies. Write on your hands, and you might find another revolutionary on a bus, at the supermarket, in math class. You had to be ready.

"Getting that flyer in the mail was the most exciting thing ever," Christina said. She sent away for several of the girl zines listed there, and as she read these other handcrafted missives, she kept remembering Kathleen's letter—"You've got to do a zine, cool dork girl!" By this point Christina had started to identify as a dyke—*bisexual* had become too trendy, and *lesbian* was decidedly unpunk.

She started listening to the sexually libertine dyke-punk band Tribe 8, and reading queer zines such as Donna Dresch's *Chainsaw* and Matt Wobensmith's *Outpunk*, which gave Christina a sense of what gleeful, untortured queer identities might look like. But all these identities included having sex, and Christina had still never dated anyone. Okay, so that was her niche: the asexual queer. She gave her new zine the self-deprecating title *Girl Fiend* and filled the pages with typewritten pieces about being a dyke who couldn't get laid or even try, feeling alienated from all her "cutehet" friends, and worrying about coming out to her parents.

She brought her first issue to a show at Wetlands in New York in July. Bratmobile and Heavens to Betsy played, with the Lunachicks headlining. Two girls made out onstage during the Lunachicks' set, which was exhilarating: Christina had never seen girls making out before. And having a zine to hand out made talking to strangers unbelievably easy. She could just go up to anyone—people a lot older than her, and people in bands—and say, "Want a zine?"

"Right away," she said, "I realized it was definitely going to make access to this world—make my ability to be more comfortable socially—that much easier." The dork girl was becoming cool.

Bratmobile and Heavens to Betsy took four weeks in June and July of 1992 to follow a meandering route from Olympia down the coast to San Francisco, across the Midwest, and up to the Northeast, where they would spend a few weeks in DC before heading back. Traveling in two cars with a plastic hamburger-shaped conveyance strapped to one vehicle's roof for extra storage, they played mostly to smallish audiences and once to nobody at all, at a business college in Illinois where everybody walked straight past the outdoor stage, barely pausing. But usually people did come, often because they had heard about the show from the female revolution flyer or had written in to get on Bratmobile's mailing list when the band was featured in *Sassy*'s Cute Band Alert.

Corin kept a tour diary, and after playing at Gilman Street in San Francisco she wrote,

> I was afraid before we played that we would be really boring, but as soon as we got on stage all the energy of what we were doing came back to me. We messed up a lot the drums fell over but we totally rocked. We left 'em screamin' for more. So did the Brats. That is the best part of tour. Seeing all the girls rocking out and feeling that energy run through you. Then I can't feel anything else. So many people came up to me and told me how they liked us and good voice and so on. . . . Spray painted love in the grrrls bathroom.

Occasionally the bands would roll up at a show and find out it wasn't all-ages, and Heavens to Betsy would refuse to play, and sometimes Erin Smith, who was still under twenty-one, would be confined to the green room after Bratmobile's set. But this was the first tour any of them had booked, and things fell into place rather easily, considering. "I felt like the small town scenes seemed a lot more solid then," Allison said. "There were fewer people in the mix—Well, that's the one person you talk to in that town, and everybody knew, and that's the band you should play with in that town."

Yet even under the best of circumstances, being on tour is a little like being stranded on a desert island with your tourmates— the background changes so frequently that it dissolves into an oceany blur, and any preexisting tensions between bandmates become unignorable. Tracy started feeling distant from Corin as they traveled in such close quarters. And Allison and Molly seemed to scream at each other a lot.

As the bands made their way toward DC, tensions were mounting there too, not necessarily within Riot Grrrl but between riot grrrls and others in the scene. Positive Force was planning an outdoor concert near the Capitol building for mid-July, which would include sets from Bikini Kill and Fugazi. The event had originally been conceived as a protest against the Supreme Court's rightward trend, with Fugazi as the only musical act, but Positive Force's Mark Andersen insisted on adding Bikini Kill to the bill. "The two most important bands in punk rock were living in DC," he said, "and I thought it was important to have them both play." Ian MacKaye disagreed; he felt that having two bands would tip the event from being a rally to being a concert. Plus, he said, two bands meant twice as much time for the cops to come and shut off the power. They might even pull the plug before Fugazi got to play.

Andersen and MacKaye had worked together on countless Fugazi–Positive Force events in the past, and their collaborations usually went smoothly, but adding Bikini Kill made the planning process more complicated. Fugazi wanted the protest's message to be about how the outcome of the presidential election was going to shape the Court for the next three decades, and MacKaye accordingly wanted the banner that would hang at the back of the stage to read "30 Years." Word came from the Bikini Kill camp (or was it from the Riot Grrrl camp? Telling them apart could be difficult) that they wanted the banner to highlight the repercussions for women. Claudia von Vacano, a member of both Positive Force and Riot Grrrl, was gunning for something like "Abort the Court." The compromise message, which nobody really liked, was "Turn Off Your TV." Turn off your TV? Anybody watching the show would be seeing it live and in person. Whose TV was even going to be on?

By the day of the show, different factions and bands were tired of one another. It didn't seem to faze the riot grrrls, though. They showed up at the concert in full regalia: Erika in jean shorts and a flowered bikini top, with the word RAPE printed in meaty, four-inch letters between her lower ribs and her navel. Next to it, she had written, a little smaller, XO, as if to say, "Am I still cute to you now? How about now?" Mary, opting for the other extreme, had covered herself up completely: A canvas military jacket shrouded her torso, and a bandana folded into a triangle, Western shootout-style, hid her whole face except her eyes, which the shiny sun visor poking out from her forehead took care of. She was proud of her look, a patchwork of different radical threats: "We were into being as militant-looking as possible," she said. The coup de grace was the banner the girls had painted for the occasion, which read KEEP YOUR FIST OUTTA MY CUNT.

Mary didn't realize until that day, when some lesbians stormed up to complain, that some women rather enjoy a fist in their cunt under the proper circumstances. But the sign wasn't meant to be read literally. It was about taking a mainstream feminist slogan— "Keep your laws off my body," a euphemism for the real intrusion— and carrying it to its extreme. "Body" in that tagline really was a metonym for vagina, so why not come out and say it? The Supreme Court wasn't giving out extra-credit points for politeness. A war was going on. In the five years leading up to 1992, nearly a hundred abortion clinics in the United States had been bombed or set on fire. A few years earlier, a circuit court in Maryland banned a gynecologist from doing any more abortions at his Bethesda clinic—because the anti-abortion picketers were disturbing nearby businesses. Let other women try their luck playing nice; the riot grrrls would tell it straight.

At the concert's beginning, Mary and Erika and a dozen other riot grrrls took the stage to invite all girls and women in the audience to the weekly meetings and the upcoming convention. The girls stood in a line, holding hands, while a girl named Jasmine read into the mic, nervously at first, from multiple sheets of loose-leaf paper. "For me, Riot Grrrl is so fucking important because it shows

me that you don't have to be a boy, or hard, or a scenester to be cool. Girls can be cool by their own rules."

The line of girls raised their linked hands and cheered.

"I'm tired of being told what I should wear, what I should say, what I should be doing with my own fucking body," Jasmine went on, her voice stronger now. "The media has told you that in order to be a real woman you must be tall, thin, blonde, white, and passive. It has told you that a woman isn't whole unless she has a male protector, that women who enjoy sex are bad or sluts, that women love to scrub floors on our hands and knees. We have been brainwashed by these myths. It is time to deprogram your head."

Close to a thousand people had gathered by the start of Bikini Kill's set. Fugazi, the show's headlining act, had become enor-

mously popular outside of punk circles; its second album, *Steady Diet of Nothing*, had just been released, and Dischord pressed 160,000 copies, a tremendous amount for an indie band. (In comparison, Nirvana's label had initially produced only fifty thousand copies of *Nevermind*.) The crowd at the Supreme Court show included a large proportion of young men in white T-shirts and backwards baseball caps—not the kind of guys one typically saw at a Bikini Kill show.

Everyone in Bikini Kill knew an audience like this could spell trouble. The band's shows were often tense, and the more macho the other groups on the bill, the tenser the situation might get. Not two months earlier, they had played at the Middle East in Boston with a bunch of male hardcore bands. A guy up front kept heckling Bikini Kill aggressively: "Hey! Get on with the show! Hey!"

"He was hassling us because I was talking in between songs and he didn't like the talking parts," Kathleen said. "I spit my gum at him and he went to punch me but got our roadie Laura instead, and she passed out." The guy was Michael Cartier, well known in the Boston punk scene as a nightclub bouncer with a short fuse. Kathleen and Billy and a girl from the audience dragged him into the alley behind the club; the girl from the crowd sprayed Mace on him, accidentally Macing Kathleen and Billy as well, and Cartier ran off.

A month later, at the beginning of June, Kathleen and Laura ran into a neighborhood friend of theirs who had some terrifying news: Cartier had just murdered his ex-girlfriend, an art student named Kristin Lardner. The friend, who was close with Lardner, told them the whole story: Cartier had beaten Lardner up during their relationship, and had been stalking her since their breakup. She had a restraining order out on him, but he went to the liquor store in Allston where she worked, waited for her to pass him on the sidewalk, and shot her in the back of the head. Then he circled back around to her body, shot her again in the face, and went home and killed himself.

People kept saying Bikini Kill took things too seriously, paid too much attention to rowdy men at shows, did too much to try to control their audiences' actions. What would those people say now? An aggressive heckler had just murdered a woman on the street.

"I felt sick to my stomach, just horrified," Tobi said about hearing the news from Kathleen. "I finally understood that the people at our shows who were threatened by our feminist politics were the same people who would pull this shit in real life—and what this really meant."

So they steeled themselves, now, whenever they had to play a show with a lot of dudes in the audience. You never knew who was in the crowd. If a guy would kill his ex-girlfriend, what would stop him from killing a man-hating feminist bitch in a band?

News of the murder was fresh in Bikini Kill's minds on the day of the Supreme Court show, especially because another roadie and good friend of theirs, Chris Bald, had been attacked by three men on the street in DC just a few nights before, pistol-whipped so severely that he came to the show with his face badly swollen. "It was very, very disturbing," Tobi said later. Everybody was on edge from the moment they took the stage.

"Just—I don't know, everybody knows what to do, I don't need to tell you," Kathleen said wearily into the mic, sick of always having to be the one to say it. But then she said it anyway: "The more girls up front the better." Because asking the girls to move forward wasn't just for their own good anymore; it was for hers. "And if anybody is fucking with you at this show because of certain reasons, and you need to come up front, come up front, and come and sit on the stage and get away from them and let us know. Because it shouldn't be one person in the crowd's responsibility to deal with fuckers."

Fighting a cold, Kathleen shouted hoarsely as much as she sang in the set. She danced like she was trying to shake something off her shoulders while it burned clear through her skin. She slapped her crotch right before singing "I can sell my body if I wanna," and scowled with real loathing at the crowd. *I know you want to see this*, her face seemed to say. *I know you wish this was the fucking Royal Palace so I would take it all off.*

> *You think that I don't know?* she sang, ferociously.
> *I'm here to tell you I do.*

(Her tank top kept slipping off her shoulder. She let it stay down.)

> *You think us sluts don't know?*
> *We know the truth about you, yeah.*

Between songs, she addressed the crowd, her voice saturated with sarcasm and hostility: "Party naked, everybody. Go

Redskins! Go Redskins!" Only during "Rebel Girl" did her mood lift: "This is for the riot grrrls," she said, and she smiled warmly at the front row while she did a little-girl dance and seemed, for a moment, to be having a good time.

When Bikini Kill's set was over, a turf battle began brewing. Boys who had been content to watch the girl band from a distance started moving forward in anticipation of Fugazi's set, staking out good spots, edging the girls aside. Several Olympia girls were in the mix—Corin, Tracy, Danni Sharkey of the cooking show—and they were accustomed to standing their ground in the front of a show by sticking together and holding hands. It didn't work this time. As soon as the music started up again, the masses of Fugazi fans began shoving and jostling, crushing some of the girls against the wooden stage. The mayhem continued unabated until the power supply cut out: DC's Park Service was providing electricity for the show, and Fugazi's amps had blown the circuit. Andersen ran full tilt to the nearest pay phone, three blocks away at Union Station, to call the Park Service and beg them to reset the fuses. The ensuing fifteen-minute lull gave the girls a chance to escape the front section and regroup further back. Erika Reinstein got out by climbing up onto the stage, flipping off the audience as she stormed to the side.

When the power came back on, the moshing recommenced. The antics were bad enough that MacKaye remonstrated the crowd: "Don't push on the stage. And boys, please stop jumping on people's heads."

Fed up, the girls took action. They hadn't been able to hold the front section, but damned if they would be pushed to the sidelines again. You don't go back to the outskirts after you've tasted what it's like to belong somewhere. The Fugazi show felt hostile, violent, threatening, but they would carve out some slice of space that felt like theirs.

They held hands and formed a circle right in the middle of the crowd, like a ring-around-the-rosy game, like a batch of witches. Some boys in the audience took it as a provocation, tried to break it up. Mary threw a punch. A boy's lip was bloodied.

So what? A bloody lip. Who knew what that guy would have done to them?

Onstage, in a pause between songs, MacKaye craned his neck, shaded his eyes from the day's hazy glare, and looked out over the sea of bodies, trying to gauge the disturbance. It seemed that the riot grrrls, so keen for advice on kicking people's asses, had figured it out on their own. "Let's not fight, please," he implored wearily into the microphone.

The girls shouted their disapproval. They'd been defending themselves! How dare MacKaye tell them not to fight back?

He tried to soften a little—"I'm not saying you particularly; I'm just saying in general"—but it didn't help. The girls were pissed.

MacKaye was pissed too. "That show was the one time where I saw riot grrrls behave like skinheads," he said. "They were fighting! Hitting men. And I just don't play music for violence, period."

Allison Wolfe was among the people standing on the side of the stage to watch the show away from the fray. During Fugazi's pro-choice "Reclamation," another song written from a female point of view ("These are our demands: We want control of our bodies; decisions will now be ours"), Allison reached under her skirt, pulled out a tampon she was finished with, and threw it onto the stage. She later told MacKaye she'd been aiming at the audience, not at him, but plenty of people heard differently. MacKaye hadn't even seen it happen; he'd only found out about it because other people told him later, "Dude, Allison threw her bloody tampon at you!"

In the late 1960s and early '70s, radical groups like the Weather Underground used to speak of "bringing the war home"—bombing government buildings in the United States, for example, in order to create a visible counterpart to the devastation in Vietnam. The riot grrrls, acutely feeling the world to be at war with *them*, were bringing that war home as well, into the punk scene. Who cared about collateral damage? Their very lives, they felt, were at stake.

That summer, as the riot grrrls picked their battles and geared up for their convention, Democrats and Republicans were doing the same, staking out positions that showed a country not yet finished taking giant rightward steps. Ever since Nixon's election to the presidency in 1968, the country's economic and foreign policies had become ever more conservative, undoing many of the progressive changes of the twentieth century. Now Republicans seemed to have decided it was time to target cultural liberalism, and the election was shaping up as a referendum on social issues such as affirmative action, gay rights, and feminism. The whole Year of the Woman thing was just part of it, and at the top of both parties' tickets this was still a Year of Men. But in another way, the tag was already apt regardless of who won seats in Congress, since both Bush's and Clinton's attitudes toward girls and women were being enlarged metonymically to stand for the candidates' positions in the culture wars. Bush would come under fire that summer for appearing to support abortion rights for teenage girls. (Asked how he would react if his underage granddaughter were to become pregnant, he said he would stand by her whatever she chose to do. "So in the end the decision would be hers?" the interviewer pressed. "Well, who else's could it be?" Bush said.) Now his party announced that right-wing commentator Pat Buchanan (who had defeated Bush in the New Hampshire primary) and Christian Coalition founder Pat Robertson would give prime-time speeches at the convention. Buchanan's opening-night "culture war" speech (in which he summed up Bill and Hillary Clinton's politics as "radical feminism") is the convention's most-remembered diatribe, but it's important to recall, too, that Robertson's attack on Clinton led off with an appeal to ideas about what was proper for teenage girls.

> *Here is what Bill Clinton wants for America: He told* People *magazine that he wouldn't let his thirteen-year-old daughter get her ears pierced. But he wants to give your thirteen-year-old daughter the choice without your consent to destroy the life of her unborn baby.*

The most passionately held political divisions in American life were being played out on the screens of girls' lives. The riot grrrls couldn't have picked a better time to hold a convention of their own.

The first nonzine article on Riot Grrrl was published in mid-July 1992, sparking a brush fire of interest in the movement two weeks before the girls' convention. (*Sassy* magazine, that mainstream purveyor of alternative culture to teenage girls, had by this point run brief items on Bikini Kill, Bratmobile, *Jigsaw*, and the Riot Grrrl DC zine, but it never attempted to encapsulate the movement in a feature article.) "Revolution Girl Style Now," by Seattle-based writer Emily White—who had sat in at the laundry-room meeting in Olympia—ran as the cover story in the *LA Weekly*, the nation's largest urban weekly. The alternative-press newswires immediately picked up the story in droves; the piece ran over the coming weeks in numerous other papers, including the *Chicago Reader* and the *Seattle Weekly*. Television talk show crews saw the piece and contacted White—Maury Povich's people wanted her to put them in touch with some real live riot grrrls to come on his show. (She refused.) And countless journalists saw the article and started hatching stories of their own.

If all the articles that were to follow White's into print over the next year had been as smart and sympathetic as hers, maybe media coverage of Riot Grrrl wouldn't have become the huge problem that it did. But for whatever reason, most adults find it tremendously difficult to take teenage girls' lives seriously. Even when girls' lives and bodies constitute a major political battleground. Even when girls are speaking truth to power in clarion, prophetic voices. Even when girls are right.

White managed to nail it. A recent Sarah Lawrence graduate, she had gone to some women's studies presentations while in college, but they didn't interest her. "It felt like they were speaking in a lot of clichés," she said, "and that the whole thing was about feeling sorry for women." During her senior year, while studying abroad at Oxford, she discovered French feminist theorists such as Luce Irigaray and Julia Kristeva, who instantly appealed to her "because of the ambiguities and the way they talk about power: that women aren't completely powerless, and that there are power structures built into femininity."

She thought of those theorists again a year later when her new boyfriend, a former KAOS DJ named Rich Jensen who was now running the financial side of Sub Pop, told her about a group of women making waves down in Olympia. White was instantly taken with Tobi's and Kathleen's fanzines: "They were just on *fire*, these women. I thought it was amazing, all of it."

She had worked at the *LA Weekly* for a year after college, and when she told her pals from the paper about this new punk feminist movement, they immediately said, "Write about it for us." Until that point, her published work had been mostly limited to book reviews. Now she spent two or three months researching the piece whenever she had a moment free from her graduate studies in comp lit at the University of Washington. In January, she attended that Olympia Riot Grrrl meeting. In April, the newspaper flew her to DC, and she went to the pro-choice march and ate a vegetarian dinner in the Embassy's living room with the members of Bikini Kill and Fugazi as the musicians discussed, in dazed disbelief, Nirvana's recent appearance on the cover of *Rolling Stone*. She talked to several older women whose efforts had fed the new movement, including Sonic Youth's Kim Gordon, Olympia-based visual artist Stella Marrs, and Jean Smith of the influential feminist band Mecca Normal. And she interviewed members of Bikini Kill and Bratmobile—Kathleen was already sick of dealing with media, but when White mentioned homocore fanzines, Kathleen could tell that "she knew what was up" and decided to give White some material. The singer wasn't entirely truthful, though; she told White that around ten Riot Grrrl groups existed all over the country, even though she knew there were only a few.

White's article was beautifully written and politically on point. She realized that what made the riot grrrls so compelling was that they were saying what so many people wouldn't say out loud: that things had gotten really, really bad for women over the past several years, and that they might still be getting worse.

> *In the public world we are entering the darkest hour of the backlash. The Riot Girls have the right kind of rhetoric with which to face this dark hour because, like many teenage girls, they phrase every setback, every dream, in the language of crisis.*

But the real crisis for the movement was yet to come. Riot Grrrl was edging its way, involuntarily, toward the cultural mainstream, and it wasn't ready to be there.

Riot Grrrl always existed first and foremost as an incantation, an idea that linked you up not only to any girls who lived near you or who became your pen pals but to the untold others out there, the thousands of girls whose names you'd never heard. The underground-conspiracy model created a sense of infinite team that could not be debunked because there was no way to measure it. Its power lay at least in part in this indeterminacy, this imperviousness to being calibrated, counted, quantified.

It was like a volume pedal, making one electric guitar sound like four.

The sound track to '70s feminism had been an acoustic guitar, a lilting voice: rigorous, unadorned accuracy.

Here, in contrast: distortion, twelve-inch speakers, monster guitar cabinet, twenty-four-inch bass drum.

All we are say—

Kathleen sang in the song "Liar," quoting carefully, like a child delivering a book report—

EEEEEEEEEEEEEEEEE!

—and was interrupted by a bloodcurdling scream: from Tobi, an audience member, anyone. Kathleen persisted:

—ying, is give peace a—
EEEEEEEEEEEEEEEEEE!
—chance; all we are—
EEEEEEEEEEEEEEEEEE!
—ying, is give peace a—

———

The first national Riot Grrrl convention took place the final weekend of July. Over a hundred girls attended, possibly more like two hundred—there was no formal sign-in where they might have been counted, just a little trifolded piece of paper with a map of the Dupont Circle area, a list of places to eat, and instructions about the Metro. Some of the girls at the convention were from DC, but many more were girls like Christina Woolner, who took a Peter Pan bus down from New York with a stack of copies of *Girl Fiend* #1 in her backpack. Scores of the conventioneers were girls who had heard about something called Riot Grrrl—mostly through Bikini Kill— and weren't entirely clear on what it entailed. They just showed up in hopes of finding out.

Later, nobody would remember much detail about the convention itself, just blurry images: 150 girls or more sitting around in a room, saying their names one at a time. The same room, later that day: a girl talking about having been sexually abused. A girl crying; a *lot* of people crying, tears of sadness but also of relief—like the meetings at Positive Force or the Martin, but many times bigger. One girl's pain was all of theirs; they all felt it. At Madison Square Garden that summer, the Democrats were speaking for girls. At the Astrodome in Houston, it was the Republicans. Here in DC, though, they were speaking for themselves.

"I felt like others understood me," Christina would write in the next issue of her zine. "I felt like I'm not the only girl who doesn't see others as stepping-stones or obstacles to climb over to reach a boy. I felt like people didn't hate me for being chubby and dorky and not knowing what to say all the time. I felt happy."

The first night, Friday, there was a show at the Washington Peace Center, a Quaker meeting house just north of Dupont Circle. The room had a drop ceiling of asbestos tiles, recessed fluorescent lights. Bratmobile played, although the band wasn't around for the rest of the convention; they were busy in the basement of the Embassy, recording their debut LP, *Pottymouth*. (Tim Green of Nation of Ulysses, who did the recording, wouldn't accept any payment except a bottle of black hair dye and a slice of cheese pizza from an Italian joint he loved.) Lois Maffeo played, with Molly drumming. And the Frumpies, a newly formed band of Tobi, Billy, and Kathi from Bikini Kill with Molly on drums, had their first show ever, a garage-y mess

of gleeful noise. Bikini Kill itself didn't do a set, even though everybody was in town. "We were already seen as the de facto leaders of Riot Grrrl and wanted to de-emphasize that," Kathleen explained.

Saturday was packed with discussions and workshops at the Peace Center. (These sessions were girls only; meanwhile, a nascent Positive Force men's group, helmed by Mark Andersen, facilitated a concurrent mini-convention for guys to talk about sexism, homophobia, rape, male sexuality, and *Thelma and Louise*.) An hourlong discussion about sexuality kicked things off for the girls at 10:30. Then, after a ten-minute break, the group reconvened for an emotional session bluntly titled "Rape."

After a lunch break came a two-hour Unlearning Racism workshop that Kathleen had organized. Girls from the group had led the other workshops themselves, but an older African-American woman from the Peace Center came in to co-lead this one with Kathleen. Melissa Klein, Jen Smith's friend from the Embassy, wrote an article for the DC-based radical feminist newsletter *off our backs* that described the proceedings in some detail:

> *A debate arose over the subject of "reverse racism" when several white women expressed hurt over jokes or generalizations made about whites by blacks. The facilitator responded that it is incorrect to label this behavior as identical to white racism because people of color lack the institutionalized power that whites have to turn negative feelings into oppression in the job market, the legal system, etc.*

This conversation called for a serious switching of gears. The girls had just spent the morning talking about and connecting based on the shared ways they were disadvantaged and put down. Now the white girls—which meant a majority of the people there—were being told that they were oppressors as well.

Some white girls in the workshop were resistant. This was probably their first time thinking about these ideas, and a few of them got defensive. *It's not my fault if . . . I didn't ask to be . . .* "I remember people saying some *dumb shit,* man!" said Jessica Miller, who helped plan the convention. "Some of the women of color were angry and getting a very poor response from one or two vocal people in the room."

The discussion turned to the issue of Riot Grrrl itself. Race had never been a major part of the girls' discussions until this day, when some started asking why there weren't more girls of color involved, and whether they ought to be taking steps to address it.

The group was mostly white but not all, mostly middle-class but not entirely. Many of the girls were involved in punk rock—itself a majority-white subculture—but nothing in their ideology made punk a requirement. Suddenly the room was full of questions. Did they want to become a more diverse group? But would recruiting young women of color just be a tokenizing gesture? Should they try to meet women of color on *their* issues, rather than trying to pull them into this preexisting group? But most of the girls at the convention *liked* this preexisting group. This was where they felt comfortable, often for the first time in years, or ever.

May Summer thought the soul searching, though well intentioned, was misplaced. "We were what we were," she said. "We were suburban young girls involved in this predominantly white scene. It wasn't Riot Grrrl's responsibility to attract and recruit other people."

But the issue couldn't be so easily dispatched. Race had always been a weak spot for feminist organizers; those who knew enough history to be aware of this worried that Riot Grrrl was doomed to repeat it. Nothing was resolved. When Jessica left the workshop, her whole body felt tense, as if she had been through a fight.

Other fights were brewing that weekend. Several professional journalists had shown up to the convention, and this media interest came as a shock. One woman was writing an article for *Spin* magazine. Another was researching a piece for the DC alt-weekly, the *Washington City Paper*, that would end up not being published. An amateur documentary filmmaker, her camera banned from the workshops, interviewed girls outside the Peace Center. And one young woman who had seemed just like another workshop participant announced casually, during a routine go-round at a workshop's start, "I'm from *USA Today*," totally stunning everyone else in the room. After so many years of feeling invisible, all this attention simply did not compute for the girls. The convention organizers certainly hadn't planned for it. They convened an emergency meeting to figure out their media policy: Female journalists would be allowed to sit in on the workshops, but not to quote anybody's comments or take photographs.

"It was really scary that we were being watched under a microscope," Corin Tucker said a few years later. "It seemed kind of unreal." That old insidious *spectacle* again, changing real life to image, experience to commodity. Why couldn't it just let them be? Some other activist groups might have been thrilled to have so much attention focused on them, but Riot Grrrl's bedrock of DIY values meant being committed to alternate means of communication. The girls didn't want to hear mainstream America's ideas about what they were doing or where they ought to be going. Some of them also harbored that general anxiety about representation common among teenage girls. Irene Chien, for instance, refused to be photographed by anybody—family, friends—for most of her teen years. She didn't think of this as political, but it reflected an understanding, however unconscious, about the perilous power of images in the lives of girls.

That evening, the girls worked off the tension at a dance party in the warehouse of the Beta-Punks, a media activist collective. Reprovision, a video collective from New York, screened footage of the recent pro-choice march. The party was girls only, except for a few guys who lived at the warehouse and couldn't be kept out; one of the guys, gamely trying to make his presence less of an affront, wore a skirt. The girls pressed up close to one another as they danced, which made Christina feel happy and frustrated at the same time. "Everyone and their sister seemed to be bi," she would write in *Girl Fiend* later, but they all seemed to be bi in a casual way that meant dating boys and grinding on one's girl friends just for fun. Where were the other *dykes*?

Jessica Miller stepped outside to get some fresh air and found herself in an alley outside the warehouse, where the backs of a bunch of city buildings opened up their fire escapes to one another. The party was in a rough neighborhood of Inner Northwest plagued with crack and crime, but the alley seemed peaceful and stilled. The way the scene was lit and its bizarre emptiness made it look like a set from *Sesame Street*: a kinder, gentler urban landscape, where everybody was friends and all the monsters were kind and the camera always found its subjects' best angle. But later that night, when Jessica returned to her car, she found that someone had smashed the front window and left a crack pipe on the front seat.

On Sunday, the convention's final day, a coed discussion about male-female communication took place on the grass in Dupont Circle—led by Mary Fondriest and Positive Forcer Brad Sigal—followed by an afternoon concert. There was no session scheduled to talk about the future of Riot Grrrl, no "where do we go from here?" plenary. The girls all had one another's addresses now, and were excited about staying in touch. They assumed the next stage would arise organically.

Choptank played the afternoon concert, as did Cheesecake, a group from Boston. Jasmine danced in the front row, wearing a Riot Grrrl T-shirt, and Erika danced beside her, a T-shirt knotted up at her solar plexus to display, once again, the word RAPE on her belly, accompanied this time by a heart. A woman was hanging around, taking pictures; some girls asked her to put away the camera, but she just stepped back and shot with a zoom lens.

Riot Grrrl wasn't a disembodied idea any more; the girls could feel it had a real weight to it. The convention was the biggest event most of them had ever organized, and they had done it not as interns for a "grown-up" organization but by putting something together themselves. The weekend fed the girls' sense that the movement was building and would only get stronger.

Yet it also showed them that the outside world was taking notice. It reminded them that to be a girl in public is always to be watched. They were experienced media critics by now; they had to be: A girl with any hope of being sane needs to develop the ability to question and take apart everything she sees.

So they knew that if they went out into public, they'd be watched. But that didn't mean they were asking for it.

A week after the convention, *USA Today* published an article about the proceedings, under the banner TEEN FEMALE REBELLION. The piece bore the title "Feminist Riot Grrrls Don't Just Wanna Have Fun," and its attitude was obvious from the first lines: "Better watch out, boys. From hundreds of once pink, frilly bedrooms, comes the young feminist revolution. And it's not pretty. But it doesn't wanna be. So there!"

Brimming with condescension and overt hostility, the piece wouldn't have seemed out of place in a far-right-wing newsletter. Its author was Elizabeth Snead, a *USA Today* staffer from the fashion beat who had pushed hard to get her editors to allow her to cover the convention. "I just remember thinking how amazing and how wonderful it was that these girls had a place that they could express these emotions," she said. But in the article, she called the girls *teen angsters*, *punkettes*, *self-absorbed*. She described a "bouncing sea of mohawked female fans in Pucci-print minis" who frighten away a lone "scrawny boy" by surrounding him, jeering, and "hopping and slam-dancing in a frenzy" until he retreats. She quoted particularly provocative lines from the workshops (she doesn't remember anyone asking her not to do so): "Another woman says that if you ask a man to touch your left breast and he touches your right, 'that's rape.' A third responds that calling all boys rapists is 'racist.'"

Compounding the insult, the article's sidebar announced, "The Riot Grrrls' punk feminist look is pure in-your-face-fashion," and outlined the movement's ostensible dress code: "unshaven armpits and legs, heavy, black Doc Martens boots, fishnet stockings and garter belts under baggy army shorts." The girls' practice of inscribing words on their bodies was mentioned in the same breath as boots and piercings, as if the word RAPE on one's stomach were nothing more than a curious fashion statement.

The article ran with a photograph of Cheesecake performing at the convention: Caitlin Bermingham, leaning back to watch her left hand on the neck of her bass; Colleen Nagle, her drumsticks arrested over her floor tom; Denise Monahan singing into the mic, looking like a '60s teen idol in a lace-necked nightie, her wistful gaze finding the right of the frame.

Behind them all, half out of focus, a middle-aged man can be seen, dressed all in black, with what seems to be a camera around his neck. He's holding it at his belly, perhaps advancing film, perhaps trying to capture an image without being caught.

SEVEN

THE MEDIA IS THE BARRAGE

Late one autumn afternoon in 1992, a handful of Olympia riot grrrls got together in a friend's apartment to be photographed for an upcoming article in *Newsweek*. Angie Hart was there, along with Julie Lary, another girl from Bremerton, and Erika Reinstein—who'd just hit town to start school at Evergreen—and a few others.

The girls weren't entirely comfortable with the idea of having their picture in *Newsweek*. After seeing the awful *USA Today* article, they were wary of being mocked by any more big publications. Still, they'd done a fun photo shoot in Olympia that summer for the *LA Weekly*, and the images that ran with Emily White's article had made them look pretty fierce, all lined up in an alley looking bored and slightly suspicious, the way rock bands looked on concert posters. *Newsweek* was no alt-weekly: They knew this. But Kathleen had vouched for the photographer, Alice Wheeler—they were old college pals, and the singer had stayed at Wheeler's house in Seattle during the fateful Kathy Acker weekend three years earlier—so the girls agreed to meet up with her.

Since graduating from Evergreen in the late '80s, Wheeler had worked as a security guard at the Seattle Art Museum while photographing the city's punk and grunge scenes for her own portfolio and occasionally for Sub Pop; she'd done the cover for Nirvana's 1988 debut single, "Love Buzz/Big Cheese" (the label paid her twenty-five dollars), and promo shots for the Afghan Whigs, but those were her only paid photo gigs for several years. In fall 1992, she finally landed a big magazine assignment. One of the photo editors at *Newsweek* was an erstwhile Seattle punk, a woman who'd seen Wheeler's work. The magazine was putting together an article about this new Riot Grrrl thing, and it needed someone in the Northwest who knew the people involved.

Wheeler met up with the Olympia girls in the on-campus apartment of one of the riot grrrls. It was one of the Evergreen housing units known as mods, more like low-end apartments than dorms. The girls squeezed into the small living room, vying for space on the institutional furniture and the thin, dun carpet. When Wheeler passed around release forms, Angie started feeling uneasy, but she set her nervousness aside.

The girls didn't write in any particular stipulations. But they would later recall telling Wheeler they wanted her to use only group photos—nothing that singled out any girl from the collective. Group shots could interrupt clichés about the poster girl, the supermodel, and could dissolve the stories implied by solo portraits, narratives of girls competing to claw their way into the spotlight, into being the beautiful chosen one.

This was Wheeler's last session of the day. She'd already gotten portraits of the few musicians who were willing to pose for her: Molly Neuman in Calvin Johnson's apartment, with the walls painted candy-pink; Kathleen in a leopard-print bustier, with INCEST? written across her chest. The girls in the mod were performance artists too: a troupe whose act, ongoing and unquittable, was to live as girls in a culture that seemed to set impossible terms for their existence. They walked a tightrope, the sightlines of all who viewed them, and they couldn't jump off; yet they could try to navigate it.

Later, they would reflect bitterly that Wheeler had used them to advance her own career. Wheeler would take issue with those terms. Sure, she wouldn't mind getting somewhere with her art. The guys she hung out with in Seattle, fellow photographers shooting grunge bands, were hitting the big time all around her, landing national gigs and making beaucoup bucks selling their photos to East Coast magazines. Her motivations weren't just about herself, though. She had grown up in Omaha in the early '80s, and when news of punk rock finally filtered into town, it changed her life; it was her ticket out. She wanted to provide that for a new generation of girls in Omaha, girls anxiously scanning the horizon for a sign that something better was out there.

As for the Olympia girls, their decision to go along was something between "Why not?" and simple trial and error. That's how you learn things as an adolescent: You think, *How will it feel if I do this?* Then you do it and you find out and you file it away as information. The photo shoot was a chance to gather data toward their ongoing mission: figuring out how media images of girls worked and how much control girls could exert in the process. This is what they talked about in meetings, what they wrote about in zines. They collected the images they saw, added them up in their heads, collaged them together on paper and talked back at the montages with handwritten rebuttals.

They knew they couldn't sit out the image-crafting process entirely, because they saw how people could wield tremendous cultural

and social power via a personal image. On a mass-culture scale, they saw this most clearly in Madonna, but even their own town ran on these images. In such a small community, where you couldn't go to the Safeway without running into a half dozen people you knew, few people wanted to wear their innermost self on the surface; too much genuine interaction would quickly rub them raw. Anyone who was going to last any length of time in Olympia learned to craft an outer persona who walked down the sidewalk and made appearances at shows and parties. That persona might wear rhinestoned sunglasses or outrageous wigs, or cultivate a quirky habit like bringing a yo-yo everywhere. The riot grrrls were trying to channel the power of images toward political ends. Ambivalence steps into the door, however, as soon as the audience for such a broadcast expands beyond acquaintances and neighbors. Ambivalence enters the living room and sprawls out on the couch when the image you're using to mark something substantial gets decoupled from its meaning. Adrift from its original reason for existing, yet still scented with some totemic version of it, the symbol becomes portable, malleable, saleable.

In the mod, Angie and Erika and the other girls were uncapping smelly markers; the chemical odor, unleashed, filled up the room. They outlined letters on themselves and one another—EXPLOIT ME. BITCH. Angie wrote PROPERTY on her stomach and MEDIA SCAM on her forearm. These words would give them control over the message their photos would carry, while cramming the image with a whole range of meanings and concepts. Meanwhile, Wheeler taped colored bed-sheets to the living room walls to serve as backdrops.

Late in the afternoon, at the end of the shoot, when the wariness had mostly worn off and they were all just goofing around, Wheeler photographed girls in smaller configurations, twos and threes, and took a few solo portraits. She was particularly taken with Angie, who had been living her idyllic, blackberry-picking Olympia life for just a few months. Wheeler looked at Angie and saw her own teenage self: dreamy and hopeful, newly sprung from the death trap that small towns could be to their tender misfits. Angie was finding liberation in Olympia, just as Wheeler had done in the mid-'80s. What was more, Wheeler saw an eerie physical resemblance. "I used to look exactly like that when I was about eighteen," she said later. "And I just thought, 'Oh, I don't have any good photos of myself.'" She laughed. "So I have a photo of her. She just was so cute, and kinda innocent."

In truth, Angie was feeling neither cute nor innocent. She was deeply uneasy. The shoot had felt like a fun hangout at first—a version of the punk pastime of the photo booth, expanded to fill a whole room and a whole afternoon—but the outsider with her camera introduced a dissonant element Angie couldn't get used to. "We didn't have the foresight," she said, "to be like, this is not a good idea—whatever feels weird and surreal about this is because it's not a good idea."

Near the end of the shoot, Angie folded her arms across her chest and gazed uncertainly out of the frame. The doubled click of Wheeler's shutter opening and closing sounded like an optometrist's apparatus, where the lenses drop into place one at a time— "Better here now at three?" *Click.* "Or four?"—as the patient strains to assess and judge. How does this look? And this? Things once obscure shake fleetingly into focus; clarity blurs to mush.

Later, back home in Seattle, Wheeler took some color prints out of their drugstore envelope and flipped through the set, trying to decide which negatives she would send to *Newsweek*. She picked out the strongest group shots, but she could tell they were missing a certain magic. The portraits of Angie, though, were quite gripping. She sent these, along with the other shots, to the magazine. Her editor could narrow it down from there.

That fall, Riot Grrrl Olympia was changing. It wasn't just the cool girls anymore; it wasn't one or even two tight groups of friends. Erika and her best friend, May, had moved there from DC to go to Evergreen, and since the town had fewer than a dozen riot grrrls to begin with, the arrival of two more was enough to shift the balance.

The DC girls were different from their Olympian sisters. For starters, most of the Olympia girls were straight-edge—especially Angie and her friends from Bremerton, where they'd watched relatives and punk peers destroy themselves with drugs and alcohol. May and Erika liked to have a drink from time to time; in DC, they had known which Ethiopian restaurant in Adams Morgan would serve them daquiris without demanding ID.

Most of the Olympia girls were vegan, too. They conducted special vegan rituals, like ardent discussions about which salt-and-vinegar potato chips contained an acid derived from milk. It was all part of the crucial task that faced the girls as they approached adulthood: figuring out how not to be anything like the adults they'd known. Cutting out items that symbolized negative values—meat for violence, alcohol for stupidity, milk and eggs for selfish excess—worked as a kind of purification spell. In addition, it sized down the world to manageable proportions: A small town gets even smaller if there's only one item you can eat on most menus, and there can be a productive comfort to that. The few acceptable objects—the cheap cookies sold in plastic-wrapped cylinders for fifty cents, the cinnamon rolls Becca baked in the Martin with arrowroot powder replacing the eggs—tended to take on a fetishistic quality.

Chiefly, though, the new divisions within the Riot Grrrl group boiled down to chemistry: May and Erika were dorky, dramatic, and loud, while the Olympia girls were fashionable and often reticent. Meetings moved on campus, to the CAB building. "It just became practical to do it there," Becca said, "because it was a common space; it wasn't at someone's house. It created more of that boundary: We're not all friends hanging out, but this is this other thing that we're doing." Everybody would circle up on the second floor in a carpeted conversation pit that had a picture-window view of the college's concrete quad, Red Square.

Discussions at the meetings became more intensely personal than they had been in a while, since the girls didn't all know one another's histories already. Erika was particularly vocal about the importance of telling personal stories—as therapy, as community building, as groundwork for political action, as itself a form of political action. Not everyone was happy about this shift. "The ones who were most outspoken about being sexually assaulted, I felt like that made them the leaders a little bit," Danni Sharkey said. "It was like you had to give them the most attention 'cause they had suffered the most. It would be hard for girls who maybe had had lesser forms of abuse. Any girl that just had gotten felt up in elementary school . . . "

Some girls seemed to indicate that until you had produced a skeleton from your own closet, you couldn't quite be trusted. "There was judgment, almost jealousy, of people who weren't putting themselves out there but still had people like them and respect them," one girl said. "Like, 'I'm on the front lines and you're not.' "

But not everybody wanted to share their most difficult experiences. "I had a lot of stuff going on also," Danni said, "but it almost made me not talk about it more, because I was like, I don't want people to feel sorry for me or to feel that that's all that I am. Who wants to be a victim for their whole life and have that be their makeup? We deserve so much better."

The group dynamics were rapidly becoming more complex. "There was such a group obligation to support each other," one Olympia girl said, "that something that got lost was thinking critically about support and thinking critically about each other. That made me susceptible to some really wack stuff. There was a bit of a contest of oppression—like who's the most oppressed person. And there was this thing of how mean can you be to the guy you're dating. You were allowed to school them and you made sure you were the boss. And there was an expectation like, 'I'm going to be mean to my boyfriend and you should not be nice to him either!' "

"If a guy said something sexist, then immediately he's the *biggest asshole ever*, and everyone's supposed to hate him," Danni said. "And I was part of that too. But now I'm just like, you make mistakes."

Since the group's initial in-crowd integrity was gone, it made sense to go further and invite new people to join. A folksinger from Oregon named Kathleen, who fell more to the hippie side of Olympia's punk/hippie divide, came to meetings often although she had a separate social circle. Other girls dropped in on meetings but didn't return after one or two times: They just didn't fit in, and they could tell. The best recruits turned out to be a trio of high school girls—Nomy Lamm, Sash Sunday, and Molly Zuckerman.

Nomy, Sash, and Molly weren't complete strangers to the punk scene. Nomy and Sash played in an all-girl band with some friends from school, and they volunteered at the Uncola, a collectively run all-ages venue in the alley behind the Capitol Theater. Nomy had seen riot grrrls around and taken notice: "There were these girls that went to Evergreen, I assumed, and were really fashionable in a Cyndi Lauper kind of way, and totally owned space at shows and were intimidating as fuck and kind of acted like popular girls." Sash had met a few of these girls through her job at the State Tri, a second-run movie theater downtown where a lot of punks worked selling tickets and snacks. One of Sash's co-workers, a riot grrrl named Natalie, told Sash and Nomy they should come to a meeting sometime.

"I had never heard of there being *meetings*," Nomy recounted. "I just knew that it was like, Oh, those are riot grrrls. I thought that you were supposed to know something, think something specific or be something specific in order to be a part of it." She knew it was a feminist group, but she wasn't entirely sure what that even meant.

Molly, a close friend of Nomy's and Sash's from school, had been a feminist for her whole life, it seemed to her. Raised by a single mom, she'd been branded a slut in elementary school for having breasts before anybody else. Men hit on her aggressively wherever she went, and she was sometimes scolded by her (female) boss at the bookstore where she worked—and even by random women on the street—for not dressing modestly enough or sitting properly in a skirt. Molly saw all these things as political: Girls and women were supposed to live within certain strictures, which got enforced in countless ways, and not always by men. When she heard about Riot Grrrl, she got her hopes up. Maybe these were her people.

The three high schoolers went to their first Riot Grrrl meeting on Halloween. Molly was on her guard from the moment she sat down in the conversation pit: These other girls were sitting on laps, petting each other's hair, and talking in sweet, girly voices. They weren't all dressed *exactly* alike, but Molly's long, black, shapeless dress, which she had to wear at the bookstore, made her visibly different. It was a feeling she knew well. This is just like high school, Molly thought. It's about being cute. This is totally not for me.

The meeting got started with a question: When did you notice you were a woman this week and why? Most of the meetings during that time were devoted to going around the circle and answering questions like this. These structured discussions drove the group and kept it together through the fall. "You could put everybody in a room together and introduce a topic," Nomy said, "and people would share with each other, and you could learn something about somebody that you would never otherwise get."

"When you're just figuring out sexism," Sash said, "all of a sudden you're like, 'Holy crap! That—and *that*—and *that*—and *that*—' Like in school, how the teacher would call on me when we were talking about *Pride and Prejudice* but not call on me when we were talking about Kafka. Or being harassed on the street or talking about self-defense classes. It was genuinely useful."

When did you notice you were a woman . . . The question pierced Molly to the core. When had she ever been allowed to *forget*? "I was feeling upset and defensive and outcast, and something about the language of the question instantly shifted something in me. I was like, *Ohhh*." When her turn came to speak, she burst into tears. To her surprise, nobody made fun of her. The riot grrrls may have looked cute and cool, like the girls who had shunned her in the lunchroom as a kid, but *these* girls—Danni and Angie, Becca and Corin and Tracy, Erika and May—they sat compassionately and listened.

The high school girls came back the following week, and when the meeting adjourned, the girls all tumulted down the broad stairs of the CAB and into Red Square. It was dusk; the parking lot lights stuttered on, each in its own time signature. The girls were heading back downtown. Molly, still unsure whether she merited a ride at all, hung back while the others claimed spots in the few cars, and she wound up crammed in a narrow backseat, her body pressed up against some other girl's body—not Nomy, not Sash, but a girl Molly hardly knew. She held her breath; she assumed anybody forced to sit so close to her would protest or recoil. "I thought of myself as a monster," she said. "That was always there: *I'm a monster, a monster, a monster.*" But the car door simply closed, sealing the girls together; the car simply drove downtown. A layer of Molly's self-hatred burned off, and its charred remains drifted out the car window.

Back at Positive Force House in Arlington, Ananda La Vita pressed some buttons on the phone and listened closely, the receiver held tight against her ear. *Of course.* Who else would be leaving messages for Riot Grrrl? Who else ever did? It was always the media now.

It was as if someone had sent out a telegram announcing that Riot Grrrl, underground support group and sometime punk event planner, was now a young feminist speaker's bureau. In the wake of the *USA Today* article, every news outlet in America, it seemed, had become obsessed with contacting the riot grrrls.

The phone messages for the DC chapter—from newspapers, magazines, television news programs, talk shows—went into Riot Grrrl's box in the Positive Force voice mail system, and since Ananda was the only riot grrrl living at Positive Force when the media cyclone hit in the fall of 1992, she was the one who had to retrieve the messages and bring the requests up for discussion. "Suddenly," she said, "every meeting had to be spent on whether or not to grant interviews to such-and-such a journalist or magazine, instead of on our own lives and other things we wanted to do and talk about."

The DC group was already at a delicate in-between moment. The girls had just planned and pulled off a national convention, and when that was over it was kind of like, okay, what now? Autumn hit and the group scattered, nearly everybody going off to college somewhere: Erika and May at Evergreen, Mary Fondriest starting school in Richmond, Claudia von Vacano back to New York City. Kathleen was still in DC, but she didn't come to meetings anymore. Mary heard from somewhere that it was the disastrous racism workshop at the convention that had driven her away. The workshop *had* frustrated Kathleen; she didn't believe she had figured out her own white privilege either, not by a long shot, but she felt like she couldn't even have a productive conversation on the topic with a lot of these girls. She started noticing other differences between herself and the rest of them as well. "At first it seemed we all had a lot in common," she said, "but then I remember way younger fan-type girls coming to this one meeting and just staring at me and giggling the whole time. That's when I realized meetings weren't really for me so much anymore." What sealed the deal was one particular night when Kathleen went to a show and overheard some girls who hadn't been at that afternoon's (supposedly confidential) meeting, discussing something Kathleen had said there. However ambivalent she felt about fame, she was now a celebrity of sorts, and her secrets had a high value on the open market. She couldn't afford candor anymore.

Ananda was the only person left in the DC group who had been at the first meeting just over a year earlier. She'd been living at Positive Force then too, so she had simply walked across the hall and into her new life. There was so much to make sense of and heal from: her parents' nasty divorce and custody battle when she was younger, and her mom's subsequent second marriage, to an alcoholic who regularly erupted into violent rages. Several times during Ananda's teenage years, he screamed maniacally at her mom and younger brother and her to get the fuck out of the house get your dyke daughter out of the house, and the three of them hurried out with whatever they could grab, peeled down the drive while he stood in the doorway, still bellowing after them like a monster in a horror movie. They checked in at motels or domestic violence shelters, or they worked the pay phones down at the 7–11 until a friend agreed to take them in for a night or two. But in the end, her mom always went back to the stepfather's suburban townhome.

Ananda couldn't get out of that house fast enough. Shortly after graduating from high school in 1991, she moved to Positive Force, paying her paltry rent with part-time jobs at a drive-through film-developing hut and at the Farm Animal Reform Movement, whose director was an old guy who wouldn't stop staring at her chest. Then Riot Grrrl started, and immediately she began seeing patterns and structures; her nightmarish family was part of something bigger, and she didn't have to accept or internalize any of it. She could grow past it.

One too-brief month later, the summer ended, and Ananda and her best friend, Claudia von Vacano, were off to New York City to start college. Claudia was doing a joint bachelor's program, art at Parsons and creative writing at Eugene Lang; Ananda was doing cultural studies at Lang. They kept in touch with the riot grrrls they'd left behind, and they even tried to start a chapter in New York, but it didn't get very big that year: The city was supersaturated with direct-action and arts-activist groups, and Riot Grrrl couldn't quite find its niche.

The following summer, the summer of the convention, Ananda

moved back to Positive Force, eager to rejoin the action. Her new room upstairs, just large enough to fit a double bed and a wall's worth of cinderblock-and-plank shelving, had massive windows that ushered in oceans of sunlight. She decorated her walls with the lyrics inserts from her favorite punk records and filled the shelves with shoeboxes of cassette tapes.

That summer was pure delight. Plans for the convention were in full swing; Riot Grrrl had mushroomed in size. Her mom had gone to live with *her* parents in North Carolina after an especially drastic blow-up at home, so for once Ananda felt her family might be safe. Mary and Claudia lived at Positive Force House that summer too, and the three riot-grrrls-in-residence luxuriated in that magic late-teenage summer spell, when your friendships are so intimate and unbearably real that they define you, consume you. Ananda's brother once shot a video of them playing around in the living room in Arlington, pouring their bodies over one another's laps on the sofa, laughing: Mary, her face shiny with sweat and joy; Claudia, vamping for the camera; Ananda, off-center, wearing a worried expression. She seemed to already be wondering how to keep this new family of hers harmonious.

When the convention was finished and the soupy summer air had started thinning out, Claudia went back to school in New York and Mary headed to Virginia Commonwealth University in Richmond. But Ananda stayed put. Unable to afford the next semester's tuition, she kept her sun-soaked room in Arlington, worked at a health food store in Alexandria, Virginia, and felt responsible for holding Riot Grrrl DC together. She was nervous about what the new year would bring. At a time when the group needed to focus on sustaining itself in the face of so much turnover, it was facing a barrage of distracting requests from the outside world.

The media had plenty of reasons for being keenly interested in Riot Grrrl. Some of the interest was absolutely surface-driven: This was a movement of mouthy teenage girls, with a flair for eye-catching visuals, who made public their private thoughts on sex, among other topics. The girls also added new elements to two major news narratives. For one thing, the past few years had seen an uptick in cultural anxiety over young women's sexuality—the campaign-trail rhetoric about pregnant thirteen-year-olds was just the most recent version. Several high-profile studies released in the late '80s and early '90s had revealed that girls were losing their virginity earlier than girls of previous generations, and having more sexual partners. Such reports on the rising tide of girls' promiscuity—this was the moralizing vocabulary of the conversation, even in major newspapers—didn't track boys' behavior, although these girls had to be having sex with *somebody*, and most of them weren't becoming lesbians. But whereas teen sex had once been merely shameful or unladylike, it was now deadly. HIV diagnoses in young people ages thirteen to twenty-four nearly doubled between 1989 and 1992; a congressional report warned in 1992 that the disease was "spreading unchecked among the nation's adolescents." "Teenagers and AIDS: The Risk Worsens," a *New York Times* headline proclaimed, while a *Newsweek* piece published a week after the Riot Grrrl convention needed say only "Teenagers and AIDS" in its headline—the rest was understood. School districts publicly assessed sex ed programs and mulled condom handouts; but however laudable these measures were, the discussions were haunted by far more enduring anxieties about sexually active adolescents, toxic bisexuals (*Basic Instinct*, released in March, having memorably channeled this phobia), and doomed underage sluts. All these developments pushed the erotic allure of teenage girls—never fully sublimated—once more to the surface of public consciousness.

In another central media narrative, about the changing political field, riot grrrls seemed to potentially represent progressive hope. The summer's Republican Convention had showcased a new, sharply conservative face of the GOP. The Christian Coalition burst into the open there after years of quietly consolidating its influence and power, and it succeeded in pushing the party's platform to the right on many issues, including opposition to abortion and reaffirmation of America's "Judeo-Christian values." Such public appeals to godliness were by no means novel, but the entanglement of Republicanism and religious conservatism had never in recent memory been this complete or this spectacular.

That fall, as George Bush, desperate for a polling boost, was addressing a Christian Coalition conference in Virginia Beach, Pat Robertson was sending his infamous fund-raising letter that characterized feminism as "a socialist, anti-family political movement that encourages women to leave their husbands, kill their children, practice witchcraft, destroy capitalism and become lesbians." The mainstream media mocked this hyperbole, but the Coalition raked in the dough, and the Iowa measure targeted by the letter—a law that simply would have added the words "and women" to the line in the state's constitution that went "All men are, by nature, free and equal and have certain inalienable rights . . . "—hurtled toward defeat. A ferocious opposition to feminism was evident throughout the new GOP—in its antiabortion stance, in its attacks on gays, in its loathing of the unmistakably liberated woman that was Hillary Rodham Clinton. Robertson's letter showed most clearly how antifeminism was fueling the religious right's ascent to the helm of the Republican Party, which was in turn setting the stage for what would essentially be sixteen more years of conservative control in Washington. For even though Bill Clinton was about to hold the White House for two terms, the Republicans in Congress—newly aware that their bread was buttered on the social-conservative side—would largely control the agenda during Clinton's presidency and the second Bush's presidency that was to follow.

The rise of the right wing was becoming big news, but any good news story needs two warring entities, and mainstream feminism wasn't having a particularly flashy moment. For six weeks that past spring, Faludi's *Backlash* and Steinem's *Revolution from Within* had been the top two books on the *New York Times* best-seller list. But *Backlash* fell off the list for good in early September, and *Revolution* came tumbling after; the following week, Rush Limbaugh's *The Way Things Ought to Be* roared into first place. Throughout the fall, as Limbaugh dominated the top slot—yielding it briefly to Madonna's *Sex*, then taking it back—the only remaining best sellers on women's issues were the self-help/archetype compendium *Women Who Run with the Wolves* and Gail Sheehy's take on menopause, *The Silent Passage*. Neither model seemed particularly game for a bruising fight against the new patriarchal Goliath of the Christian right, and feminism's institutions didn't seem up for the struggle either. "If you had to choose between the National Organization for Women and the Christian Coalition, just in terms of wanting to win," a political science professor told the *New York Times* that fall, "you'd choose the Christian Coalition." The Christian Coalition had the numerical advantage, too: In its brief three-year existence, the right-wing group had amassed 350,000 members. NOW, a quarter-century old, had only 275,000.

Riot Grrrl was far smaller than either of these organizations. But these young feminists, ready for battle, were just what the media narratives needed. And so the interview requests poured in.

ABC News? No way.

Sally Jessy Raphael? Don't even call back.

Spin? Well, maybe . . .

The request from *Spin* had thrown the girls for a loop. Despite its being a cheesy corporate alternative rock magazine, or maybe even *because* of that, it might be a good way to reach girls across the country. Plus, the freelance writer contacting Riot Grrrl DC was a young feminist activist from New York who clearly wanted to spread the word, not mock the girls or belittle them. Ananda and the others set aside their misgivings and gave her the go-ahead.

Twenty-six-year-old freelancer Dana Nasrallah had first learned of Riot Grrrl several months earlier, when she traveled from New York to DC with her video-activist collective to shoot a Bikini Kill show. The band impressed the hell out of her. Kathleen just seemed so *free*. "It was very empowering," Nasrallah said, "to see these women making up their own rules and trying to help one another." She was excited, too, to see young women articulating a sexually liberated feminism to counter what she saw as the "antiporn militancy" of older feminists. She had written only one or two articles for national magazines, but she knew an editor at *Spin*, and he gave her the assignment.

Spin in 1992 was something of a liberal propaganda machine. Aimed at the eighteen-to-twenty-five-year-old set, the magazine waded into political marshland wearing the thick hip boots of idealism, openly coaxing its readers to take action. Celia Farber wrote a new article every month on the AIDS crisis, and she traveled to Wichita, Kansas, to report on Operation Rescue's antiabortion crusade. In interviews, musicians discussed not only new hits but news headlines—the rapper Sister Souljah, for instance, talked about being publicly castigated by Bill Clinton for a comment she had made about the Rodney King riots ("If black people kill black people every day," she'd said, "why not have a week and kill white people?"). Polls plumbed readers' opinions on issues such as abortion, gay rights, religion, and premarital sex, revealing that among female respondents, one-fifth had been forced to have sex, an equal proportion didn't feel safe on campus, and a majority felt the issue of sexual harassment wasn't taken seriously enough. Readers of both sexes generally cared about the state of the world but didn't do much about it:

Ritual protest central to my life: 0.9%
Regularly involved: 14.4%
Maintain idealism but don't speak up often: 50.0%
Don't maintain idealism but complain sometimes: 13.1%
None at all: 21.6%

Spin's target audience, the generation that was just beginning to be tentatively labeled "Xers," constituted a powerful demographic in 1992. Many analysts believed that young voters held a critical key to the presidential election. The number of young people who bothered to vote had been dropping since 1984, and those who did cast ballots had been trending rightward. Figuring out how to reach the youthful abstainers and reverse their conservative drift might be a recipe for a Democratic victory in the fall.

The music industry was getting in on the action: Its new Rock the Vote initiative had signed up ten thousand young voters in time for the New Hampshire primary, and MTV had launched its own million-dollar Choose or Lose campaign, through which the channel broadcast a ninety-minute forum with Bill Clinton. (Political involvement did not necessarily equal progressive values or even intelligence: In one Choose or Lose spot, Aerosmith's lead guitarist licked whipped cream off a woman's chest while talking about the freedom "to wear whipped cream as clothing." The spot also included a cameo from a giant condom.)

Choose or lose, indeed: To be young in 1992 was to feel that the world's fate could be determined in the next seventy-two hours, and that the outcome might not be too favorable to human survival. With the December 1991 breakup of the Soviet Union, the threat of nuclear annihilation had finally faded, but other terrifying forces, seemingly more cosmic and geologic than strictly political, had come to light. AIDS was painting everybody's sexual awakening with somber mortality; global warming and skin cancer meant the sun was suddenly deadly as well. Magazines and newspapers printed ominous maps of North America striped with creeping red fever-rashes. Temperatures and sea levels were rising; incomes and standards of living were plummeting. For the first time in the nation's history, young people told pollsters they expected to do worse than their parents had done.

Despite *Spin*'s attention to such issues, the magazine remained largely a boy's club, with men outnumbering women on the masthead three to one, and the resurgence of feminist activism had gotten scant respect in its pages. When Kathleen chose not to be interviewed for a Bikini Kill article in early 1992, the magazine ran an unflattering photograph of her grabbing her breast, mentioned romantic connections between the band members and the boys of Nation of Ulysses, and lashed out at her:

Hanna, however, doesn't exactly have mass-media savvy—she declined to speak to SPIN *and, with that, gave up the opportunity to reach thousands with her motivating voice. At a recent CBGB Bikini Kill show, many guys panted at the prospect of seeing Hanna topless (she had doffed her shirt at a previous gig), turning a potential act of defiance into an oglefest. Some of the older females present saw the show as just a Poly Styrene/ X-Ray Spex retread.*

Incensed, Kathleen tweaked the lyrics of "Don't Need You" at a subsequent show in New York: "Does it scare you, *Spin*, that we don't need you? RROWR!"

Nobody from Bikini Kill or Bratmobile would talk to Nasrallah for her article, so she went for the grassroots angle. She attended the Riot Grrrl convention in DC, where she picked up a slew of zines, sat in on workshops, and interviewed girls in small groups. She even did what journalists are supposed to never do: She brought a draft of the article to the subjects of the piece (in this case a Riot Grrrl DC meeting), solicited feedback, and made the requested changes before filing.

The girls didn't know that the article still had to go through layers of editors who not only cared much less than Nasrallah did about the revolution but may even have felt personally threatened by it. Several years later, a jury in New York would determine that the *Spin* offices in the early '90s had been a hostile environment for women. The allegations of wrongdoing were plentiful: One editor suggested to a woman seeking a promotion that perhaps she might advance to "executive sex kitten"; another told a female writer, "Girls can't write"; the editor-in-chief, Bob J. "Gooch" Guccione, Jr., had a habit of dating much younger interns. But the verdict in this sexual harassment suit, *Bonner v. Guccione*, filed by the magazine's former research editor, wouldn't come down till 1997. Nasrallah, a freelancer who rarely went to the *Spin* offices, knew little of the chaotic workplace atmosphere, and the two editors working directly with her on the article—one man, one woman—were, she said, "super PC." She didn't know what she was up against, and the riot grrrls certainly had no idea.

Once other people at the magazine got involved in the editing process, though, Nasrallah quickly realized she had gotten sucked into a contest that she was bound to lose. One editor, objecting to Nasrallah's political analysis, pulled most of her personal views about what made Riot Grrrl important, replacing those parts with relatively tame zine quotes such as "I was one of those people who's always worrying about what a boy thinks. Being friends with women has helped me stop that." A copy editor wanted the word "grrrl" to be spelled "girl" throughout. (Another editor helped Nasrallah win that round, pointing out that the magazine would never correct the spelling of the band Phish.) After the piece had been scrubbed of her excitement and optimism, what remained was a curiously dry patch of prose, more like a newspaper story than a piece of cultural reportage. Riot Grrrl was defined matter-of-factly as a collection of metrics: over a hundred zines, one convention, a half-dozen chapters, a mosh pit reclamation at a punk show, articles in certain newspapers. The energy was gone.

"I remember fighting, trying to maintain the purity of these girls' voices and images," Nasrallah said. "I was so frustrated that I couldn't make everybody happy, get this word out and make the riot grrrls happy and make the editors happy. I remember feeling sick a lot."

The struggle over the piece's layout was the worst of all. The art director decided that the piece should run alongside a photograph of a topless girl with her hands covering her breasts and the word BITCH written across her chest. Nasrallah, aghast, managed to squeeze out a compromise: The rail-thin model would wear a shirt, and the paintbrushed words dripping down her bare arm would be

RIOT GRRRLS. But in a teaser that ran next to that issue's letter from the editor, the BITCH was back: A photo appeared of the model with that word written just above her eyebrows.

Nasrallah's article was published in the November 1992 issue, of which nearly a quarter was devoted to current affairs, including an eight-page election special. A record producer listed "25 Things You Should Know About George Bush When You Go to the Polls." A half-page article profiled the direct-action feminist group Women's Action Coalition, hitting all the stale points: hairy legs, check; feminists who "screamed" their slogans, check.

And then there was Dana Nasrallah's three-page article, titled "Teenage Riot," after the Sonic Youth song. The subheadline proclaimed, "Revolution is in the air and, yes, it smells like teen spirit."

When the DC girls opened the magazine and read the piece, they were aghast: This was not the article they had read and fine-tuned and finally signed off on. It was obviously sympathetic to the girls, didn't quote any critics of the movement, didn't call anybody self-absorbed or mock anyone's unshaven legs. But the piece emphasized fashion more than they would have liked (with "a little black dress with big boots and a shaved head" cited as a typical outfit) and included condescending language (girls "tittering" in a workshop at the convention).

The girls hated the article's dryness. They were offended at having their ideas characterized as a "crazy salad" of different sources, which sounded nonsensical to them. (The riot grrrls—and probably most of the article's young readers—had never heard of *Crazy Salad*, Nora Ephron's 1975 book about women that had borrowed its title from a line in a Yeats poem; the girls just couldn't understand why they were being dismissed as a bunch of lettuce.) They hated the brooding photo that ran with the piece: "Something was very passive about that picture," a girl from the chapter explained later. "The point was, it wasn't us. It was a paid model, right back in the system that we're trying to fight."

Above all, they hated the fact that they'd been had. They'd signed off on one version, and then something else was published. "I had to make a lot of compromises," Nasrallah admitted. "I empathize with them. If I was them, I wouldn't have liked the article either."

It wasn't just that they didn't like the article; it was what that article *meant*. They finally had to admit that they'd never had any control at all where the mainstream media were concerned. They'd been willing to be wrong about this, maybe even a bit hopeful, but each repetition drove home the truth a little more. There was no way to play the magazines' game and win, because the magazines owned the casino.

For several months that fall the riot grrrls of DC made no zines, set up no shows, attended no national rallies. Nobody remembers making a specific decision to pull back like this, but they were unmistakably withdrawing from the world at large. It was a season, instead, of sleepovers and intensely personal meetings, as the mostly new crew of members focused on building trust and rapport. Jessica Miller, who had gone off to college in Ann Arbor, heard from a friend still in DC that "a lot of things had changed," she recalled, "that the meetings had just become solely support group and there was no political action." Between all the interview requests to reject, the sexual situations to discuss, and the alcoholic dickhead father figures to defuse, who had the time or the emotional resources to be out in the streets? The girls were taking care of one another.

Some of the newcomers couldn't help feeling that they had arrived a bit late at the party. Twenty-year-old Seanna Tully, a recent ballet-academy dropout turned Riot Grrrl devotee, was proud of her new identity, proud to wear her nickel-size Shrinky Dink necklace bearing the words RIOT GRRRL in typewriter font and three hand-drawn stars. But she was acutely aware that her pendant marked her as a Janey-come-lately: It had been made not at the inaugural plastic-baking session at May's house that past winter but at some later crafting moment, perhaps the one that summer in Irene Chien's Potomac kitchen. "I had first-generation-Shrinky-Dink envy," Seanna laughed later, aware of how silly it sounded, but her comment pointed to something real: how easy it is to idealize things that happened in the past, or are happening to somebody else, as more enticing than what you could make out of your own life.

The riot grrrls were determined to counter that tendency, but the suspicion that you've missed the boat is a powerful and resilient one. In 1991, the Violent Femmes were singing, "I was born too late, I was born too soon," in a biting send-up of pop-music (which is to say classic teenage) clichés. That song, "American Music," hit number two on the Billboard Modern Rock chart, but it wasn't the year's alt-rock megahit; that place went to an earnest pre-grunge paean to the global village, pushed out with a cheekful of synth brass and compressed drums, combating the born-too-late crowd with all the smug entitlement of a prep-school sophomore. "Right Here, Right Now" was by far the British band Jesus Jones's biggest success, not only topping the Modern Rock chart in the summer of 1991—just as the first Riot Grrrl meetings were taking place—but going all the way to number two on the multigenre Billboard Hot 100. The song starts off with a cheap shot at the populist optimism of the 1988 song "Revolution." Jesus Jones dispatches Tracy Chapman's wishful refrain in the very first line: "A woman on the radio talks about revolution when it's already passed her by." The singer, Mike Edwards, pauses before the word "revolution," as if reluctant to sully his tongue with the sounds, then spits it out as fast as he can. The chorus, of course, goes:

Right here, right now
There is no other place I wanna be
Right here, right now
Watching the world wake up from history

But this wasn't about vowing to craft the life you'd always wanted, a revolutionary existence of historic proportions. It was about being content to watch big things happening somewhere else. The song, as everyone knew, was about the end of the Cold War. The youth of the '90s were so often pitied for not having, or scolded for not caring about, big issues as their '60s counterparts had done; but in fact, the song crowed, young people were living in a time of global transformation that utterly dwarfed all those piddly protests of old. The Gen X hubris of this hornpipe is clear from line two: "Bob Dylan never had *this* to sing about," emphasis added here but only because for Edwards to add it himself would have risked puncturing the triumphalist *passivity* that the song so emphatically embodies: "I was alive but I waited, waited." The triumph of capitalism trumps all the principled movements against its ugliest excesses. And best of all, one can own this alleged victory just as surely by hanging around on one's sofa, watching the news, as by taking active part. In the video for "Right Here, Right Now," rebellion is itself ephemeral, figured as video projections of newsreel scenes—tanks, summit meetings, protests—painting the bodies of the musicians just as psychedelic color wheels batiked Hendrix and Slick at the Fillmore in '68. In this new slacker age, all one needed to do to dispel apathy was to *notice* that something was happening, to watch it on a screen, to passively serve as its screen. O ye MTV viewers, why bother rebelling at all? True youth rebellion is always elsewhere, and verily, 'tis better that way, without the chaos and collateral damage and inconvenient principles that always seem to mar such movements in close-up. This is social conscience, 1990s style. You're not on the right landmass to take an active part, but that's no problem; you'll just catch the tape at 11, or on the Sunday night rerun of *Week in Rock*.

Watching the world wake up from history . . . No need to exert any effort, no need to *try* to awaken from the nightmare of history. Just watch. *Waiting, waiting.*

One of Nasrallah's few victories in her battles with *Spin* had been persuading the magazine to print Riot Grrrl DC's address, along with a note that zines cost a dollar plus two postage stamps. (*USA Today* had falsely claimed the zines were free; zinesters had to ignore hundreds of requests.)

The DC group's post office box soon flooded with mail. But the chapter hadn't made a zine in forever; they had nothing to send these people. Letters piled up for months. Seanna snagged a tall filing cabinet that her childhood ballet teacher was about to throw away, and she brought it to Positive Force House and stashed all the letters away in its heavy metal drawers.

Ananda wanted the group to make a new zine to send to these girls, but the others in the group didn't seem ready to put one out yet, and she was itching to write about the media issue while it was still fresh in her mind. In her room at Positive Force that November, she plugged in her electric typewriter and fired it up: The machine hummed softly, and the pinwheel whirred into motion, poised. Easing her page's bottom edge behind a roller, Ananda felt the smooth uptake as the paper slipped through her fingers.

She hit the caps lock key and shout-wrote,

EVERY DAY THERE'S SOME FUCKING MAINSTREAM MAGAZINE, PAPER OR TV SHOW THAT I HEAR IS COVERING RIOT GRRRL.

In the eloquent two-page critique that followed, she dissected the coverage:

> The latest has been ABC NEWS. Fortunately we turned down their offer and hopefully they will take no for an answer, but from experience, chances are they will do something anyway and it will be like all the others: showing us as this "item," this quaint new market-able "discovery" of a fashion or music trend that a bunch of rebellious teenage girls are into. . . . One thing I am particularly upset about is how they take something that has no actual definition, and they attempt to define it. Riot Grrrl is about destroying boundaries, not creating them. But these mags make us look like we're one 'thing,' that you have to look a certain way or be into a certain type of music or believe certain things in order to be a riot grrrl, when there are no such requirements. To girls just being exposed to Riot Grrrl, it makes them feel like they have to be that way to be in our "club." As a result a lot of girls are turned away! or we will look like "sell outs" to them. Riot Grrrl is open to ALL girls. It is about a lot of things, like support for each other as girls. Music is just a <u>medium</u>. Just like this zine is. You do not have to be "punk" to be involved! For girls who are already involved, reading about our-selves in these publications puts these sub-conscious boundaries in our heads too. It is

a weird experience to read a tidy description
about what I am, what I see Riot Grrrl as, in
the perspective of a mainstream paper; usually that description will put an image in my
head of what I'm supposed to be like and I'll
probably find myself starting to be like that
description whether I mean to or not. Seeing
ourselves described by these mainstream writers puts boundaries in our minds. I think
this is really dangerous. We can counteract
it by: keeping alive the "underground" aspect
of Riot Grrrl—keeping alive our communication
with each other. We can't let these papers
dominate our images of each other.

Spin had been the final straw, showing the girls that spreading
their message via mainstream media would never work the way they
wanted. Well, now they knew. They just had to decide what to do
with that knowledge.

One option, they knew, was to opt out. Bikini Kill had always
turned down most mass-media interviews, and the more offensive the
pieces that came out, the more tight-lipped the band became. This
approach was looking smarter and smarter to the riot grrrls of DC,
who were confronting the unmanageable contradictions of growing
up female by embracing unruliness and contradiction without apol-
ogy. Two-inch columns of ten-point type could never convey this
faithfully; stabs at pinning the girls into a tight girdle of journalistic
prose missed the mark entirely. The cut-and-paste lexicons of their
zines and manifestos, the tearful confessionals of their meetings,
the inarticulate screams of frustration that punctured such songs as
Heavens to Betsy's "Firefly" and Bikini Kill's "Liar": These were the
only vocabularies with a prayer of encompassing the girls' truths.

The DC chapter decided to impose a media blackout: no more interviews, no more photos, no more access. The decision happened not through a formal vote but just through loose consensus; it was clear that everybody agreed. "We wanted to spread the message, but we were interested in alternative ways of doing it," Ananda said. "We needed space to get our bearings and to put a halt to a fucked-up process and dynamic that was sucking all our time and energy, before it did too much damage."

Trouble was, the process had already been set in motion. It was too late to stop it now.

EIGHT

"THE PRESS NEEDS A MOUTH FOR A MOVEMENT"

Riot grrrls from DC had scattered, starting new groups wherever they landed: Richmond, Los Angeles, Boston, Ann Arbor, Oberlin, Western Massachusetts, Minneapolis, New York. Communication among these groups was scant, limited to a trickle of letters from friend to friend. News of the DC chapter's struggles with media attention filtered out to the others, but there was no mechanism for holding a nationwide discussion about whether to declare a media blackout. Autonomy was the ideal: Everybody would do what she pleased. Within reason, of course.

This suited Jessica Hopper just fine. Sixteen and ambitious, she was part of the Minneapolis–St. Paul group that got going in the fall of 1992, but she'd been a riot grrrl before those meetings began, and she was allergic to groupthink. Raised (on antisexist bedtime stories) by her mother, who worked as a newspaper photo editor, Jessica had been a feminist practically since birth; at twelve, she'd founded a pro-choice club at her junior high school, selling T-shirts with sinister coat hangers rendered in puffy paint. Jessica's Riot Grrrl awakening came in 1991, when she was fifteen and Bikini Kill's first cross-country tour with Nation of Ulysses brought the bands through Minneapolis. Inspired by the racks of fanzines at the record store where she worked at a self-devised internship, Jessica had recently resolved to start a zine of her own. She'd come up with a title, which meant she was serious: *Hit It or Quit It*. Bikini Kill's set at the Seventh Street Entry blew her away. She interviewed Kathleen Hanna over slices of pizza after the show, and the two of them talked for hours. Kathleen told Jessica about the Halloween show they had just played in Seattle with Nirvana and Mudhoney, and how troubled she was by her friends' sellout lifestyle. She talked about her body-writing strategy: "I write the word SLUT on my stomach because guys always think that. When you take off your shirt they think 'Oh what a slut' and it's really funny because they think that and then they look at you and it says it." Kathleen also told Jessica about the Riot Grrrl activity in DC, encouraged her to get a group started in Minneapolis, and sent her home with the second issue of the *Bikini Kill* zine, a copy of Tobi's *Jigsaw*, and a list of other zines to check out. Jessica published the first issue of *Hit It or Quit It* soon after, with an introduction that bore the influence of this new reading material:

```
A lot of the music bullshit I read is to-
tally male dominated and grrrls' issues and
grrrls' music is totally ignored.
```

She began trading zines, tapes, and letters with people on the East and West coasts: Bratmobile's Erin Smith, who sent copies of *Teenage*

Gang Debs; Allison and Molly, who sent *Girl Germs*; Ramdasha Bik-ceem, a high school girl from New Jersey who made a skateboarding zine, *Gunk*, that was cited on all the lists of grrrl zines.

Jessica never tried to start a Riot Grrrl chapter in Minneapolis. Her zine, and the pen pals it brought her, were all she needed: They gave her backup, context, and inspiration, which helped her do her own thing. A one-girl insurgent army, she wrote "Revolution girl style now!" on her school notebooks, preached at all-ages matinees against boys dominating the mosh pit, and even dabbled in vigilantism: She carried her camera to shows in a metal elementary school–style lunch box, in accordance with the punk fashion (hers bore a Snoopy design beneath all the band stickers), and if boys got too rowdy, she hit them with the lunch box. One unfortunate boy who crossed her path at the wrong moment during an L7 show left the club that night with a bloody nose. Her ferociousness surprised some people who had never thought to consider a slender, five-foot-one girl a threat to life and limb.

Hit It or Quit It was a hit. Her circulation reached four hundred within a year, and the local alt-weekly, *City Pages*, called her "a teenaged Lester Bangs," comparing her to the drunken prophet who had revolutionized rock criticism in the '70s and early '80s before dying at thirty-three. In October 1992, less than a year after Bikini Kill's first stop in Minneapolis, *City Pages* ran a full-page article about Jessica and her fanzine, praising *Hit It*'s "distinctively fresh and feisty charm." The article also discussed the emergence of the Riot Grrrl network and printed the time and address of the new Twin Cities chapter's upcoming meeting.

Jessica hadn't founded the local group; that credit went to Elizabeth Anthony and Susan Davies, two DC riot grrrls attending Macalester College, a small, liberal school in St. Paul. They had been friends in junior high in Maryland and reconnected when they wound up across the hall from each other in their first-year dorm. That was in 1991, and they were still unaware of the punk feminist stirrings that had just begun in DC and Olympia. Elizabeth had dabbled in the DC scene, but the Twin Cities punk style was more extreme than what she was used to. The Minneapolis–St. Paul aesthetic was one of dirty dreadlocks, chunky facial piercings, and thick canvas pants covered in silk-screened patches. Elizabeth's thrift-store cardigans and hot-pink hair were tame in comparison. Susan—with her dreadlocks, piercings, anarchist beliefs, and fierce nickname "Sin"—had an easier time fitting in with the crusty punks who hung around the Emma Center, a storefront anarchist community space in a working-class neighborhood in Minneapolis.

Elizabeth first heard of Riot Grrrl during spring break of her first year of college, when she visited New York City and saw a flyer from the group Ananda and Claudia were then trying to get off the ground. Sin got connected to the DC girls on a school break the same year. She had already noticed a change at shows in DC: "The strong presence of the women there, up front," she said, "dancing, not acting like they were out to impress anyone, not standing behind all the guys slamming around, and really talking about some intense issues in a personal way. That really inspired me." She met Erika Reinstein through a shared high school friend and wound up at a sleepover party with some of the core DC activists, including Erika, Claudia, and Kathleen.

Over summer vacation in 1992, Elizabeth and Sin started going to meetings at Positive Force. At Elizabeth's first meeting, the girls were talking about a sexual assault one girl had reported. The offending male was in a band, and the girls were discussing what they should do about it. Should they call a boycott of the guy's band? What would that entail—refusing to attend any shows the band played? Encouraging other bands not to share bills with them? Boycotting other bands that failed to honor the picket line? In the end, the girls decided to tell people not to buy the band's records. Elizabeth was impressed.

"I was just like, good, you shouldn't be able to attack someone with impunity," she says. "That was the idea: You don't do that without there being some consequences. It was a big deal."

Riot grrrls everywhere dealt constantly with this question: how to address sexual violence within their communities. It came up disturbingly often, and a satisfactory solution was always out of reach. At college campuses around the country, from Brown University to Evergreen, students were posting lists of alleged date rapists in women's bathrooms, warning one another of known sexual predators. This was a start, but the riot grrrls wanted to figure out what else could be done. They knew that 95 percent of rapes never yielded a conviction, and that if a woman pressed charges, the defense attorneys would advance on her like jackals: "What were you wearing? Why did you invite him into your apartment?" Even in punk scenes, the guy involved would often dispute the assertion that an assault had happened, and people in the scene would start taking sides, or abstain from taking sides, saying they didn't have all the facts. To the riot grrrls the latter position seemed like a cop-out. Why would a woman ever lie about such a thing? The riot grrrls would believe all girls, but they would *especially* believe all riot grrrls, because all riot grrrls, no matter where they lived, were bonded together. They trusted one another. They were all on the same team.

Elizabeth and Sin went back to Macalester in the fall of 1992 and called the first meeting of the Twin Cities Riot Grrrl chapter for a Sunday afternoon soon after. Gathering at the Emma Center, the group grew to about twenty members, including anarcho-punks, rock musicians, students from area colleges, and some girls from the local arts high school. One of the high schoolers was Jessica Hopper, who had met Sin at a Nation of Ulysses show. Jessica was still diminutive, precocious, and highly motivated, and her knack for self-promotion was getting ever sharper. She used *Hit It or Quit*

It to help her connect with and become pen pals with older musicians, and she traded mail with Kathleen Hanna, Jon Slade and Chris Rowley from the British band Huggy Bear, and the volatile Courtney Love, who had made herself plenty of enemies in the Twin Cities scene in the mid-'80s before moving from there to the West Coast. Jessica had learned to play bass; she was always trying to form bands, and she wrangled shows for her groups—the more famous the headlining act, the better. Jessica's reputation preceded her to Riot Grrrl. She was known in town as a social climber and a trend chaser; some of Elizabeth's male friends told her the teen was just coming to meetings to build up "punk points." Elizabeth defended her. Of course boys were going to try to tear down an enthusiastic younger girl who was sticking her neck out. Sure, there were reasons to be wary of Jessica if you were looking for reasons. She didn't open up in meetings the way the other girls did. And she *did* seem careful to make sure everyone knew how cool she was, mentioning her friendship with Love, bragging about how she was supposed to have been the bass player in Hole but her mom wouldn't let her drop out of high school. Still, Elizabeth reasoned, Jessica was probably insecure around this group of older girls. She just needed support and girl love. She needed to see how rewarding a female community could be.

Bikini Kill came through Minneapolis again that fall. Jessica arranged for the band to stay at her best friend's house, and she was looking forward to spending some quality time with the musicians, especially Kathleen. But she felt a change from the previous year. The members of Bikini Kill now struck Jessica as curt and selfish: eating all the food in the house, making a lengthy long-distance phone call and not offering to reimburse her friend, buying blank T-shirts from Jessica's friend but presumptuously demanding extra freebies.

"They were my teenage icons—I didn't think about them as

being human people," Jessica said. "I was totally put off. This wasn't the kind of experience I'd had with them before."

The St. Paul show was huge, with hundreds of kids, it seemed, gathered inside the club and more spilling out into the alley. The power kept blowing out. Bikini Kill sounded tight as hell. But to Jessica the effect was less than thrilling. "I felt removed from it suddenly," Jessica said. "So much of my sense of Riot Grrrl was built up around these people personally, and how I felt that they were being in the world. I let go of some of the idea of Riot Grrrl right then. I thought, these people are just as fake as anybody."

Riot Grrrl Twin Cities was a hive of activity. The girls put together an exhibition of female artists at the Emma Center. They booked benefit concerts to raise money for domestic violence organizations. They made mini-flyers about body image and slipped them between the pages of the teen girl magazines at drugstores and newsstands, so some young girl might open up a *YM* or *Seventeen* to find a slip of paper promising her, "You don't need lipstick to be beautiful!" or urging, "Love your body the way it is."

Elizabeth added her address to the list of Riot Grrrl chapters that was traversing the country in zines and on flyers. Letters poured in to Elizabeth's campus mailbox from girls all over the country, especially from the Midwest. The letter writers wanted information about what Riot Grrrl was, advice about how to start a chapter, or just some reassurance that there was *hope* for people like them. One girl writing from North Dakota lamented that nobody in her town even knew what a feminist was. "It was kind of like they just wanted us to know they existed out there," Elizabeth said. She divvied up the mail among the chapter's members, and everybody who wrote in got a response.

The girls also started plotting an action at the Hooters restaurant at the massive Mall of America nearby. At Hooters, waitresses flashed their pushed-up cleavage while wearing skintight orange hot pants and tiny low-cut tank tops that bore the restaurant's logo: an owl with round, wide eyes drawn to look like a pair of breasts. In recent years, this *Playboy*-lite chain had become a staple in cities nationwide, casting itself as a wholesome, all-American place for red-blooded males to ogle ex-cheerleaders' asses. Had the world gone mad? Had the '70s never happened? How had this overgrown tit-joke become integrated into mainstream culture?

The riot grrrls wanted to voice their disgust, but they needed a flashier tactic than the predictable standbys like picket lines and letters to the editor. They focused on a sign in the restaurant that read:

MEN: NO SHIRT—NO SERVICE.
WOMEN: NO SHIRT—FREE FOOD.

The girls decided they would call the restaurant's bluff by showing up, taking off their shirts, and demanding free dinners. How would the restaurant react to a group of females who displayed their bodies without the friendly, flirtatious attitude of the Hooters girls? In the same spirit as Kathleen Hanna's bare-belly SLUT, could they use their bodies as a tool to fight the system that valued them only *as* bodies? They never found out. The "No shirt" sign disappeared from the restaurant before they had a chance to enact their plan. The girls congratulated themselves: Someone must have tipped off the joint! In any case, the sign was gone.

Many boys in the Twin Cities scene, as elsewhere, were suspicious of the new group. What were these girls doing at their all-girl meetings? They must be talking about *us*, some guys concluded. They're deciding which boys are okay and which boys to blacklist. This paranoia had some basis in reality, as Elizabeth knew. She often thought back to that meeting at Positive Force where the girls had discussed boycotting an alleged abuser's band. And she'd heard about a group of women at the University of Maryland who had made an art piece that took the rapists-on-the-bathroom-wall idea one step farther, posting a list of forty-five hundred male students under the heading "Notice: These Men Are Potential Rapists." Elizabeth thought the project was pretty clever, but she didn't bring such tactics to the Twin Cities. Striking a more diplomatic tone, the Minneapolis–St. Paul chapter held a coed potluck to show their goodwill toward men, but only one guy showed up, and he wasn't even one of the complainers; he had been supportive of the girl-only-space idea from the beginning.

Even if the boys in their scene couldn't be coaxed to a potluck, the rest of America continued to be extremely interested in Riot Grrrl. And as journalists hit brick walls with the girls in DC and Olympia, they branched out. Elizabeth got a message from *20/20*, and then someone from Disney called: They were working on developing a Riot Grrrl cartoon, and could somebody please give them a call back to answer a few questions?

Elizabeth told her comrades about these calls and they laughed the whole thing off. Man, if you gotta ask, you'll never know. This humor masked an anxiety, though. "The press really seemed like vultures to me," Sin said, "waiting for someone to give them something juicy they could sell." The girls' personal images and words had acquired an exchange value. Grunge was already the leviathan fashion trend of the season: *USA Today* ran a piece titled "Fashion Designers Rummage Up Grunge Chic," *Vogue* was working on a grunge feature for its December issue, and "flannel" shirts were even now draping the waists of sullen runway models in New York. (The shirts were actually sand-washed silk, Marc Jacobs' representative hastened to explain to the press.) Grunge was the perfect couture statement for a serious economic recession and uncertain political future; never mind that a utilitarian style—born of the Northwest's weather conditions, economic marginality, and thrift stores—was becoming a status symbol for deracinated fashion elites. Meanwhile, a teenage Kate Moss was scowling, hollow-cheeked and sullen with a definite tinge of victimhood, out of Calvin Klein ads. Winds of commerce blew ever more insistently at the cellar door of the underground. The riot grrrls, gathered together for warmth on the hardpack floor below, listened to its howl. They had found one another, fellow refugees from a mass culture that didn't speak to them—or, rather, spoke to them *too much*, that was the problem, that it was *full* of messages for them: You're too fat too ugly too awkward too loud too queer too different wrong wrong wrong wrong wrong . . . Together they shut out these destructive voices, creating a culture that would nourish them. Now the mainstream was after that too.

Clearly the media's incursions must be beat back. The Twin Cities chapter discussed at length, but never held a formal vote on whether to honor the media blackout. There didn't seem to be any need. Elizabeth thought everybody was in agreement that they wouldn't give interviews for any corporate media coverage of Riot Grrrl. She thought the girls were all on board.

Jessica Hopper, perhaps predictably, was not on board. To her, the discussions about the media blackout seemed overly idealistic. In her mind, any press attention for Riot Grrrl, however imperfect, could help empower and inspire the girls who read the coverage. "I didn't want to be cloistered," she said later. "It was like, we can have a media blackout, but nobody even knows we're here."

That fall, Farai Chideya, a twenty-two-year-old staff writer at *Newsweek*, started leaving messages on Jessica's answering machine. Chideya had set out to write an article about Riot Grrrl, but news of the blackout had spread widely by then: Almost nobody would return her calls, and the few who did refused to speak for attribution. Then Chideya learned of Jessica from the *City Pages* article. At first, Jessica ignored the journalist's calls. The other girls hadn't given her too much grief about doing the *City Pages* interview, but that piece had been about her and her fanzine, not about Riot Grrrl as a whole. Plus, there was a big difference between a local alt-weekly and a national newsmagazine. She believed that a *Newsweek* article might be able to change thousands of girls' lives—not to mention her own—but she also knew people would be seriously pissed off if she participated.

In Chideya's third message, the reporter, desperate by now to find somebody who would talk on the record, spoke at length about her own life. She was a feminist, she told the answering machine tape. She had done performance art in college. She was really into feminist zines. She wanted girls in Idaho to know about Riot Grrrl. She thought she could write an article that would make a difference in the world.

So Jessica Hopper talked. It was strictly on background at first. "She was always so media-savvy," Chideya said. "*She* was interviewing *me* to see whether she wanted to go on the record." They spoke on the phone for four hours, and Jessica FedExed the reporter a big package of zines, *Hit It or Quit It* as well as others. And finally, to seal the deal, she went on record in an hour-long phone interview.

On the day that the November 23, 1992, issue of *Newsweek* hit the streets, a regular Wednesday night Riot Grrrl meeting took place at the Emma Center. Jessica arrived late; she had stopped off at a newsstand to buy the magazine.

The other girls had already picked up a copy of the issue—Jessica had warned them that an article might be coming out—and they were aghast at what they saw. "Revolution, Girl Style" occupied a two-page spread in the Lifestyle section, complete with a photograph of Jessica (the caption dubbed her a "prototypical Riot Grrrl"), a portrait Alice Wheeler had taken of Angie Hart that autumn afternoon in the Evergreen mods, and a photo of Love, whom Jessica had described to Chideya as "Riot Grrrl's patron saint." That designation stemmed only from the fact that Love had passed out copies of *Hit It or Quit It* at Hole shows in England. The musician actually had an open antipathy for Riot Grrrl and anybody associated with it—especially, it seemed, anybody associated with it who had been close with Cobain before she had met him, namely Kathleen and Tobi. Love had recently left a long, rambling answering-machine message for a girl named Nina Cunzio, who was trying to get a Riot Grrrl group started in LA: "We should totally have meetings at my house, I'd love that a lot," Love had said, sounding to Nina like somebody on drugs. "But you gotta lose this Kathleen Hanna bullshit." Nina never called back. In just a few months, Love would write a vicious column in *Melody Maker*, blasting Riot Grrrl and Bikini Kill.

The *Newsweek* article was sympathetic overall, not quite as smart as the *LA Weekly* piece but infinitely better than the *USA Today* hatchet job. Chideya called the movement "a new feminist voice for the video-age generation," a force that was out "to make the world safe for their kind of girlhood: sexy, assertive and loud . . . They may be the first generation of feminists to identify their anger so early and to use it." Yet for each reasonable assessment the article contained, another line seemed to make generalizations about its members—like the sentence that pegged Jessica as "typical" of the girls due to her being "young, white, urban and middle class"—or make light of the movement: "Riot Girl is feminism with a loud happy face dotting the 'i.'"

The Twin Cities riot grrrls sat in the Emma Center, passing around the article and simmering. How could Jessica have done such a thing—spoken for the entire movement, to a national magazine, without even consulting with the rest of them? It felt like a gargantuan betrayal of trust, like Jessica had just been using all of them to gain more exposure for herself and her own projects, no matter who else got hurt along the way.

They decided Elizabeth would facilitate the meeting to ensure it stayed civil. But that plan quickly went out the window. A girl named Amanda Taylor was particularly incensed at Jessica for sending Chideya some issues of Amanda's zine without asking permission. *Newsweek* had reprinted a particularly personal quote from it: "SLUT. Yeah, I'm a slut. My body belongs to me. I sleep with who I want." The moment Jessica walked in the door, Amanda was on her feet, shouting. *How dare you? What were you thinking?*

The others piled on, adding their counts to the indictment. Jessica thought a lot of their objections sounded elitist. She remembers people expressing worries that girls who hung out at the mall with brand-new plaid flannel shirts tied around their waists because that was what they'd seen on MTV would start coming to meetings. "We're just going to be part of these girls' grunge trend," somebody complained. After half an hour of being yelled at, Jessica got up and left the meeting. A few girls who had heard about the group from the *City Pages* article got up and left with her.

As weeks went by, more problems with the article emerged, and even though Jessica denied any connection to the offending portions, she became associated with them just the same. The piece had identified Kathleen Hanna as a former stripper—a fact that Kathleen, although she spoke freely about it at shows, had never told her family. And it reprinted a Polaroid photo of the three women of Bikini Kill in bathing suits on a beach in Hawaii. It was a personal photo, something the band had never wanted to have out in public.

Elizabeth Anthony saw the article as "the worst possible thing that could have been written." Within the context of their own lives and communities, this movement meant everything, but when it was time for writers to spell out Riot Grrrl's importance for the country as a whole, they fell back on easy stereotypes about appearance or sexuality, or else leaned on mainstream youth-culture signifiers like MTV, things whose importance may have been axiomatic to readers but had little to do with what mattered to the girls. The system was weighted against the issues that they cared and cried and bled about; it was stacked so that the way their lives *really were* never had any relevance at all. What was relevant in the media's eyes was a cute girl with famous friends, a band in bathing suits on a beach. The riot grrrls had thought they were all united in their resistance to that structure. But now one of their own had played directly into that system, putting other girls' privacy and principles on the line. If riot grrrls couldn't trust one another not to sell them out, who *could* they trust?

News of the blow-up in the Twin Cities group spread quickly to the other chapters. Some girls heard that Jessica had been kicked out of Riot Grrrl for breaking the blackout, but Elizabeth left her several phone messages, encouraging her to come back to meetings. "I was trying to strike this conciliatory note: 'Please, we'd like to have you come, we'd love to talk to you, we're sorry about what happened.' Even though I don't know how sorry I actually was. But I knew it was important not to be nasty, because she *was* another girl." Above all, Elizabeth wanted to hear Jessica's reasons for having talked, and she wanted a chance to explain to Jessica how her actions had hurt people. Jessica never called back.

The Minneapolis–St. Paul chapter limped along for a few more months, but the heart had gone out of it. Elizabeth was mortified that the defector had been from her chapter, that "this had happened on our watch," she said. She felt like her group had let all the others down. She felt, too, that she had failed Jessica: a girl so insecure, Elizabeth thought, that she had turned to the national media to feel important, even at the cost of selling out her sisters.

Jessica wasn't in the mood to defend herself or apologize. The girls' reaction had confirmed her suspicions about them: that they weren't serious about spreading feminism, that they just wanted to keep it to themselves, that they wanted to live safe lives in small underground communities without making the compromises necessary to graduate to the real world. And that she would get a lot farther without them holding her back.

Whatever warmth had lingered with her zinester and musician pen pals mostly dissipated. But she was unrepentant, at least publicly. In the first post-*Newsweek* issue of *Hit It or Quit It*, Jessica wrote, "The press needs a mouth for a movement and it's D-u-m-b to think that if you don't talk it goes away."

NINE

"WHAT IS RIOT GRRRL, ANYWAY?"

Angie Hart didn't normally read *Newsweek*, so the first time she saw the enormous photo of her that ran with "Revolution, Girl Style," she was at the motel in Olympia where she worked as a maid. God, she hated that job. Some days she'd get in at 8 in the morning only to have her boss tell her that there were no rooms for her to clean. He couldn't call to tell her that *before* she'd taken the bus all the way downtown for nothing? It was him, or maybe his wife or their obnoxious teenage daughter, or maybe all three of them in concert—she wouldn't remember exactly—who showed her the magazine opened to her full-size photo, her entire torso and head and her suspicious scowl and the word PROPERTY on her belly. "Look!" they said. "Is that you?"

It was useless to deny it. She was mortified. She'd felt certain that Alice Wheeler would use only the group photos, that the solo portraits were just for fun. *Help out another woman artist*—what bullshit. "It was a lesson in—gender is a joke," Angie said. "It was this false sense of, I can trust this person because they're a woman and I'm a woman and we're talking about feminism." She felt betrayed not just by the photographer, whom she had only met that one time, and not just by Jessica Hopper, whom she'd never even heard of before reading about her in this article, but by the idea that women and girls wouldn't screw each other over beneath the banner of Revolution Girl Style Now. The gang of girls holding hands up front at a show, that solidarity she had reveled in? It wasn't such a guarantee of safety anymore if you thought the girl next to you might be about to slug you in the kidneys.

When Angie had a chance to actually read the article after work that day, she couldn't believe how patronizing it was. No, it was worse than that: It was *minimizing*. Life in Olympia, life in Riot Grrrl, had been the size of the whole ocean, of all the sky in the universe. But now, tacked down to the slick, flimsy page, their revolution looked prosaic, quaint, limited. Which version was true: her own, or the one coolly regarding her from the pages of a magazine?

A long-exposure photograph registers all the light emitted by moving objects but not the objects themselves: Cars melt to rivers of headlamps; boats are red tracks on a lake. The *Newsweek* article did the reverse, conveying just the concrete leavings of a precious magic that had changed Angie's life and the lives of her friends— making it seem like the externals *were* the thing. Pissed-off teen punk feminism was being sold to America as the latest way to be, the newest identity to slip on. And what was a *Newsweek* reader's guide to how to adopt this identity? What was the visual key? It was Angie.

"I just felt consumed," she said—that is, that others were consuming her. Other riot grrrls could complain that their personal experience was being warped into a trend, but in Angie's case this became visible with particular starkness.

That article marked the end of the fun for her. She stopped going to meetings; her rage bloomed and wilted her, leaving her shut down. She hardly discussed the article with anyone.

The other girls in Olympia—Allison and Corin and Tracy, Danni and May and Erika, and all the rest—did discuss it. They weren't mad at Angie; she clearly wasn't to blame for what had happened. *Newsweek* could just as easily have made a poster child out of any one of them. They were angry with Wheeler, of course, and they were livid at this Jessica Hopper, whoever she was, for talking. *Her* betrayal was the worst of all, because it had come from within the movement. They were committed to every girl as an individual making her own valid choices, to the idea that, as one flyer said, "THERE ARE *NO RULES*—EVERY GIRL IS A RIOT GRRRL." But just one rogue actor could ruin it for everyone else. Maybe it had been too idealistic, after all, to think girls could come together and support one another without someone trying to get over. Maybe the leadership vacuum was just too tempting.

The *Newsweek* article, which came out right before Thanksgiving in 1992, felt like a culmination of the madness that had been going on all fall. The big difference was that the girls had managed to beat back all the previous incursions, but this time the media got its story. The previous incursions had been unsettling nonetheless. For instance, Danni Sharkey had been stalked by a television producer at a punk show in Tacoma. None of them had ever heard of the producer, and years later they wouldn't even remember her name. Maybe she had somehow seen Danni's two cooking-show episodes that had aired on public access the previous spring. But Danni wasn't making public appearances anymore; she was just an ebullient junior at Evergreen and a dedicated riot grrrl. She'd never had a group of female friends before, and now that she'd found this gang, she felt confident, capable, and powerful—all the things she had never felt growing up. The change was so personal and precious, there was no way she could translate it for the outside world.

She couldn't make much sense of the producer's request, anyway: I'm creating a punky new magazine, she said, and we want Riot Grrrl to be a feature, and it's going to be on TV.

A magazine . . . on TV? As if each of these big-media evils weren't bad enough on its own, somebody had to go and combine them? And of course they wanted Riot Grrrl.

"We're not interested at *all*," Danni had told the woman on the phone.

I'm a woman struggling too, Ms. TV-magazine persisted. You should be helping me out. I'm on your side.

Danni wouldn't hear of it. But the woman didn't seem to understand the word *no*. So she went to that punk show in Tacoma and asked people if they'd seen Danni. Most people, sensing the fishiness, feigned ignorance, but the producer still managed to find her quarry and run through the pitch again. Danni started thinking maybe she could turn this woman's persistence to Riot Grrrl's advantage. She stonewalled some more, but at the group's next meeting, up in the sunken seating area in the CAB building, she laid out her idea.

"Let's ask them for a lot of money," she said, "and if they give it to us, we'll do it."

The riot grrrls were into it. They figured that since their image was going to be sold to Americans with or without their cooperation, they might as well get paid. They drew up a list of everything their chapter needed to buy—tape recorders, photocopies, audio equipment—and added up all the costs. After the meeting, Danni called the producer back and gave her the news that the Olympia riot grrrls would help her out for the price of a thousand dollars—the largest amount of money the girls had been able to conceive of asking for.

The producer acted appalled. "How dare you try to blackmail me?" she said.

Danni stood firm. "Aren't you going to make a profit off this?" And that was the last anyone in Riot Grrrl Olympia heard from Ms. TV-magazine. Days of wheedling and pleading, stalking and setting terms, with nothing to show for it on either side.

That's what it meant to be a riot grrrl in Olympia in the weeks leading up to the *Newsweek* article: to be hunted, a chase that was ultimately fruitless for everyone involved. To dodge incessant calls from the Jenny Jones show and Sally Jessy Raphael. To have a reporter from the *New York Times* barge up to you at a show and ask to buy your zine of raw, personal stories that you had written for only your friends to read—never thinking that anybody else would *want* to read it.

At meetings, complaining about the media threatened to overtake all other discussion topics. For a crew of girls angry about how everybody seemed to think girls existed for onlookers' enjoyment—*C'mon, beautiful, how about a smile?*—the media chase fit into a disturbing pattern. "I feel like I have so little control of my life as it is without some reporter saying who I am," Erika wrote in her zine that fall. "I feel marginalized enough as it is without the corporate media making matters worse."

"It was just so much easier to focus on the media abusing us," Danni said, "instead of talking about being abused or assaulted or having trouble with guys or being a lesbian or whatever. Immediately it was all just about how everyone wanted to get a piece of us."

It certainly did seem that way. *Spin* had come out with its dumb article about girls who shaved their heads and believed in salad, or something ridiculous like that, with an awful photograph of a live Riot Grrrl Barbie in skivvies. Then a *Newsweek* journalist started hassling them for interviews; somebody from the magazine called Allison Wolfe's house three times in a week. It all confirmed what many of them were reading in school, about how mass media turned real life into spectacle in order to sell it back to people as a meaningless, glammed-up, depoliticized version of their own lives.

Riot Grrrl had started as a way for girls to resist the outside world's attempts to define them. Paradoxically, it had wound up *intensifying* those external definitions. Now, in addition to fighting what everybody said girls were supposed to be, they had to contend with lies and generalizations about riot grrrls. Misconceptions abounded even within their own scene. The group did have a marvelously supportive crew of male allies: "The guys were like, 'Can I drive you to your meeting?'" Danni said. "I don't think they had a choice, really."

"They all wore little barrettes in their hair, and they always had our backs," Michelle Noel said.

But others in the scene—male and female alike—could be heard saying that riot grrrls hated all men; that the meetings consisted just of shit-talk about boys; that the girls were trend-jumpers who were trying only to be cool; that they were elitist and exclusive. "It felt like anywhere you went, you were open to criticism about Riot Grrrl," Michelle said. "It was a constant feeling of judgment."

These calumnies needed to be countered. But crafting a public relations strategy was new territory for the girls of Olympia, where ideas and trends normally traveled easily and effortlessly from one end of the scene to the other, like electrical pulses racing along a copper wire. They had tried to broadcast in typical Olympia ways—being visible in public, putting on events, making flyers, talking themselves up—but the messages were getting mangled somehow. The mainstream media (and, surely, some boys' resistance to girls being in charge) had caused static on the line.

One afternoon in early November, the girls gathered at Becca Albee's apartment in the Martin, planning to assemble a flyer that could clear up the misconceptions about their group. They had twenty contributions, though, too many to fit onto a single sheet of paper, so they made a zine out of the pages they had brought: percussed on different manual typewriters all over town, written in careful lowercase print, reeled out of computer printers, embossed in thick block letters, bordered with rows of hearts or stars or photos.

The final product was a pocket-size zine titled *What Is Riot Grrrl, Anyway?* This was a question they'd been hearing a lot from outsiders, but for the first time they were asking it of themselves. Before this, they simply *were*. Now the media attention, combined with the group's diminishing cohesion, was raising new questions: Just what is this thing we're doing? Who are we, that the *New York Times* and *Nightline* and Jenny Jones want to talk to us? What do we believe, if it's not what *Spin* says? What are we, anyway?

In response, they didn't hammer out a position paper, as their radical '70s predecessors had done, or vote on resolutions, as the established feminist organizations in the early '90s were accustomed to doing. They created a forum for each girl to have her say, and the sum of these would be their statement. Each mini-essay in the zine reflected a different girl's wish list: what she needed out of the group, what she had managed to get. To someone who had always longed for friends, Riot Grrrl was

```
GirlPower  GIRL♥LOVE  Sisterhood  Friendship
BESTFRIENDS.
```

A girl who needed a space free of derision found the meetings to be a time when nobody was

```
laughing at the way I look or the way I sit
or my style of dress.
```

For someone trying to move forward from a history of abuse,

```
Riot Grrrl is a hand to hold & a fist in his
face.
```

One girl, summing up the zine's overall message, wrote:

```
Riot Grrrl is whatever I want it to be. It's
whatever you want it to be.
```

Above all, the girls wanted their readers to know that each one of them was unique. Their insistence on individualism and multiplicity, on Riot Grrrl as being without any intrinsic meaning or substance, says a lot about what they were defining themselves against: namely, definition itself. "We know there's not one way, one light," went the Bikini Kill song "Jigsaw Youth," "one stupid truth . . . " Journalists kept trying to make declarations about what the movement *was*, which ensured they would keep missing the crucial way that Riot Grrrl, not only in Olympia but everywhere, served as the ground for a relief print of each girl's everchanging desires.

This "whatever I want it to be" individualism reflected not just a postmodern love of multiplicity (though, yes, there was definitely that) but also what America had become over the past twenty years, and especially over the Me Decade that had just ended. The roots of this pose were even older, though. Legions of '60s idealists, stung by seeing their aspirations for a new society fall short—and horrified by the Kent State and Orangeburg massacres of antiwar protesters on campuses, the US government's COINTELPRO campaign against activist organizations, Black Panther Fred Hampton's FBI-arranged assassination, and the seemingly unendable carnage in Southeast Asia—had withdrawn from political organizing in the '70s to focus on matters of lifestyle. Progressives moved to communes, cultivated personal growth, and sang to their overalls-clad offspring that in this land every girl grows to be her own woman. As conservative backlash became the status quo, personal issues, which the women's liberation movement had cast as a starting point for a new kind of public politics, became a *destination*—the only possible location of a politics of liberation. "The personal is political" became "The political is personal": Gloria Steinem, in the introduction to *Revolution from Within*, posited this inverted formulation as signaling a holistic, psychological approach to realpolitik, but it indicated as well a narrowing of the radical imagination. In America by 1992, some revolutionaries felt they had little hope of changing anything but themselves.

The riot grrrls were steeped in this brand of personal politics, yet they fought against it. What many of them longed for, in addition to individual self-expression and interpersonal support, was precisely *movementness*; many pages in *What Is Riot Grrrl, Anyway?* gave voice to this dream of collectivity, speaking in a manifesto's lexicon of *we*s and *us*es. There was

```
we are coming together in full force because
we know the world treats us like little-
girlsdumbslutsstupidwhoresuglybitches-
oldmaidshelplesscreaturesPROPERTY. and we
know what we really are. (sometimes).
```

and

```
because we need a place to feel free + safe
to talk, to do, and to plan the revolution
which is taking place daily.
```

and

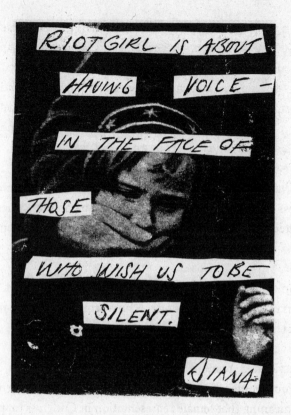

RIOT GIRL IS ABOUT HAVING VOICE — IN THE FACE OF THOSE WHO WISH US TO BE SILENT. DIANA

Erika collapsed the movement/individual distinction altogether: "OH fuck it! i'm in riot grrrl cause *i am a riot grrrl!*"

In the zine's centerfold, Michelle tackled the media issue most directly:

Riot Grrrl is not a product for the media to sell. I am opposed to mainstream media coverage, although some riot grrrls may argue with me. The media has made us into a fad so that we can easily be put in the back of people's closets with the macramé and parachute pants when we aren't "the next big

> thing" anymore. Hopefully some girls/women
> will see through the fad image and catch the
> important stuff. It's funny how some people
> try to write off true movements like femi-
> nism, veganism, ecology, etc., as faddish
> . . . . I guess it's scary to recognize new
> ideas/eras that threaten your way of life.

Toward the end of her piece, she deftly tied Riot Grrrl's growing trendiness to something similar happening in politics, where the abbreviated shelf life of women's power was being made even more explicit:

> "The Year of the Woman" ha ha. The shit's
> coming down for good. They won't forget us
> next year.

The vaunted Year of the Woman had, in fact, come about; twenty-four women had won seats in the House and four in the Senate, meaning that female representation in Congress topped 10 percent for the first time in history. It was far from parity, but it was progress. Meanwhile, a victorious Bill Clinton assembled his transition team and promised to appoint a diverse Cabinet that "looks like America." The country was about to be run by a Democrat for the first time in a dozen years—which is to say, for the first time since any of the riot grrrls were old enough to care about politics. In its first year, Riot Grrrl had fed into and off of a decade-old barricades mood in leftist activist circles: People were *dying*, after all, in villages in Central America and in AIDS hospices in California, because of actions or inactions of the country's Republican rulers. Now the tide seemed to be turning—weakly, perhaps, but turning nonetheless. For the riot grrrls, strategizing about things outside their own lives and experiences had abruptly become less urgent. Clinton's election was no magic bullet, but it had bought the girls some time to find their own voices before plunging full bore into the task of fixing the rest of the world.

Well, this wasn't quite true for all of them. "Riot Grrrl is a girl gang with secret plans to destroy Olympia," read one unsigned page in the zine, relating an event that nobody remembers having occurred:

> This one night at a Riot Grrrl meeting some girls started talking about all these rapes that started happening at the college here. We got so mad at the total way the school and the media ignore sexual abuse and harassment. And how shitty it is to live in fear. So we made up a secret plan and carried it out that night. We laughed and held hands and ran around in the dark and we were the ones you should be looking out for.

The other girls in the group remember Erika discussing her wish that Riot Grrrl would grow more radical. Talking to one another and supporting one another was revolutionary in a certain sense, sure, but if they were serious about dismantling sexism and male privilege and the subjugation of girls and women—that *was* what they ultimately meant by revolution, wasn't it?—well then, Erika believed, talking would have to be coupled with action.

After making *What Is Riot Grrrl, Anyway?* the chapter formed a media working group, and about half the core members joined—not exactly what Erika had in mind, perhaps, but a step in the right direction. There was some communication with the DC group about officially calling for a media blackout, now that Jessica Hopper had shown they couldn't just assume everybody would do the right thing. Within the Olympia group, at least, there was no dissent. "I think any girl that would've been supportive of [talking to the media] would have felt like she shouldn't be there," Danni said. The committee convened at Nomy's house one evening to write a letter asking the other Riot Grrrl groups to respect the blackout too. Nomy drew a picture of a cartoon princess at the bottom, and they mailed it out to all the addresses they had.

This was the first time any riot grrrls had tried to set policy for other groups. "Looking back," Nomy wrote in an e-mail, "I think it's interesting that we (RG Oly and RG DC) made this decision and then wanted everyone else to abide by it, when supposedly Riot Grrrl was a decentralized movement. There was no reason to expect everyone else to go along with the blackout, without having some investment in the decision-making process." At the time, though, it made perfect sense to them. Individual autonomy just wasn't practical in this case.

That winter, as the mainstream-media madness died down somewhat, the girls started doing their own biweekly radio show. KAOS's new program director, twenty-two-year-old Diana Arens, was a couple of years older than the group's other members, and she had first gone to a meeting at the suggestion of Calvin Johnson, who was one of her good friends and dependable allies at the station. She was frustrated that only one-quarter of the station's DJs were women; her goal was 50 percent, and she and Calvin thought some of the riot grrrls might want to do a radio show. When she first showed up at a meeting, she expected that she'd be intruding on a tight-knit crew, just inviting them to submit a show proposal and then fading away back to the station. But she got drawn in to the group right away. These girls were fearless, wildly romantic about the power of their friendships and the force of their desires. "It's pretty irresistible, really, to have a girl gang," she said.

Diana trained the girls to do radio and saw to it that their show got a prominent time slot, Thursday nights from 8 to 10, which had recently become available when a popular bluegrass show went on sabbatical. (After Riot Grrrl Radio's debut, the station was deluged with angry callers who'd tuned in expecting their beloved banjo picking.) It was a big deal to give the show such a good slot. All the other rock shows were relegated to late nights, after 10, and new DJs usually had to work their way up from the 2 A.M. shift. But Diana wanted all of Olympia to hear the riot grrrls. "It was important to, I thought, the whole community," she said, "to have unprofessional-sounding young women on the radio."

The show, a mix of casual political banter and songs by female musicians from Bratmobile to Queen Latifah, was hosted by a rotating cast of riot grrrls. For one program, produced when Kathleen was in town, about a half dozen girls, including Kathleen and Erika and Corin, dedicated the airtime to playing ostensibly antisexist songs performed by all-male bands—mostly hardcore outfits whose songs were nearly always about some social issue or another—and critiquing the bands' sexual politics. In addition to recapitulating the objections to Fugazi's "Suggestion," the girls also tore apart the band Positive Greed for singing that a man who wanted to get laid was "not a stud" but rather a "whore" ("A whore isn't something bad," Kathleen said. "A lot of this white straight-edge boy thing singing about sexism is so incredibly stupid to me, I just can't even deal with it!"), and lambasted another band for the disparity between its pro-girl lyrics and its members' womanizing ways (one girl pronounced them "the biggest bunch of one-night-stand use-women boys I've ever met").

Boys singing about sexism, Corin said on the show, constituted "a real issue of containing a struggle, containing a resistance movement. If the people in power discuss it, then it's contained and they've brought it up, but they don't have to really deal with the issues."

"People in this town who pose the position of not being sexist, not being racist, the I'm-in-the-struggle-with-you boys," another girl chimed in, "they're like the wolf in sheep's clothing."

The studio phone was lighting up with angry calls. "We just had a phone caller and he said that those women deserved to be raped," someone announced. At the end of the program, Erika took the microphone. "I'm so psyched that we had this show," she said. "Obviously it's affecting people. I'm not psyched that somebody called me up and told me I deserve to get raped, but you're obviously really scared."

"And we *want* you to be scared," Kathleen added.

Near the end of the school year, the Olympia Riot Grrrl group hit upon the idea of teaching workshops to one another. Danni, who was studying audio engineering, taught a session on how to run the mixing board at a show, and another on how to make a four-track recording. Nomy Lamm, who was a heavy girl and walked with a fake leg following an amputation in childhood, had started reading a book about fat oppression called *Shadow on a Tightrope*, and she gave a workshop about the topic. It engaged her so much that she began working on a zine titled *I'm So Fucking Beautiful*, which would become one of the movement's best-known publications and eventually land her a spot as a Woman of the Year in *Ms.* magazine.

Meanwhile, May and Erika were holding lengthy discussions about strategy for the movement. It seemed to them that Riot Grrrl was at a crossroads. The mainstream media issue had been a massive distraction, but it also showed that an audience existed for the movement's ideas; to let all this interest go to waste would be a shame. Although the two of them believed in the media blackout, they also felt that by refusing to give interviews without having an alternative way to spread their message, they were losing potential recruits. Every month that they didn't broadcast their own voices nationally was a month that a girl in Montana might read a crappy article someplace and conclude she wasn't cute or thin or rich or punk enough to be a riot grrrl, or that the way to be powerful was to dye her hair and wear bright lipstick and combat boots.

May and Erika wanted to get proactive about building the movement. Taking a course called "The Search for Justice" had given them a new framework for their experiences: They realized they'd spent the past year and a half helping create an autonomous grassroots movement of marginalized people. They also started to understand that such movements never got very far by pure happenstance. At some point, somebody had to seize the reins and start thinking about the long term.

The idea of a distribution service for feminist zines had first been floated in early 1992, by Kathleen Hanna and Allison Wolfe, but it had never gone anywhere. Now Erika and May began laying plans. They were concerned that the zines, which had always been the most powerful component of Riot Grrrl to them, were getting lost amid all the controversy about mainstream media. Plus, all the ephemeral things the Olympia group was doing to counter the mainstream-media attention dissolved as soon as they hit the air. Most weeks, nobody made recordings of the radio program; Dana Younkins was the only one who had tapes of the public-access television show; no documentation existed of any of the parties or concerts the chapter had organized. There was certainly something to be said for the value of life lived in the present, not distorted right away into an object for nostalgia. But a rich and inspiring culture was disappearing every day. At this rate, all that would live on would be the music of just a few bands—enclosed in CD jewel cases, shiny and confined as the Cheshire Cat's smile after its body had vanished. What about everything else?

May and Erika hammered out a project proposal and submitted it to their professor. Getting Riot Grrrl Press off the ground would constitute the entirety of their academic work for 1993's spring quarter—

the capstone to their "Search for Justice" coursework. They made a flyer that announced the formation of the project and encouraged girls to send in their zines; they mailed it to all the girl zinesters they knew, and these girls ran the flyer in their own zines as well.

Its called RiOt Grrrl Press, and here are six reasons why its important RIGHT NOW

* self representation. We Need to make ourselves visible without using mainstream media as a tool. Under the guise of Helping us spread the word, corporate media has co-opted & trivialized a movement of angry girls that could be truly threatening & revolutionary. & even besides that it Has distorted our views of each other & created Hostility, tension, & jealousy in a movement supposedly about girl support & girl love. In a time when Riot Grrrl Has become the next Big trend, we need to take back control & find our own voices again

xoxoxoxoxoxoxoxoxoxoxoxoxo

* RG PRESS will make &'s zines available to people who wouldn't necessarily get them otherwise. Yeah, that's right. Networking. There are a lotta people IN THIS world & there are probably several who would benefit from and/or enjoy reading our zines BUT Haven't had the opportunity. There are also a lot of radical activists & groups that we really need to network with NOW ok?

We will take the Burden off of (usually) young women who can't afford to distribute their zines, or whose zines aren't well known. First it'll get the word out to everyone who gets the catalogue and PLUS we'll be doing all the SHit work of copying and dealing with $.

* * * * * * * * * * * * * * * * * * *

* It's gonna Help Feminist Movement IN general because it will create another vehicle of communication for & nationally & internationally.

* It'll Be easier to get Back issues of zines. IF you've ever tried to get a Back issue of fantastic fanzine From me (erika), you know what i'm talking about.

pleasepleasepleasepleasepleasepleaseplease

* It will Help Riot Grrrl Chapters have Better communication with each other by acting as a central place for obtaining addresses & such.

bi: May & ERIKa

Contact Riot Grrrl Press at P.O. Box 1375, Arlington VA 22210

Erika and May knew, too, that the journalists who managed to get interviews with Bratmobile and Bikini Kill and Heavens to Betsy were always asking about Riot Grrrl, and that the musicians were never sure what to say. Most of them hadn't been to meetings in months, if they had ever gone at all, and they didn't want to appear to speak for a movement that they had such a tangential relationship with. Erika and May urged them to talk about Riot Grrrl Press instead, and some of them did.

But Riot Grrrl Press would not begin in Olympia, where after seven months Erika and May continued to feel like outsiders. They left town at the beginning of April to take the project back home, to DC.

TEN

EVERY GIRL IS A RIOT GRRRL

By early 1993, Riot Grrrl DC's membership turnover was complete. All the founding members were in other towns, and none of the DC girls had ever known a Riot Grrrl movement that was *not* of interest to the outside world. This was part of its identity now: Riot Grrrl (n.) An underground radical feminist movement that the media want to exploit.

The DC group wrote its own version of a blackout letter, asking the girls of other chapters to think carefully before they spoke to the media, and suggesting that the chapters keep in better touch with one another. For instance, who would like to put on this summer's convention? Nobody stepped up.

Of course, articles kept coming out anyway, throughout late 1992 and early 1993.

Los Angeles Times: "Mean, Mad and Defiantly Underground."

Seattle Times: "Feminist Fury."

Buffalo News: "In-Your-Face Feminism."

Washington Post: "From the Youngest, Toughest Daughters of Feminism—Self-respect You Can Rock To."

That last one, printed in midwinter, was by Lauren Spencer, a young *Spin* staffer who had been asked to write something for the *Post* on four days' notice. It was for the Outlook section, normally a realm of op-eds and personal essays, rather than for the *Post*'s famously catholic Style section, which might have been more fitting. Spencer suspected that the Outlook editors had had a last-minute slot to fill. This meant nobody would expect her to deliver a piece of in-depth reporting; she just had to give her impressions on the subject. Which was fine with her, because nobody was talking. She wrote that a "new, rocking breed of feminist" was "proliferating enough in Washington and other cities to upend one of the pop media's favorite themes: that feminism is the fast-depopulating province of the middle-aged." So far, so good. She also wrote that the movement was "drug free" and "vegetarian inclined," and that it appealed largely to "affluent suburban teens," "young women in clunky shoes from Sidwell Friends, Wilson, Walt Whitman and Churchill." This specificity annoyed the girls, many of whom weren't drug-free, weren't affluent, didn't go to any of the elite schools listed, and what did their shoes have to do with any of it?

Cosmopolitan covered the movement that spring, in a piece titled "The New Activists: Fearless, Funny, Fighting Mad" that also discussed direct-action groups No More Nice Girls, the Women's Action Coalition, and Women's Health Action and Mobilization (WHAM!). Its celebratory attitude toward the feminist revival was a stark contrast to the article *Seventeen* ran a month later. America's most widely read teen magazine asked, "Will Riot Grrrl refocus feminism or fry in its own fury?" in the lead-in to a piece titled "It's a Grrrl Thing," peppered with a by-now familiar mess of generalizations:

- "a crowd of girls with chopped-off hair in plaid vintage dresses and D.M.'s [Doc Martens boots] moshing in the pit"
- "a lot of Riot Grrrls don't shave and deliberately give each other bad haircuts."
- "you'll see Riot Grrrls in fishnet stockings and army shorts, cinch-waisted dresses with combat boots, or miniskirts with long underwear. Grrrls also like to 'accessorize' with black Magic Markers . . . "

The article also hit a new note in the Riot Grrrl media chorus: intramural cat fight. The piece was structured around the narrative of Jessica Hopper, feminist naïf who had innocently spoken to *Newsweek* only to find herself ostracized forever by a pack of vindictive girls. "I was just speaking for myself," she told *Seventeen*, "about my band, Andromeda Strain, and my fanzine. But of course Riot Grrrl came up because I was so heavily involved with it."

Now here was a juicy story—grrrl's inhumanity (inhumynity?) to grrrl. According to the article, Riot Grrrl was bound to burn out quickly, doomed by such cruelty as it had shown Jessica, in addition to its "punk superiority trip," its "condemning the Y chromosome as the root of all evil" (a particular sacrilege in the boy-crazy universe of *Seventeen*, where the Y chromosome was the root of all that was good and holy), and the girls' entirely inexplicable wish not to be covered by mainstream media. Oh, and how did they ever expect to get anywhere with those *abysmal* haircuts?

"Ultimately," the piece concluded, "the movement's militant slant may intimidate some young women otherwise drawn to the Riot Grrrl ideology." This was total nonsense, because of course there *was* no Riot Grrrl ideology without militance. The whole point was no compromise.

Seventeen's article didn't shock the DC riot grrrls; no slander could surprise them anymore. It was depressing that the media had resorted to pitting girls against one another. But realistically, what else would the magazine have run? What other take on Riot Grrrl would have fit in with its editor's letter gushing about the models who appeared in each issue, its house religion that centered on the sacrament of attracting boys' attention, its ads playing on hatred among girls? (A bathing suit advertisement featured a photo of a string bikini and the tagline "Who Cares If The Women Talk Behind Your Back. So Do The Guys"; a makeup ad called a girl with clear-looking skin "the sort of girl you love to hate.")

The surprising thing wasn't that *Seventeen* printed an attack on Riot Grrrl; it was that the same issue also ran a summary of a nationwide survey about sexual harassment in schools. The surprise was that the magazine didn't collapse from the fundamental contradiction of criticizing the riot grrrls for being antimale militants while also reporting that thousands of *Seventeen*'s young readers had been grabbed, pinched, and forced into sex by male classmates, teachers, and administrators. Forty percent of the respondents said they endured abusive treatment every day. An equal number said they'd reported harassment to a school official and gotten no response. The conclusion of the piece with the survey was not that girls should riot or start a vigilante campaign or organize to get offending teachers fired or even make posters to hang around their school; it was that they should write to the NOW Legal Defense and Education Fund. Let the grown-ups handle it.

Elsewhere in the issue, readers' letters described inappropriate touches from male family members and classmates as being "on my bottom and on the top" and "either or both places." That girls were supposed to oppose rampant sexual harassment but never so much as name or discuss their own body parts—all while picking the proper Outrageous Lip Color, Expert Eyes Shadow, and Foaming Facial Cleanser—sums up astonishingly clearly how incoherent the rules about being a teenage girl really were.

MTV called the Riot Grrrl DC chapter that spring, asking to bring a camera crew to one of the group's meetings. It was out of the question, of course. But the DC girls wanted to get the message out somehow. They didn't have access to a community radio station or college television studio, so they began carefully collaborating with certain media outlets. They did a feature with the feminist newsletter *off our backs* that consisted of a transcribed conversation between three teenage riot grrrls and an *oob* collective member. "As I grew up it was sort of a tacky thing to talk about feminism—there was something really passé about it," one girl told the interviewer. "Riot Grrrl showed me there were other girls that thought that to be a woman, you didn't have to be like the cover of *Cosmo*." The piece ran with a list of zine addresses and information on how to contact the DC chapter directly.

The girls also cooperated with the British pop culture magazine *i-D* to produce an article anchored by the single most arresting image the movement ever produced.

The girl in the middle, Angela Seguel, was twenty-one at the time this photograph was taken. It was taken at possibly the only Riot Grrrl meeting she ever went to, or one of the very few; she didn't *not* consider herself a riot grrrl, but she lived in a group house of indie rock boys in Mount Pleasant, which was geographically far from Positive Force House. Anyway, Angela had already done her time in the service of the revolution. Living in Seattle during college, she'd done the ACT UP thing, the Queer Nation thing. ACT UP was the main community gathering place for young insolent queers, but some people in the Seattle chapter were conducting

very personal battles with the disease—you were supposed to say "living with AIDS," yet they were so clearly dying of it. And being around this had come to wear on her: facing death all the time, screaming, fuming, going to jail, and throwing shame at the opponent. Angela didn't even have any close friends with the disease. It didn't feel quite personal enough to her.

By the time Angela moved to DC, in the summer of 1992, the summer of the Riot Grrrl convention, she was burned out on activism. In DC punk she found a welcoming community without the rage. All the women in the Mount Pleasant punk houses knew one another. Some of them considered themselves riot grrrls, some didn't; it hardly seemed to matter. In little more than a year, the elementary reforms of Riot Grrrl had been absorbed into the marrow of DC punk, transforming the scene and making the movement itself far less necessary for women who were sufficiently plugged in. It was normal now for women to play music and to stand up front at shows. Even the *Post* took notice, reporting that fall that "girls are starting their own bands in unprecedented numbers," citing female and coed groups like Slant 6, Tsunami, and Velocity Girl. Many more groups played only a few shows and recorded, at most, a single cassette tape, but that was *enough*. In this, DC had finally caught up to Olympia: Playing a show was becoming as much a rite of passage for the girls of the scene as it had always been for the boys; music was for everyone, not just the most skilled or the most macho; and a band was any song you ever played with anybody even if only once.

Riot Grrrl seemed to have inspired the women of the DC scene to become purposeful about supporting one another. They took their relationships with one another seriously, reveled in them. "There was a lot of love between the women that I knew," Angela said, "whether they were Riot Grrrl–involved or were just in the indie rock scene." She hadn't had any close female friends since she had come out as queer during college, when every hug she might offer became shaded by a cloud of suspicion. In DC, to Angela's great relief, those walls came down. "It wasn't a sexual thing," she said, "it didn't have to be, but we could be really close. We could snuggle with someone in bed or on the couch or hold someone's hand. Like girls do."

Angela felt invested in Riot Grrrl even though she hardly ever went to meetings, and when Susan Corrigan, the British writer for *i-D* who wanted to cover the group, lodged her request, Angela thought they might be able to make it work. As she saw it, the point of the blackout was to keep articles from coming out that a) presented Riot Grrrl as a fashion or trend and b) made girls reading the articles think Riot Grrrl was something that belonged to girls who were older/younger/ cuter/thinner/richer/punker. And in this case, it seemed possible that the best way to keep another of those articles from coming out might be to take a more active role in the process.

Seanna Tully, who had been a faithful meeting-goer ever since quitting ballet and had been a strong proponent of the blackout from the beginning, agreed this might be a good time to make an exception. "We looked at this magazine, we passed it around," she said, "and we decided that we were just going to do it, and we were going to basically try to control it as much as we possibly could, and present it as well as we could."

Most encouraging of all, Corrigan said the girls could do their own photo shoot. Angela knew, from her time in ACT UP, that a carefully orchestrated image could say a lot. The specific idea of writing on her naked body for *i-D* grew out of an earlier photo shoot she had done at her house. She was sitting in her room one night, menstruating and writing and thinking about how women are always supposed to hide the fact that they bleed—not just things like fearing bloodstained clothes or knowing it's not polite to acknowledge the bleeding, but even the way pads and tampons come shrouded in pastel camouflage, and the way a woman is supposed to hide the fact that she's bringing a tampon with her to the restroom. Thinking of all this, Angela took off her clothes and smeared blood on her torso. She checked herself out in the mirror. It looked pretty good. Fierce, warriorlike. "I just felt like— I'm just bleeding," Angela said, "like: Here! Here it is!" She called her roommate in to take photos, and she published them in one of her zines. It was a big deal to her to display her body; by the time she got to DC, she had spent years being thoroughly ashamed of it. She'd been told since kindergarten that she was fat. Her mom made her follow diet after diet and counseled her in fitting rooms to pick whatever skirt was the most slimming. Even when she spent the night with one of the boys who had in her post–Queer Nation life begun to seem endlessly fascinating (though barely less untrustworthy), she wanted the light off, the sheets drawn up: She was petrified of having her body *seen*.

She got naked for her zine and then for *i-D* magazine because she figured that if you're scared to death of something, it was best just to do it, and see that you didn't die. And it did make her feel better. When the article came out, she was proud of her part in it.

"Who Are the Riot Grrrls?," published in the April 1993 issue of *i-D*, was two pages of images—the photo, plus cut-up graphics from zines and flyers—and two pages of text, with easily half the text made up of paragraph-long quotes from Angela, Seanna, and a few other girls from the meeting. Corrigan had faxed the girls a draft of the article, they had signed off on it, and the magazine printed that version with only minor changes. At last, the girls had managed to communicate broadly that what the movement *was*, was none other than their lives.

Yet even as the DC group reached out to the larger world, it was losing its hold on some of its most long-standing members. Whenever girls from the original crew came around, they felt out of place. Joanna Burgess, who had stayed behind in Virginia while her best friends (May, Erika, Mary) went off to college, skipped meetings for weeks at a time, partly because she had to be at her record-store job and partly because when she did manage to attend, she often felt like the people there were either uninterested in getting to know her or just plain unfriendly. Another girl came home from college for spring break and was surprised that she didn't know anybody at the meeting. She tried to plan a slumber party anyway, hoping that would bring back the old spirit. But on the appointed night, the DC area was paralyzed by a snowstorm. The sleepover never happened.

Members of Riot Grrrl's scattered freshwoman class mailed each other letters that spring, wistful keenings of diaspora. They wanted their revolution to continue. But they weren't that excited to meet the waves of newcomers that kept arriving at meetings—drawn by word of mouth or by the article in *off our backs*—who were getting progressively younger while the first crew were growing up.

When May and Erika came back to town at the beginning of April, to spend their spring and summer academic quarters in DC getting Riot Grrrl Press going, their presence galvanized things in a way that nothing else had in a long while. Suddenly life was full of action again: They held a Riot Grrrl topless croquet match on the National Mall, to commemorate a judge's ruling that it was legal for women to go shirtless in public. They set up Riot Grrrl Press tables to sell zines at shows. And once, at a huge alienating jock-filled Fugazi/Slant 6 show at the University of Maryland where some jerky boys booed Erika's onstage announcement about Riot Grrrl, the girls went into the women's bathroom and inked WRITE RAPISTS' NAMES HERE on the wall; one girl from the college asked to borrow Erika's marker and wrote a name up on the wall right away.

They finally tackled the morass of mail that had been building up ever since the *Spin* article came out. It took six hours to open all the envelopes, unfold all the handwritten notes, mound up all the dollar bills and postage stamps and, most frustrating, one-dollar checks made out to Riot Grrrl that were useless since the organization didn't have a bank account. Girls had written angst-filled letters lamenting their isolation in rural outposts and conservative suburbs. They wanted to find pen pals, to know whether anybody else within a hundred miles of them had by any chance written too. Some wanted to know how to start a chapter in their own town. What would they have to do? Was there a path to affiliating formally? Some wanted lists of zines, lists of bands; lots of college students wanted information for term papers.

The girls made a new zine to send to these supplicants, writing emphatically, "You don't need our permission to start your own Riot

Grrrl in your own city." They headlined one page "How to Start a Riot Grrrl Chapter," but wrote only vague instructions, which read in their entirety:

```
If you want to start one, you've already
begun, all that's left to be done, is to do
it. We in D.C. have weekly all-♀ meetings.
Mostly people know of us by word of mouth.
You could also make flyers announcing what
you're doing. do it do it do it do it do it
do it do it. and keep in touch with other
Riot Grrrl chapters!
```

This instruction manual takes up only half the page. On the bottom half, someone has hastily sketched out a bunch of hands, reaching in from the sides of the page toward the center. Each hand has five digits, but most lack discernible thumbs. Some of the fingers narrow to spiky points; others are bulbous, like petals on a grade-school daisy. The hands grope toward one another with palpable energy but never quite manage to make direct contact.

Over three nights in April, in Joanna's childhood bedroom in Reston, where she had been living all year, she and Erika made a collaborative zine called *Fix Me*. Jo was ecstatic to have Erika back, to watch her typing on an electric typewriter while Jo sang along to her Belly cassette: "Take your hat off, boy, when you're talking to me." It was the sweetest feeling imaginable, to hear her own voice take up its real estate in the room / *this little squirrel I used to be* / pushing away the matte suburban silence outside the doublepaned window / *slammed her bike down the stairs, they put silver where her teeth had been* / hedging the yellowed darkness of the street outside / *baby silvertooth, she grins and grins* / and then to look at the page Erika had been typing and see this:

```
there's a sense of urgency in the air right
now it's been growing for some time like
we're all starting to get it i mean REALLY
GET IT things are burning collapsing we are
watching rome fall we are doing it ourselves
we feel true love true soul friendship con-
nections we are dying in each other's arms
we are dying for change.
```

At the end of April, when a national march for LGBT rights took place, riot grrrls came to DC from all over and marched together, as part of a huge queer-punk posse. It was only a year since the Riot Grrrl group had made a spectacle on the same stretch of protest turf, at a pro-choice march, but so much had happened since then: the convention, the media feeding frenzy, everybody scattering and reconvening, new groups springing up. This year's Riot Grrrl contingent was triple the size of last year's. Mary Fondriest's sign was four times as long as her old KEEP YOUR FIST OUTTA MY CUNT banner, and even more militant: I AM QUEER AND PROUD (it said) AND I WILL BEAT YOU UP IF YOU SAY ANYTHING BAD ABOUT ME OR ANY OF MY QUEER FRIENDS. And the girls' body-writing reflected the changes the past year had brought, with one girl writing on her arm: NOT YR FUCKN TREND.

The political situation had changed tremendously as well. Organized feminism had stood on the National Mall a year ago and vowed to take power through electoral politics. But the ballot-box victories weren't translating into the hoped-for changes in policy. After three months in office, Bill Clinton's footing had already begun to falter: Around a third of Americans disapproved of the way he was handling his job, by far the worst showing any modern president had made so early in a term. In a *Washington Post* article that spring, reporter Joel Achenbach wrote, "The Failed Clinton Presidency. It has a certain ring to it." Clinton's failures *were* legion: He had been badly defeated on gays in the military, right at the start of his term. He'd had to withdraw two attorney general nominees, both women, over concerns about nannies they had hired. (Meanwhile, the male secretary of commerce was allowed to pay back taxes on *his* domestic help and keep his job. For all Clinton's stated commitment to women's opportunities, the nation as a whole still saw child-rearing as women's responsibility, and women who shirked that responsibility were liable to get smacked down.) The Freedom of Choice Act was headed for defeat; First Lady Hillary Rodham Clinton was launching a losing bid to reform health care; and off in Virginia Beach, quietly for now, the Christian Coalition was sharpening its knives, strategizing about how to win conservative control of Congress in next year's midterm elections. Clinton's presidency, which had been supposed to reverse right-wing rule, was merely hampering it temporarily while the religious right and the Republican Party strengthened their alliance and laid the groundwork for long-lasting political dominance.

Once again, the riot grrrls—with their sense of heightened stakes, of crisis—had a prophetically dire take on the moment.

```
Frankly, this place is burning down, it's
on fucking fire and I don't have time to talk
about the furniture or the winter coats in
the front closet.
```

That particular voice belongs to Mary, who came back to DC at the end of the school year in 1993 and moved into a two-bedroom apartment in Arlington with Erika, Joanna, and their friend Jill, sleeping two to a room. (May moved into a different apartment, a five-minute bike ride away, with her boyfriend, a gentle, long-haired punk photographer named Pat Graham.) The girls' place, part of a sprawling redbrick complex called the Buckingham, was cheap and run-down, with tawny wall-to-wall carpeting and endless infestations of roaches and mice. Once, as Joanna was putting newly refilled ice cube trays in the freezer, a mouse scampered across the top of the refrigerator, fell off the front edge, and toppled headfirst into one of the ice cube compartments. Later that day, her roommates found the mouse half mummified in ice, half sticking up from the tray.

Luxury living this was not. But it was their home. As the DC summer unrolled itself stickily onto the city, the crew decorated the apartment's walls with flyers and a copy of the EVERY GIRL IS A RIOT GRRRL photo, and they lived frugally there, subsisting largely on pasta dressed with margarine, vinegar, and nutritional yeast flakes; for an occasional splurge, they treated themselves to slices of pie at the Steak 'n Egg Kitchen.

The apartment was headquarters for Riot Grrrl Press. Girls from all over the country sent their zines to be included in the inaugural catalog, and piles of mail littered the apartment. Some girls mailed in their thick cut-and-paste originals, even though they weren't supposed to, and May, who had taken a job at a copy shop, would make clean masters when her supervisors weren't looking. She gingerly copied the patchwork pages whose paper corners were curling up as rubber cement lost hold. Where pieces of text threatened to break free from the whole, she would press the corners back down and make new, uncreased, double-sided copies that could go through high-speed machines without a glitch. The machines all around her clacked in a comfortable rhythm, sucking in blank paper and spitting out printed pages with a steady, sibilant *sip-flup, sip-flup*. The flats would all get organized into folders back at the Buckingham, slotted into the tan two-drawer file cabinet or the plastic trays set atop it.

May spent a fair amount of the time at her friends' apartment, but she would usually go home at the end of the night to her and Pat's little shack at the back of the Simple Machines house. While she set up house with her boyfriend, her best friends were becoming ever more critical of heterosexuality. Their criticism sometimes crossed the line into vitriol: "If I hear about another YET ANOTHER heterosexual couple I'm going to vomit," Erika wrote. One day, one of May's friends was over at her and Pat's house, looked at May holding a dish, and said, "Such a cute little wife." May was incensed; she began to suspect that her little inlet of Riot Grrrl wasn't as supportive of women making their own choices as it once had been. "It may seem like I'm the one who sold out," she wrote in a zine, "and I get a lot of shitty het privilege in society but I lose a lot of power in society too and I think when womyn are putting down other womyn for wearing lipstick, having male partners, or god forbid raising children *they* are actually buying into the *lie*."

As May drifted away—by the end of the year she would have separated herself completely, newly absorbed in other schoolwork and ready to move on—Erika and Mary became closer. Throughout the first year of Riot Grrrl in DC, the two had been friendly enough with each other, but in the second year they hardly saw each other. Now they were sharing a bedroom, and an intense connection sprang up between them; it wasn't romantic, not in the conventional sense of the term, but they felt like soul mates. The two girls tallied up all the things they had in common: single moms and difficult dads, body odor and acne, lip rings and nightmares, and the experience of having grown up without much money but not knowing exactly what to call that—working class? Lower middle class? Temperamentally, they were similar too. "We're both really loud and obnoxious, and that was what we cultivated together," Mary said. "We were really erect, willing to make fools of ourselves and take up a lot of space and take on leadership roles." Like

Erika, Mary made zines that explored histories of family abuse and drew battle lines for conflict with boys. And like Erika, Mary was a gifted writer, given to swerving between messianic urgency and bitter, profane confrontations ("Fuck off and die straight whitey punk . . . . We will kill your kind").

Their apartment was like a chem lab for homemade radical feminist theory, and if being in the company of other restless, ambitious minds helped motivate the girls, it could also be discouraging. "All my friends are brilliant writers," Mary wrote that summer. "I feel like we can all be brilliant together, but when it comes out around outside forces, our geniuses get judged against each other—this usually happens with white boys. And I feel like I'm standing in a shadow." As much as they wanted to kill the J-word jealousy, as an old Bikini Kill zine had exhorted, a feeling of competition just wouldn't die. Joanna felt it too: She confessed in her own zine, *Cherub*, that when she tried to write and sometimes even when she tried to speak, she felt like she was "parrotting those around me."

To counteract this, the girls made a point of crediting one another in print as positive influences, often even referring in zines to each other's actual, physical presence, as if their friends' being there had helped the zine come into being. Which was largely true. Their zines were products of particular circumstances, not mythical objects with eternal life. By nodding to the friend in the room, the girls insisted on their creativity as communal; by referring to the moment of writing, they demystified the product.

At the end of the summer, Mary and Erika made their first zine together. Like its title—*Wrecking Ball*—the zine's writing was threatening and fearsome, with an undeniable momentum. It opened up with a pair of blistering manifestos. Mary's, titled simply "The Manifesto," kicked off with "1. There's no such thing as good, so there's no such thing as good boys," and later proclaimed "7. FUCK unity. We're tired of explaining ourselves to well-meaning

COLONIZERS (see #1)." Erika's list, on the opposite page, began on a note that sounded uncharacteristically accommodating next to Mary's stark typed lines.

1. i hate boys 4ever ♡ xo ♡
2. i don't always ok?

For the centerfold they printed pictures they had taken of each other naked, in deadpan porno poses: Mary kneeling and leaning back on her hands, thrusting her breasts up; Erika sitting with her legs slung open. They had each been the one girl who went too far; now they had each other, united in their shared abandon, augmenting each other's brightness like a blinding double star.

Having already poured so much energy into exploring the meanings of being subjugated as girls, they'd both spent their first year of college thinking about race and class. As they tried to write about being both privileged and oppressed, their language sometimes fragmented, as in Mary's manifesto where she wrote:

It's time for us/you privileged to figure out for our/your selves how to LISTEN and make connections.

Mary and Erika, having grown up in modest townhomes with single moms and periodic child-support checks from fathers they seldom saw, felt increasingly aware of the range of class backgrounds within Riot Grrrl and wanted to see it acknowledged more openly. They were keenly aware, too, that Riot Grrrl had dropped the ball on the issue of race, which had brought up so much animosity at the convention. The summer of 1993, a year after that disastrous workshop, some girls of color took the floor at a

Riot Grrrl meeting to talk about how they felt that white girls in the movement were ignoring race, but that discussion didn't go much better. Erika wrote about the meeting in *Wrecking Ball*:

> All these grrrls got defensive so it was
> really stifled, which sucks . . . I should've
> taken more responsibility to confront white
> grrrls in the meeting, but I was hoping
> they would follow my example and try to
> be better listeners instead of speaking up
> every five minutes to reassert the fact that
> they are working on their racism.

Mary and Erika felt they had a duty to educate other white girls and to make sure the topic stayed on the table. They printed reading lists in their zines: Angela Davis, bell hooks, Audre Lorde, Trinh T. Minh-ha, Toni Morrison, Alice Walker. They weren't the only ones concerned about race: Ananda La Vita made a zine called *White Girls, We Need to Talk*, which argued on its front cover:

> Our movement is predominantly white for spe-
> cific reasons—because we have not spent enough
> energy or time incorporating race + class
> awareness into our "feminist" (gender only)
> awareness. Because we have not spent enough
> time or energy addressing the particular
> concerns of nonwhite girls. We have not made
> this movement feel inclusive for them.

Girls of color were discussing, among themselves and with white girls, their sense that Riot Grrrl was, in fact, "too white" for them to feel at home there. But it was Mary and Erika who had the means to push the discourse in the movement as a whole. They were among Riot Grrrl's strongest writers, their zines some of the best known. And they were becoming ever more visible as the people running Riot Grrrl Press. Having built the only central institution in a decentralized phenomenon, they had created leadership positions for themselves in an otherwise leaderless movement.

By the end of the summer, they had printed the first Riot Grrrl Press catalog, a listing of almost ninety zines. Erika was out of town when the catalog was ready to go, so May did the lettering on the cover and Mary wrote the intro, making sure to note that May was "sitting next to me doing mail at this very moment." At the end of the intro she wrote,

```
p.s. we still say if you are a reporter FUCK
OFF RIGHT NOW. This is self-representation.
```

and under that, she wrote

```
p.p.s.
```

and left the rest of the page blank.

Mary and Erika weren't done having their say. They were just getting warmed up.

ELEVEN

"THIS IS HAPPENING WITHOUT YOUR PERMISSION"

In October 1992, two years after Bikini Kill started playing shows, the band recorded its first full-length album and released its debut record, a self-titled six-song EP, on Kill Rock Stars. The elder statesmen of rock-crit applauded the new EP: Robert Christgau gave the release an A minus in his *Village Voice* column, and Greil Marcus put it in his Top Ten in *Artforum*, hailing the "hard, cruelly funny band" for music that sounds "like a house burning down." But *Rolling Stone* savaged the record: "The EP *Bikini Kill* has plenty of yowling and moronic nag-unto-vomit tantrums over stock school-of-Sabbath riffage; like almost all noisy bands lately, this one is better at melody than at ugliness but usually opts for ugliness." The negative reviews didn't bother the musicians, but other aspects of the press coverage Bikini Kill and Riot Grrrl had received over the past two years were wearying, especially for Kathleen. "Most articles posited me not only as the leader of Riot Grrrl but also as the leader of Bikini Kill, and it made me feel really depressed and embarrassed and alienated," she said. "I was getting set further and further apart from everyone."

The worst article to come out that winter, in her opinion, was the *Washington Post* Outlook piece, which cited an earlier item in a small music magazine referring to Kathleen's history of sexual abuse. Nobody from the *Post* had called to ask permission to run the allegation, and Kathleen was knocked flat by seeing something so personal, printed without warning, in a major newspaper—a newspaper her relatives who still lived in the area were likely to read.

The most painful thing about the *Post* article was the sound of her phone not ringing in the days that followed. Nobody called to say *I saw that article, it's so intense that they printed that, are you okay?*

Bikini Kill was taking a short hiatus, and Kathleen wasn't in constant contact with her bandmates; they probably never even saw the piece. She was still friendly with some people from Riot Grrrl, but those relationships were starting to seem pretty lopsided. In working to create community for other girls, she had wound up without one of her own.

Kathleen didn't want Bikini Kill to be about what she had or hadn't overcome. People were always treating the work of women artists as autobiography, conflating female artists' personas with their personal lives. (A music critic in Hawaii, for instance, had written of Kathleen that "it was sad to see a woman so desperately confused.") But this band was about all girls, from the girls at Safeplace in Olympia to the girls who still stood at the margins of every rock club, staring gravely at the stage or at their feet until Kathleen asked them all to come up close and she saw how their faces transformed, boredom and defensiveness melting away, engagement and excitement taking hold. It was about the girls who wrote to her, unwieldy mountains of handwritten letters telling how isolated and silenced they'd felt before they found their way to the stage shouting "I'll resist with every inch and every breath I'll resist this psychic death," and how they'd gone home and started bands with their friends and screamed, for the first time since childhood, as loud as they wanted. *They* were the story of Bikini Kill. The songs were for them.

Kathleen had had a mission from the beginning, and in early 1993, she was astonished at the progress she saw. Girl zines had proliferated so fast there was hardly time to read them all. Many times she'd play a show someplace and someone would leap at the mic to announce an upcoming Riot Grrrl meeting. When she looked out at her audiences now, she saw girls with words and hearts inked hopefully on their skin, roaming the rock world in boldly signifying packs.

But if the front rows held girls passionately singing along with every song, there seemed to be an equal number of men just behind them who shouted "Show us your tits" and howled "Shut up!" whenever Kathleen paused between songs to talk to the audience. She engaged hostile hecklers, occasionally at length. She wanted everybody's eyes on the offenders; if they were being abusive, they needed to realize the whole crowd was aware of it, because she knew polite silence too often led to more abuse. Around the release of the EP, Kathleen told a critic her influences were "fourteen women in Montreal"—the engineering students killed in 1989. And she had never forgotten the heckler in Boston who'd turned out to be a murderer. When she asked girls to come up front at shows, it wasn't just to give them a better view but to create a buffer zone between her and the men in the audience. Often, when they were finished playing, she'd ask some of the girls to walk her to the van so she wouldn't have to navigate the club's back hallways and alleys alone.

———

While Kathleen was living in DC and facing the lonesome downside of fame, Tobi went back home to Olympia. She had always felt alienated by the private-school pedigrees of the punks in DC, their three-story Victorian group houses that were far bigger than anything her family could ever afford. She'd been homesick for Olympia's steady rains, its enormous fir trees, and the kids she'd known since high school. Amazing new bands had formed while she'd been away, bands like Unwound and Karp, which played spastic sets in basements through busted PAs while the kids freaked out and danced themselves sweaty and hot. *This* was punk rock. But still she worried. Was her beloved underground truly thriving in these deafening basements, or was this only a brief flaring up of something that was about to die forever?

In the two years since the International Pop Underground convention, Nirvana's *Nevermind* had become the megahit record of the decade; Nation of Ulysses had broken up; and Bikini Kill had become shockingly well known, an object of fascination and vilification both in the national media and in Olympia. Tobi poured her thoughts into a new zine in mid-February, sitting at her typewriter for hours on end, amped up on coffee and determination. Where to begin? She was annoyed at the media's insistence on equating Bikini Kill with Riot Grrrl; the latter no longer interested her much, she wrote, except as "just one small example of how something which was once mine and genuinely meaningful to me has been taken from me and has been made into something quite else than was initially intended." Her ideas about angry grrrls and revolution girl style had been hijacked by the media, and she'd watched her articles of faith and fervor become unrecognizable, embraced only by "posers or maybe just well intentioned and hopelessly enthusiastic extremely isolated young girls living in small town america who read dumb articles in dumb magazines written by dumb people." *Poseurs* was the word cool kids everywhere were flinging at those who got their music news from *Spin* or *Sassy* and their plaid flannels from the Gap; compared with this, Tobi's image of "well intentioned" girls was a little more sympathetic, but still dismissive. "This was not being mean, like 'Oh I'm so much cooler than these people,'" she said later. "I was trying to say look, we exist in the underground, we oppose capitalism." She was disturbed to see girls being sold on "Riot Grrrl" as yet one more piece of what she termed "lame corporate youth identity bullshit": a commodified readymade to be passively donned and buttoned up like a rain slicker.

I'm all for grass roots girl power movements, but this riot grrrl thing to me has been so taken out of context by the media that it almost seems ridiculous to insist on calling yourself one and I just wonder if it could possibly mean anything at this point . . . . The main problem to me is that it's all about identity, and an illusive one at that, rather than on action—everybody's talking about what kind of girl, nobody's starting a riot.

And it was all connected to Nirvana's becoming the biggest band in the universe. She wasn't *mad* at her friends in that band, not exactly. But their decision to go mainstream had changed everything, in ways they had never wanted.

The fact that anyone even wrote about any of this stuff is all a part of the mining of the northwest underground that has been taking place ever since it became Superhip to come from the land of grunge to do with Nirvana's

> making top forty history and this is exactly
> what I mean when I say that decisions made
> by individuals in a band become ever so much
> more than that, regardless of intention.

Now that Bikini Kill was getting attention too, Tobi wanted to make sure her bandmates were totally clear on the costs of selling out. But some compromises couldn't be avoided; for instance, as the band planned an upcoming UK tour, people told them the British music press was so powerful that if Bikini Kill refused to do interviews with the two British weekly music tabloids, *Melody Maker* and *NME*, venues would hesitate to host the shows, and people wouldn't show up. Tobi agreed to cooperate with the magazines. She was excited for the trip, especially because they would be touring with her new favorite band, a British group she'd been trading letters with but never met: Huggy Bear.

Over in England, Huggy Bear was conducting its own tormented negotiations with the limelight. Having been together for just over one year, the group had already become one of the most talked-about bands in Britain. Niki Elliot, Karen Hill, Jo Johnson, Chris Rowley, and Jon Slade—these three girls and two boys were *the* British face of Riot Grrrl from the get-go. In their first round of interviews—after which they swore off cooperation with the press—they'd explicitly aligned themselves with the movement: Jo was photographed for *Melody Maker* in July 1992 with RIOT GRRRL written on her knuckles (Niki wrote PRIK TEEZ on hers), and in a roundtable on women in rock that the *Maker* printed in September, Niki said, "We're not just doing Huggy Bear. We're also involved with this thing called Riot Grrrl, which is happening in America right now."

Yet they were still rather unclear on what the movement was. At first they'd known only what they could glean from their old friend Everett True (né Jerry Thackray), a critic and editor at the *Maker* who took periodic research trips to Olympia and brought back cassettes and zines from the mysterious land across the sea. That was how they had become pen pals with Tobi, and her communiqués shed a bit more light. But there was no music online then, no established transatlantic underground link other than individual carrier pigeons like True. The Huggies were avid for any information they could get, and they loved what they heard coming over from America, both the music and the politics. Riot Grrrl's uncompromising gender analysis, its mashed-up contradictory clamor, felt to them like the perfect aesthetic, a second coming of the Futurists and Situationists whom they admired but whose brand of avant-garde chaos had entirely disappeared from British punk rock, ridding the form of everything that had initially made it appealing to the members of Huggy Bear.

They were especially impressed by this American underground that communicated directly with a community of listeners, bypassing the mediating force of magazines and newspapers. This scarcely existed in Britain anymore. For much of the mid-'80s, the UK had had a thriving indie pop scene, with tons of zines coming out of cities from Glasgow to Bristol to London. But that seemed all but finished now. "You can tell the underground's dead over here," Jo told *Melody Maker*. "There's no new fanzines. No one's excited enough or driven enough to embarrass themselves by committing to print." Plus, Jo lamented, there was no stigma attached to the notion of selling out. London bands were rarely unknown for longer than six months: The *Maker* and *NME*, each itchy to scoop the other and herald the next hot group, kept up a steady churn, launching act after act into the small nation's obsessive, fickle spotlight. And the bands participated, each one of them, because there was no alternative network, no other way to spread the word or hear of anything new and exciting.

In October 1992, Sally Still, a veteran musician (and friend to Everett True and the Huggies) who wrote for the *Maker* under the pseudonym Sally Margaret Joy, became overcome with enthusiasm for Riot Grrrl and wrote a four-page cover feature about it. "Right now, in America, there's a whole movement of girls devoted to people like you," she told British readers. "This article should bring its distant throb closer." There was no organized Riot Grrrl activity in Britain yet, but Still avoided admitting as much. "British contact address to follow soon," she vowed, and ended the article with this:

HOW RIOT GRRRL WILL BE DIFFERENT IN ENGLAND
It already is.

Sally Still called the first meeting soon after, inviting several friends—including Jo and Niki from Huggy Bear—to make a British Riot Grrrl zine and hand it out at shows. Meetings occurred sporadically in late 1992 and early 1993, at people's houses or at Bunjies, a basement café in the West End full of arched catacombs that felt like the perfect place for a secret, rebellious rendezvous. Among the girls who found the zine and got drawn in were Tammy and Jen Denitto, American-born sisters in their early twenties. "At the time in music," Tammy said, "there was mostly boys. You didn't see girls in the papers, you didn't see girls on the TV." Inspired by the new group, the sisters became regulars at the meetings, and they started their own zine, *It's Unofficial.* "The idea was that if you thought you were a Riot Grrrl, you *were* one," Jen said. "You didn't need to sign up to anything. You just got out of bed and you said, 'I am.' I had the idea that if you told two friends, and your two friends told two friends, you could really change the world."

Tammy and Jen formed a band, Linus, and also organized a cooperative post-office box that they named BM Nancee—"nancy" being British slang for wimpy or gay. They put out word that any girl who wanted to launch her own zine could get mail at the Nancee box instead of divulging her home address. About a dozen girls in London did so, and many more from around Britain sent a slew of excited letters.

Riot Grrrl groups began forming in the smaller towns of northern England and Scotland. But in London, it wasn't taking off. The city's scene was so closely tied to the national culture industry that the idea of making culture outside the established channels was a nonstarter. This was a city, after all, whose first Riot Grrrl zine had been made by a *Melody Maker* reporter—how underground could *that* be?

Even Huggy Bear, who were so committed to DIY culture, remained a constant in the *Maker*'s pages, thanks to Still's and True's cheerleading. "You'll want to catch them before they've become untouchably famous and adored," Still wrote of the band, "and you know what, there isn't much time." Shortly afterward, in the fall of 1992, Huggy Bear recorded a four-song 7", "Rubbing the Impossible to Burst," and put it out on the indie label Wiiija. The band insisted on pressing only two thousand copies of the record, which were gone in an instant. By the end of the year, most Huggy Bear shows, at pubs that held a couple hundred people, were selling out. In December, the group opened for Sonic Youth and Pavement in Bristol, playing to a crowd of five thousand. In January, the group's second 7", "Kiss Curl for the Kid's Lib Guerrillas," reached number one on *NME*'s Indie 45s chart.

In February, with Bikini Kill's UK tour a few weeks away and a split Bikini Kill/Huggy Bear LP in the works, Huggy Bear released its third single, "Her Jazz." The band had written many sorts of songs already: hasty miasmas of feedback and noise, grandiose boasts ("You wanna fuck me!" Chris cried repeatedly in "High Street Jupiter Super Cone," over garage-glam guitars), lullabies of half-whispered brutality. "Her Jazz," which was to spend seven weeks in *Melody Maker*'s indie singles Top Ten, sounds like the hit that it was: a sarcastic bruiser of a pop rocket, built around a driving power-chord twelve-bar blues with ominous-sounding diminished fifths, a single verse that exhausts itself by going on for eighteen lines before the first chorus comes in to relieve it of its duties, and a jagged-leaf bouquet of auxiliary sections that spring up in that one verse's wake. The lyrics traffic effortlessly in aphorisms, tailor-made for zine covers worldwide: "I'll run you over! Watch me," Niki snarls, and "This is the sound of a revolution," and "This is happening without your permission," and, chanted twelve times in each chorus, "Girl boy revolution"—followed sometimes by a believer's "yeah," sometimes a cynic's "tease"; for, as the onstage ire between real-life lovers Niki and Chris often demonstrated, a Girl Boy Revolution was an even more complicated proposition than the plain old Revolution Girl Style Now.

Melody Maker (though neither True nor Still) called the song "bollocks . . . quaint, sloganeering, posturing cartoon anarchist nonsense." But *NME* named "Her Jazz" its single of the week, lauding it as "perfectly fulfilling the rock 'n' roll essence of capturing a moment in time." And the magazine *The Face* called the band "one of the more promising and conspicuous sets of young guns on the London indie scene."

Two days before Valentine's Day, the band played the new track live on Channel 4's *The Word*, a blokey late-night television program that alternated musical guests with tasteless segments on topics such as famous actors' early porno gigs and a man who dangled heavy weights from his genitals. Ever since the Sex Pistols' obscenity-strewn appearance on Bill Grundy's *Today* show in 1976, bands behaving badly had been a major trope of British television, and *The Word* was no different: Kurt Cobain had announced on-mic in 1991 that Courtney Love was "the best fuck in the world," and the following year L7's Donita Sparks dropped trou midsong, playing the final guitar solo of "Pretend We're Dead" while naked from waist to knees.

When Huggy Bear played "Her Jazz" on *The Word* in February 1993, the members were separated from one another on circular islands, like lily pads—Jo in huge white sunglasses, playing guitar; Karen bashing her drums; Jon and his bass tucked away in back, hardly moving; Chris practically fighting over one mic with guest vocalist Amelia Fletcher of the indie pop band Heavenly; and Niki, a clunk-shod figure on her pedestal, outlandish magenta wig flapping, her poses awkward: fingertips to shoulder, furious hunch into empty space. She performed as unhinged and enraged, dancing around so jerkily that the cameras couldn't keep her in frame.

At the end of the song, the show launched right into its next item, a videotaped interview with a pair of *Playboy* models called the Barbi Twins. As the tape played, Jo and some of her friends—Tammy, Jen, Sally Still, and others—regrouped, fuming. They'd been under no illusions about the nature of *The Word*, but it was disappointing how easily the structure could absorb their provocations without so much as a blink, and then move on to a couple of self-described bimbos.

They edged up to the fake-living-room stage where the boyish blond host, Terry Christian, was preparing to move things along. When the Barbi Twins segment was finished, Jo shouted—loud enough to be heard by over a million viewers across Britain—"So, Terry, you think all fucking women are shit, do you?"

"Oooh!" Christian said, as if a three-year-old had just stepped on his foot.

"Crap!" the girls hollered. "Crap! Crap! Crap!"

The host's smile held fast to his face. "So did you like those young ladies?"

The girls booed boisterously; others in the audience applauded or woofed, Arsenio style. Cut to aerial view of the studio: The place was in an uproar. Militant fists beat against the air.

"I think somebody's out to make a name for themselves," Christian simpered, barely audible over the crowd. He said it again, but by this time the screams from the audience had jumped an octave, turning from outrage to alarm. No cameras panned the floor now. Nobody in Brighton or Birmingham saw bouncers pounce on the girls and drag them from the studio.

Chris Rowley, left behind, shouted something inaudible that, whatever it was, pulled Christian off message. "Come up here, mate," the host challenged the musician, the violence beneath his grin peeking through like wallpaper glue. A beat. Christian rubbed his hands together as if washing them clean. Showed a dozen teeth, his lips rolling tensely.

"We'll be back after the break," he then said, smooth again. And wasn't that just the problem? They always *were* back after the break. No matter how great the rupture, the regularly scheduled programming always prevailed.

But the programming also served as a vehicle *for* the rupture, and the kids who saw it were electrified. "My God!!!" one *Melody Maker* reader wrote in from Derby. "I've just seen Huggy Bear on 'The Word' and they were WAY more exciting than Nirvana . . . I just can't help worshipping them!" Another reader, from Devon, gushed that the show "made me feel proud to be a babe with attitude—they were THERE, saying what *I* would have liked to."

A week later, the chaos was the cover story of the *Maker*: a huge photo of Niki's face pulled apart midyell and the headline "This is happening without your permission!" Huggy Bear was *the* story in British indie rock. The *Maker*'s letters page, week after week, ran thick with rants pro and con; one crop of missives bore the headline "Sorry—No More Letters About Anything Else, So Here's Some More About Huggy Bear." "Every time I went to a show," Gary Walker, who ran the Wiiija label, said, "at least one person came up to me to say, 'Why'd you sign that fucking band? They can't play for shit.'"

Even before the *Word* fiasco, the *Maker* had prophesied, "Expect mayhem when Huggy Bear join Bikini Kill on their tour of Britain." Now a ruckus seemed unavoidable, and others were preemptively piling on: Nils Bernstein, the publicist of Sub Pop, sent a fax to an extensive list of British music journalists and editors, arguing that Bikini Kill was getting attention only because the band was (mostly) women, and that the group didn't deserve any coverage at all.

Bikini Kill weren't looking for trouble when they crossed the Atlantic. The whole point of their several-month hiatus leading up to this tour had been to recuperate from the nonstop action of 1992, and in going to England they all felt as Tobi did: excited to be hanging out with another radical feminist band, especially one that was making such a desperately gloried racket.

The bands toured together for two weeks. Girls up front was the rule, as flyers distributed at the concerts made clear:

> At this show We ask that girls/women stand near the front, by the stage. Please allow/encourage this to happen This is an experiment.

The shows got confrontational at times. Some men seemed keen on starting a brawl, others keen on watching one, and people came to the venues the way teenagers go to a school stairwell where they've heard their classmates might be about to fight. More than once, Huggy Bear or Bikini Kill halted a set to demand that men stop shoving or that a man harassing girls by the stage be removed to the rear. In Newport, Bikini Kill was booed; in Derby, Jo got beat up in the venue's lobby by the girlfriend of a guy whom Kathleen had booted from the club for dancing violently up front.

But the tour was fun overall. Bikini Kill played five hundred–capacity halls with multicolored stage lights and powerful sound systems, they recorded a session with BBC producer John Peel, and they met Gina Birch and Ana da Silva from the Raincoats. An amateur British filmmaker, Lucy Thane, trailed them the whole tour, shooting not only the musicians but the girls in the crowd, who were only too happy to go on camera, jammed up against the sinks in the ladies' loo, to talk about how Bikini Kill had changed their life. "For fuck's sake, I'm a female and I can *do* this!" a girl in Glasgow said. "It's my time, it's wonderful," gushed another.

Upon returning to the United States, Bikini Kill went into the studio again, this time with Joan Jett in the producer's (and backup singer's) role. Ian MacKaye had introduced Jett to Bikini Kill, and she was instantly impressed by both the music and the zines. She was particularly heartened that a rock 'n' roll feminism was catching on; she could have used some of that in the late '70s, when she was a teenage guitarist playing in the Runaways. "The Runaways had *nobody*," she said. "I felt like a feminist, but I felt completely dissed by other feminists, 'cause they were like, 'Well, you can't dress sexy.' Number one, I'm *not* dressing sexy—even though I did have my pants open from time to time. But what do you mean? You're saying women can't have sex? You don't *tell* me that girls don't get horny and don't wanna fuck! You know why girls 'can't play guitar' and 'can't play rock 'n' roll'? Because rock 'n' roll is *sex*. That's what I grew up with, and that's what I wanted to make. So meeting people like Kathleen and Allison and all those girls, it was really incredible, because I felt like maybe people were starting to get it."

Bikini Kill had recorded a full-length album that past October, titled *Pussy Whipped*, but it wasn't due out till the following fall, and they had already written new songs to record with Jett—glammy, triumphal anthems that explored pleasure and play. "Turn that song down / Turn the static up / CMERE BABY LET ME KISS YOU LIKE

A BOY DOES," "New Radio" exulted. "Let's wipe our cum on my parents' bed." And for the introduction to "Demirep," Kathleen and Jett sat cross-legged on the floor, facing each other, and played a hand-clapping game they'd both learned when they were little girls: "Miss Mary Mack, Mack, Mack, all dressed in black, black, black . . . " These two songs, along with a new version of "Rebel Girl," would be released on a 7" in September 1993, a month before *Pussy Whipped*.

After the sessions, in late April, Rock for Choice flew Bikini Kill to LA to play a benefit, and the band booked a short run of shows there leading up to the evening. At Macondo Cultural Center, a Latino community space in Hollywood that hosted punk concerts, the band was stronger than ever. A tangible levity edged Kathi's and Tobi's habitual cool; Billy could hardly stop grinning, and Kathleen was positively jolly. "I'm gonna show you my cellulite now," she said at the start of the show, and stepped out of her skirt, leaving just a cropped yellow T-shirt and the bottom half of a black bikini. The girls in the audience whooped and applauded. "This is cellulite, this is what it looks like, and you don't see that in a magazine." She bent over and smacked her butt cheek a few times. "You don't see this on MTV."

Kathi tore into the bassline of "Don't Need You," joined a few beats later by the others. The sound onstage was abysmal; it was nearly impossible for them to hear themselves, let alone one another. The three instrumentalists faced each other in order to play in time, with Kathleen out in front by herself, half-naked. She jumped up and down, shimmied brightly for a measure or two, then shouted, her voice pure fire:

Don't need you to say we're all right
Don't need you to say we suck

She held one hand up to her ear, straining to hear her own voice. Whoever was at the sound board couldn't help. But despite the technical issues, everybody was relaxed and cheerful. Even Kathi cracked a smile between songs, and Kathleen's dancing had a soaring ease to it. Several people were shooting video in the front row, and they had all asked the band's permission first. It was a good show. And then—

I'm your self-fulfilling porno queen, yeah,

Kathleen was singing, when she noticed, by the side of the stage, a guy taking pictures of her from behind. She reached her arm out and covered his lens with her hand, shaking her head no.

I mimic out your every fucking fantasy,

she went on, but he was shooting again; even when she faced away from him, she could see the flash of his camera going off. She turned back, put her hand over his lens again. "I said no," she said firmly, in time with the music. "NO."

Oh whoa, whoa whoa whoa

He was still at it. She swatted at him, pointed to the door. "Out. *Out!*" She pushed the guy away from the stage.

I can almost reach mine now, my sugar

Then a short instrumental break. The guy hadn't left. Kathleen went to the side of the stage and shouted at him, ending in a chant: "Get him out! Get him out!" She took center stage once more, glancing back to make sure he was finally gone. She danced, but all the joy had gone out of it.

The song ended. Kathleen faced the audience, catching her

breath. "If I say that I don't want to be photographed, and I put my hand up in front—if you keep photographing me anyway"—she was livid, taking breaths between almost every word—"three times in a row, when I put my hand up, and I go like *that* to you"—she asked a front-row fan if she could demonstrate, and tapped the fan on the shoulder—"I'm *sorry*, but I'm not a bitch for that." She gave a strained, sarcastic smile, shaking her head, still livid. "I will not have pictures of my ass taken by some white boy over here who I don't know. So write about *that* in your fuckin' fanzine."

Five nights later, the band played a sold-out Rock for Choice benefit to an audience of four thousand at the Hollywood Palladium. King Missile, Stone Temple Pilots, and Kim Gordon's side project Free Kitten were also on the bill, but the biggest buzz was around Bikini Kill. Kathleen performed in a dress with the words KILL ME printed on the chest, and some men shouted boos at the band. The *Los Angeles Times* ran a review noting that "while much of the audience seemed unsure of just what to make of this Olympia, Wash., band, there was a small contingent of female fans that seemed wholly enthralled—as if they had found music really mattered."

People thought either that Bikini Kill were ruining music or that the group was the greatest band ever. Reams of fan letters filled the Kill Rock Stars mailbox, but there was also frightening, graphic hate mail; one letter writer described in detail how he wanted to mutilate Kathleen. Even among fans, some lavished the band with adoration while others were beginning to act as if the group owed them something—like the girl who asked Tobi before their set if they would play "Feels Blind" and hit the drummer when she said no, or the girl who requested a hug and punched Tobi for declining. "It goes without saying that guys were assholes, but the girl stuff was harder to dismiss," Tobi said. "It complicated things, really."

After the LA shows, the whole band went back to Olympia, but the town felt even more claustrophobic to Kathleen than it had before, more finger-pointy, more whisper-ridden. One girl came up to her at the Safeway near her house and said, Kathleen recalled, "something to the effect that I must think I am really cool, but I'm not, I'm just a conceited bitch who is ruining the punk scene, blah blah blah. The basic gist was that I was a really mean stuck-up person who thought I was super cool, but I really was a piece of shit."

She fled to Portland, Oregon, and moved into a house of female artists including Radio Sloan, a brilliant guitarist and audio engineer, and Johanna Fateman, who made a zine called *Snarla* in collaboration with Miranda July, an artist friend of hers. Kathleen traveled up to Olympia every so often for Bikini Kill practice, and her bandmates came to her sometimes, but she was happy to focus on new projects in Portland: putting on women-only shows in her basement; making a video, *Stupid Punks*, and a zine about fandom, *My Life with Evan Dando*; recording a punk rock–opera album, *The Fakes*, with Tim Green, her old friend from Nation of Ulysses; and starting a band, the Troublemakers, with Johanna and their friend Molly 16. Tobi, Kathi, and Billy were keeping busy, too, mostly with the Frumpies, their band with Molly Neuman. They recorded a 7", "Alien Summer Nights," and began plotting a West Coast tour. And Tobi started up a cassette-only label called Bumpidee.

In early July, Mia Zapata, the lead singer of the Seattle grunge band the Gits, was raped and murdered by a stranger a few blocks from her house. The Olympia musicians knew her—Bratmobile had played with the Gits in LA a few days earlier—and the murder shook them up badly. Zapata's death was awful news in and of itself, but Tobi and Kathleen also couldn't help but think of the scary hate mail Kathleen was getting. Was she in genuine danger? When Kathleen heard about the killing, she was in Seattle, helping Joan Jett write and record Jett's new record. Kathleen wrote much of "Go Home," a song about being stalked—by a person, a memory, a fear—that would appear on Jett's new album, *Pure and Simple*. Kathleen felt thrilled to watch somebody else singing the words she had written. "Get that voice ah-outta my head," Jett sang into the studio mic. "I will stab it dead—dead. I will kill it dead—dead."

Working with Jett was Kathleen's first major-label experience, but the big guys were starting to come calling for Bikini Kill. "Kathleen had a hot band," Jett's manager, Kenny Laguna, recounted. "Every label in the business wanted them! Warner Brothers, Capitol, Interscope: everyone." Kathleen didn't think Bikini Kill should abandon Kill Rock Stars, but she was curious about getting wider distribution for her ideas. Plus, she explained later, "I wanted to say to myself, 'I looked into it and it wasn't the right thing,' as opposed to just assuming things." Tobi didn't even want to look into it, though; she saw what Nirvana's success had done to them. "I was very saddened to see that that success did not make them happy," she said. "I knew that things were really really bad: Kurt was on drugs and the band was falling apart." She had always suspected that capitalism tended to wreck art: Now she had proof.

Laguna urged Kathleen to at least meet with the labels. You don't have to do anything you don't want to do, he said. Get a free plane trip out of it, stay in a nice hotel. "I thought we could talk them into it," he admitted. "They could have had over a million dollars." After weeks of cajoling, Kathleen and Billy and Kathi let the label executives fly them down to LA for a week for meetings and fancy dinners. Tobi stayed home; just before the trip, Cobain had killed himself in Seattle, and her old friend's death shocked and grieved her. "There was no way I was going to set foot in that world at that time," Tobi said. "It was just too depressing."

But Kathleen wondered: How much could she get out of these labels without giving anything in return? She was close to broke. Bikini Kill still hadn't released a full-length record, let alone a CD, so the band had seen scant royalties so far. Seven-inch records and ten-inch EPs didn't pull in the dough for any band, indie label or not. She asked the major labels to send CDs of their other bands, supposedly so she could check out their rosters; then she sold the discs to record stores and paid her rent with the loot for the better part of a year. She persuaded a label to fly her and her two roommates to New York, telling the honchos that Johanna was her hairstylist and Radio was her manager.

In the end, Bikini Kill stayed on Kill Rock Stars. "I got a postcard from Kathleen: 'Thank you for all your help. We've decided our community would ostracize us if we signed,'" Laguna said. "I think they were dead wrong. I used to make fun of them. I'd say, 'Nineteen girls in Olympia would be upset if you went with a major, that's it.'"

"Signing to a major label was not just a matter of 'integrity' or 'purity,'" Tobi said. "Our vision was of creating a feminist youth culture that was participatory and would change society. We wanted all girls in all towns to start bands. We didn't just want to be 'the feminist punk band' that people would come and see on tour." But that was what they were becoming. They played more shows, wrote more songs, took breaks when they could afford to. They were becoming better musicians, better songwriters, better performers. At the same time, audiences were starting to see them as stars. "Pretty soon we were all over twenty-five and our biggest fans were under sixteen," Tobi said. "Selfishly, I wanted stuff to change and for there suddenly to be all these women in bands around my age who could be peers. Instead there would be a long line of kids at a DIY show making us sign autographs."

Yet at least young listeners now had the *option* of idolizing an overtly feminist, majority-female band. This was progress. Even if it wasn't exactly what the musicians had wanted, it was changing the sound track of adolescence for good.

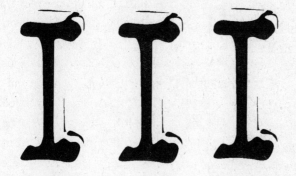

III,

1993-94

TWELVE

THE SOUL OF EVERY GIRL

There's no way to map out with any certainty the scattered cartographies of rebellion that were forming by 1993. The punk feminist revolution was spreading like windblown seed, sprouting in the tertiary cities and suburbs and rural routes of North America, growing differently in each place depending on the local climate. Some girls started zines; some formed bands; some just dug in their closets and pulled out the little-girl barrettes they'd heard riot grrrls wore, and admired themselves in the mirror with bright plastic butterflies poised on their temples, proud of this new look that said they were doing something different from what everyone wanted them to do: They would not grow up the way adults intended.

We know that seventy-five thousand people eventually bought *Pussy Whipped*, which came out in late 1993. But we don't know how many copies were dubbed on boom boxes and dual cassette decks for how many friends or pen pals, or how many people were riding in the car to school one morning when somebody hit Eject on the Lemonheads singing, "Into your arms, oh whoa into your arms I can go," and swapped in Bikini Kill's "Alien She":

> *She wants me to go to the mall*
> *She wants me to put the pretty—the pretty pretty pretty pretty*
>   *lipstick on*
> *She wants me to be like her she wants me to be like her*
> *I want to kill her*
> *But I'm afraid it might kill me*

These girls weren't aware that Bratmobile's Erin Smith had told the British newspaper *The Guardian* that "Riot Grrrl by name is destined to flop. The whole thing has become diluted. Like now it's popular, it's not cool any more." They didn't know that Tobi Vail thought it had become pointless, or that Molly Neuman had drafted (though never published) a piece for *Jigsaw* titled "Revolution Girl . . . You Disappoint Me." They just knew that "Fuck you too, cool schmool" was exactly what they wanted to scream in the cafeteria every day, and that when they heard Kathleen bellow, "Dare you to be who you are! Dare you to do what you will!" they felt an electric charge through their whole body, like they really *could* do anything.

A census of all these girls can't be taken, but some of them can be tracked down: the ones who founded chapters, left traces, met enough other girls to make themselves traceable. One of these was Ann Carroll of Omaha, who found out about Riot Grrrl from the *Seattle Weekly*'s reprint of the Emily White article and would eventually organize the movement's second national convention, deep in the heart of Nebraska. Things that were cool or new or underground rarely filtered through to Omaha, but a pal of Ann's who'd moved to Olympia mailed the article to Ann's best friend,

Andee, and Ann knew immediately that this was what she'd been waiting for.

She had already founded and given up on several activist clubs at her high school. She'd been director of Omaha Youth for Peace, which when she took the reins was little more than a social club. Members would joke, "Are you going to Youth for Pizza tomorrow?" Ann did her best to refocus the group. For the first time in years, YFP had an openly waged American war to oppose: Operation Desert Storm got underway in January 1992, during her directorship. The night the United States attacked Iraq, the group gathered at Ann's house to watch the news on TV, and throughout the war, networks showed cruise missiles descending like videogame weapons, the targets exploding in pristine black-and-white silence. Peace activists viewed these "surgical strikes" as a facade, a sign that the government was selling the Gulf War to American viewers as a kashered conflict, its gore siphoned tidily away. Nebraskans for Peace, YFP's parent organization, held rallies, and the youth showed up. But nobody was paying antiwar protesters any mind, and Ann had to admit her efforts weren't doing much good. YFP was getting less serious, not more. New people were showing up to the meetings just because MTV said that being active was the "alternative" thing to do, Ann thought. When the Youth for Pizza voted to mount a campaign opposing censorship, the cause du jour for with-it youth, Ann wanted to discuss whether curbing free speech might be acceptable in some situations—depictions of violence against women, for example, or expressions of racism. But everybody else just wanted to toe the party line.

Fed up, Ann quit her post with YFP and resigned herself to living out of step from an age in which all politics was televisual and all counterculture was nostalgic. At her high school, the usual strains of sartorial rebellion—punk, goth, hippie—each claimed a handful of adherents, with all the freaky dressers hanging out together in a meaningless blur of black lipstick and jingle-bell anklets. They were historical reenactment societies, all of them; throwbacks to the past, just like the aging beatnik men who ran the three-story landmark of a used bookstore downtown where the outsiders went after school, flipping through mildew-scented records in the basement and wandering the dim labyrinths of books upstairs. YFP had its meetings at this store, whose very name, the *Antiquarium*, accepted this fate of being terminally out of date; embraced it, even. The beatniks sat at the cash register with their shoes off, greeting everyone with "Good morning," no matter what part of the day it happened to be; the passing of time was irrelevant to them. But it plagued Ann, who was certain that all the world's important cultural moments were in the past. "There'd been the hippies, and the beatniks, and punk had already happened," she said. "I had decided that there was no room for anything new."

Then the *Seattle Weekly* article appeared in Andee Davis's mailbox. Ann had graduated from high school by then and was living downtown, attending the state university part time. The old friend who'd sent the article, along with some flyers and zines, wasn't a riot grrrl herself but went to Evergreen and had a hunch that this was something that would appeal to Ann and Andee.

Riot Grrrl seemed genuinely new to the two of them, enough so that it hadn't been drained of its political import or reduced to a set of superficial styles. Of course, in the eyes of the original riot grrrls, that was precisely what was happening. At the same time that millions of *Newsweek* readers were learning about Riot Grrrl via the now-disgraced Jessica Hopper, Ann was thinking excitedly that it was "something not very many people knew about; it was a secret club, almost." And in Omaha, that's just what it was.

Ann and Andee started seeking out the music associated with Riot Grrrl—"That first Bikini Kill record was like this life-changing thing for us," Andee said—and they wrote away to all the girl-zine addresses they could get their hands on. They started zines of their own and collected multiple pen pals, including, as it happened, Jessica Hopper. Even if Ann and Andee had known that Jessica had fallen from grace, even if they had known that Jessica was *so* not a riot grrrl any more that she was talking to a *Seventeen* reporter about how mean the girls had been to her, it wouldn't have mattered: Ann and Andee still would have befriended Jessica. The idea of ostracizing anybody was unthinkable to them. And Minneapolis, six hours from Omaha, was practically around the corner compared with all the other rebel girls clustered on or near the coasts. They couldn't afford to be too choosy. "We really thought: Friends everywhere! Boy girl revolution!" Ann said.

In early 1993, as Bikini Kill was touring the UK and Erika and May were starting Riot Grrrl Press, Ann and Andee took a spring break trip to Minneapolis and stayed with Jessica at her mother's house for a week. They thought they were finally meeting another riot grrrl—her zine had been listed on one of the flyers in the care package from Olympia—and Jessica was happy to have found a few riot grrrls who still wanted to hang out with her. "They were the funnest feminist girls I had met yet," Jessica said. "I was like, damn, I wish they lived here."

Jessica was only sixteen then, several years younger than Ann and Andee, but she was bossy, cocky, and cool. She shoplifted during their visit, pocketing sunglasses with such exaggerated movements that Ann and Andee couldn't believe she never got caught. At a restaurant one night, she pulled a tampon out of her purse, stuck it in her mouth like a cigar, and pretended to smoke it as she sauntered through the restaurant to the bathroom. Back at her mother's house, she had her new friends call the local newspaper to report that Jessica's band, Andromeda Strain, had been added to the bill of an upcoming Fugazi show. She thought it would be awkward to make the call herself, since she wrote for the paper sometimes.

Every other Twin Cities band would have given their Gibson SG to play that show—the club booker's phone was ringing off the hook with musicians begging for the opening slot, and the list of possibilities had grown to fifty bands. Jessica leapfrogged over the lot of them by calling Fugazi's label directly. "It worked," she said. "*And* pissed off every band in town, because we were terrible."

The Omaha girls might as well have driven down a rabbit hole on I–35 somewhere around Fertile, Iowa (population 382), and emerged in a parallel universe, a wonderland of self-promotion and outrageous self-confidence and being buddies with celebrities. "We were getting bombarded with this whole other world," Ann said. Jessica talked about being friends with Huggy Bear and Courtney Love and Kurt Cobain, and about how Love had named Jessica a Woman of the Year in *Melody Maker*. The mantle of the celebrity couple's fame seemed to hover around Jessica's head.

The three girls made a brief zine together during the visit, titled *Teenage Bullet*: fast, impossible to pin down, deadly. The back cover featured xeroxed hands stretching their fingers down from the top of the page like Fourth of July bunting. The hands were, of course, adorned with words. One hand said SEX POT; another, TEEN BULLET GIRL. The hand on the far left was Jessica's. Written on it were the words MEDIA WHORE.

A month after returning from Minneapolis, Ann and Andee called the first meeting of Riot Grrrl Omaha. A half dozen girls became regulars at the weekly meetings at Ann's apartment. The girls talked about their lives, discussed sexism and self-defense tactics, planned feminist propaganda, and talked about their boyfriends. Ann was dating a Deadhead environmental-activist guy who was six years older than her and felt alienated by her feminist zeal; their friend Monica had a boyfriend who hated the idea of Riot Grrrl and attacked her for associating with a project he saw as discriminatory.

(He once confronted Ann on a city bus, saying, "If you saw things with your third eye, as I do, you would understand that I have as much of a feminine side as you.")

They propagandized around town, going to rock shows to hand out zines about eating disorders, and toting spray bottles of thinned-out wheat paste to the Old Market, a key hangout spot for young Omahans, to post their flyers on the walls.

WATCH OUT Because next time you yell Hey Babe you might be left WONDERing what hit you. A Public Service Announcement from Riot Grrrl Omaha

Many of the flyers they posted were subsequently scribbled on, crossed out, ripped down. Somebody wrote on one, "I wish every riot grrrl was dead." The girls were undeterred; they had already known that sexism was pervasive and violent, and this only proved them right.

The Omaha group never got very big. In addition to the core, there were a few people from the suburbs who saw the flyers, showed up for awhile, then drifted away again. But Ann and Andee were trading letters and zines with scores of girls, mostly younger than them, from around the country. Their own zines took on a kindly, encouraging, advice-giving tone; Ann and Andee slipped easily into their role as mail-order priestesses of feminism, writing at the apses of their loose-edged epistolary congregations. "I am a Riot Grrrl because I believe that the soul of every girl matters," Ann wrote on a flyer, determined to reach each sheep in the flock.

Acting locally was harder to manage. When the girls heard that some fraternity members at the university had raped a woman and then hassled her for reporting it to the police, they felt desperate to strike back. It was maddening to know how likely the guys were to go free. "We were trying to think of what was the absolute most offensive thing that we could do," Andee said, "and we decided we were going to make bloody pads and stick them to the frat house." But the group never carried out the plan. Maybe just having the revenge fantasy, together and out loud and in vivid gross detail, was enough. If they knew they could do something, if they could make a plan and had enough people in the

room to carry it out, then they would know they weren't powerless. Riot grrrls across the country revered penis-severing Lorena Bobbitt and lesbian serial killer Aileen Wuornos as folk heroines; they wrote zine pieces about antirapist ass-kicking girl gangs that never existed.

RIOT GRRRL D.C.
P.O. BOX 11002
WASHINGTON D.C.
20008

WHY DID JOHN WAYNE BOBBIT GET OFF? ARE WE GONNA LET LORENA GET THROWN IN JAIL?

SPEAK OUT!!

Follow-through on these fantasies was comparatively rare. The girls invoked, praised, and defended the *idea* of the feminist vigilante far more often they became her. In some places, though, especially on the coasts, girls were taking action by lodging their accusations in public, combining the classic feminist move of "breaking silence" with the contemporary activist tool of public shaming that ACT UP had popularized. A girl in Seattle wrote RAPIST on the car of the ex-boyfriend who had assaulted her; when she saw other girls talking to him at shows, she'd pull them aside and say, "I think you should know that that guy you're talking to doesn't treat women very well." A girl in DC wrote in permanent marker on the seats of the Metro that her stepfather—she used his full name—was a wife beater; another shouted an offender's name into a silent moment during "Suggestion" at a Fugazi show; still another performed a spoken word piece at a punk show about an accused rapist who was at the show. She didn't have to name him; everybody knew who she meant.

Some observers were concerned. A boy could be vilified and pilloried in the public square without a fair hearing—without any hearing at all. But it was worse, the girls felt, that men so frequently did hateful things without facing the slightest consequences. Most of these girls had no regrets, but a few did have compunctions later on. One Olympia girl who made a zine excoriating her former boyfriend for being manipulative expressed remorse years after the fact. "I'm not saying I didn't feel abused by him, because I did," she said. "But now I'm able to have more responsibility for how I interacted with that. I got to play the victim and he got to play the offender."

For the Omaha girls, it was hard to know how to react when violence infiltrated the group itself. Monica had moved in with her boyfriend, and one night, in the middle of a fight about Riot Grrrl, he threw a glass jar at her. The physical abuse got worse from there, but she told nobody. "I even stopped attending riot grrrl meetings for quite a while," she wrote years later, "convinced that my friends were, indeed, a bunch of man-haters." When the remaining girls tried to reach her, she iced them out. They spent many meetings talking about Monica: How could they have failed her so completely? Was she lost to them forever?

Around the same time, in Arcata, a university town in northern California, a cofounder of the local Riot Grrrl chapter was approached by a young woman who'd been driven to tears by a guy in one of her classes. He harassed this woman mercilessly, but when she tried to file a complaint with the university, she told riot grrrl Kirsten Frickle, she received no response. "They won't do anything," the woman said.

"Well, *we'll* do something," Kirsten said. She was twenty-five and had known some terrible men in her life—the faraway father of her young son, for one. She went with another member of the Riot Grrrl group to wait outside the guy's class, and when he came out of the room, they approached him. "So, we hear you like to harass women."

"Yeah," the guy said. "I like harassing women. It's fun."

Kirsten's friend whipped out a Polaroid camera and snapped his photograph. The two of them made a flyer that included the guy's photograph and his name and the caption: HE THINKS SEXUAL HARASS-MENT IS FUN. WE THINK HE IS UNACCEPTABLE. They posted the flyers all over town. Kirsten heard later that the flyers had caused the guy some trouble in a custody dispute he was in the middle of; she heard he'd even lost his job. She had no doubt that he deserved this, and worse. "In that thirty-second confrontation," she said, "you knew he was a jerk on purpose and he liked to rile people up. He had a rapist mentality." Somebody called her and threatened to press slander charges, but Kirsten couldn't be cowed that easily: She was a journalism major, so she knew the law. "Slander is spoken, libel is written," she informed the caller, "and it's not libel if it's true. You don't have a leg to stand on."

Kirsten had a closer relationship to the media than most of her movement cohorts in other towns. She'd done a stint as arts editor at the campus newspaper, *The Lumberjack*, so the process of shaping and trimming reality into a story, and the distortions inherent in that work, didn't faze her. The media played an important role in helping people understand the world, she believed, but readers had to be responsible for maintaining a healthy level of skepticism. When Kirsten first heard about Riot Grrrl from the *LA Weekly* article, for example, she automatically assumed that the piece, smart and well written as it was, didn't convey the whole story. But the article included the mailing address for the Olympia chapter, so Kirsten sent a letter and got a note back from Nomy Lamm telling her to go ahead and create a Riot Grrrl in Arcata, and to make it whatever she and the other girls she met wanted it to be.

Just as Kirsten was posting flyers around Arcata, Angie Gross was putting up similar signs in Eureka, fifteen minutes away. Together they founded an Arcata-Eureka chapter that drew a dozen or more steady members, high school and college girls. "We were our own little pocket," Kirsten said. "It didn't seem like we had to be super connected." They didn't even know about the media blackout. It was irrelevant to them; no national media were tracking down girls in the redwood forests. The only reporter who expressed interest was a student staffer from *The Lumberjack*, and that piece turned out fine.

The girls who got Riot Grrrl up and running that same year in Vancouver, British Columbia, didn't start out with as much skepticism about things they read in print. They were a full decade younger than Kirsten, with no journalism experience. Ingrid Gerberick was fifteen when her cool artist dad showed her the article about Riot

Grrrl in *Spin*. Ingrid brought the piece to school and showed it to some of her friends; they wrote a letter to the address in the magazine, and eventually a letter came back from a DC girl who had just received a scholarship to go to the University of British Columbia the following fall. She encouraged them to get things going; she would join up with them in a few months.

Riot Grrrl wasn't the Vancouver girls' introduction to feminism—they were already learning about it through their parents and classmates—but it gave them a way to put those ideas into action. They started holding regular meetings in Ingrid's dad's studio building, and they immediately began making zines, which they passed out at all-ages hardcore shows, attracting more girls to the meetings.

The first gatherings were mostly griping and zine-making sessions, but gradually the discussion topics became more substantive: abuse, eating disorders, sexual pressure, molestation, rape. Sexual abuse loomed especially large. The girls discussed not only overt incidents but also abusive undercurrents and overtones they'd sensed in less dramatic encounters but never held up to the light. "It was people being able to name things that they had never conceived of [as abuse] before," Ingrid said, "and understanding that all those things *had* been really fucked up."

Unlike most other Riot Grrrl chapters, whose zines came out once or twice a year at best, the Vancouver girls were prolific publishers, making an issue every other month for over a year. Vancouver took the Riot Grrrl zine model and refined it, filling issues with essays on sex and self-esteem, poems, drawings, and diverse inspirations—one zine reproduced a page of Anne Frank's writing and a work by the radical gay 1980s artist David Wojnarowicz. Riot Grrrl zines commonly reproduced offensive graphics from magazines and added sarcastic retorts, but in the August 1993 centerfold from *Riot Grrrl Vancouver*, composed of images clipped from skateboarding magazines, juxtaposition and collage performed the critique with nearly wordless grace.

Still, the girls didn't leave every manifestation of sexism to speak for itself. When they received an irate letter from a concerned mother (she wrote that the zine "disrupts the natural family order where the woman and children are indeed submissive to the male"), they printed it in their zine along with a point-by-point rebuttal. Maybe they could have just let the letter slide, but Riot Grrrl wasn't about letting things slide. They were all high on outrage, on the surge of strength it brought. So they sallied forth to battle, armed with their improvised weapons. Which sometimes were and sometimes were not equal to the task.

One girl wrote in the Vancouver zine about a man who had waved his dick at her as she was heading home from school—on three separate occasions. Most recently, he had asked her, "Like it, wanna suck on it?" "If this happens to anyone else out there, tell him to fuck off," the girl wrote, and invited anyone who had had a similar experience to call her. But this man didn't just need to be dissed in a zine; he needed to be arrested, put into sex offender classes, possibly even kept far away from girls for the rest of his natural life. This was just one instance of how talking about an offense, though an important first step, was often not enough. The feminists of the '70s had eventually gone from raising consciousnesses to building institutions: rape crisis centers, domestic violence shelters, women's self-defense classes. Realizing how important these things were, the Vancouver riot grrrls printed lists of them in the zines. Longing for a world without rape, they scarcely could imagine a world before rape hotlines. On ground hard-won by their feminist predecessors, the riot grrrls teetered on tiptoes, straining to reach the next ledge up.

Throughout the spring of 1994, Riot Grrrl Vancouver met almost every Sunday. The girls wrote their meeting agendas and minutes in a small spiral notebook, its blue cover mostly taken up with a xeroxed sticker from Riot Grrrl NYC that read, "Overthrow cockrock and idolize your girlfriend." The girls put on frequent all-ages punk shows, providing a venue for local girl bands and bringing more established groups up from Washington State and Oregon. They helped put on a Rock for Choice benefit and organized a festival called Girlapalooza. They celebrated Valentine's Day together and drove three hours to Olympia to see Bikini Kill play.

They were aware that Riot Grrrl in other cities had had some trouble with the mainstream media, and they figured they should come up with a policy in case anybody were to show up wanting to write about them. But this was a difficult question. How could a chapter that owed its very existence to *Spin* magazine deny interviews to other publications? They knew how even a mediocre article could change girls' lives and even reshape an entire scene, and it would have been nearly impossible for the Vancouver girls to hear about the movement any other way. Underground US bands rarely played in Vancouver, since getting the necessary permissions to perform in Canada was costly and troublesome—Bikini Kill, for example, never played there. Even mailing zines across the border was a hassle.

In April 1994, a year and a half after Jessica Hopper had violated an implicit media ban that was made explicit only afterward, a member of the Vancouver chapter wrote in the communal notebook, "1st R.G. POLICY FOR INTERVIEWERS ETC." This heading was followed by: "THEY MUST PROPOSE BEFORE"—before what? There was no answer, only a jungle of psychedelic doodles, spirals and scalloped whorls and heavy-lidded staring eyes, drawn on the page with a blue ballpoint pen and such a heavy touch that the reverse of the page became an undulating, ink-stained braille.

Six weeks later, the meetings stopped. The girls who were involved had already met one another; they'd found the relationships they needed, and the structure was extraneous now. Besides, the media issue underlined how confusing it was to try to stay accountable to girls in other cities whom they might never meet. The rest of the notebook was a static flip-book of blank pages interrupted only by empty blue lines.

While girls in some cities were forming Riot Grrrl groups, others took inspiration from the growing network but opted to create their own entities. Girls in Chicago discussed creating a Riot Grrrl chapter but ended up calling themselves Girls Empowered Resisting Labels and Limits (GERLL) and setting up a zine distribution project, similar to Riot Grrrl Press. A group of punks in Rapid City, South Dakota, made a series of collective zines and convened regular meetings under the name Empowerment Through Sisterhood—"just because there wasn't much communication, if any, with riot grrrls anywhere else," Jessica Catron, a founder of the group, explained.

In New York City, a vibrant group took root that was quite

different from anything else that used the Riot Grrrl name. A year after Ananda La Vita and Claudia von Vacano's first attempt to start a chapter in the city, several New Yorkers attended the Riot Grrrl Convention in DC. On returning home, they founded what became an enormous Riot Grrrl group, with meetings that dependably drew twenty people and could swell to as big as fifty. The group drew an unusually wide range of ages, too, from fifteen-year-old high school students to women in their thirties.

New York's was also among the queerest of all the Riot Grrrl chapters, and not just the bisexual-with-a-boyfriend model so common in DC and Olympia. Easily over half the New York group identified as dykes, and even many of the apparently straight members came out of the closet within a few months of joining. Riot Grrrl NYC meetings and events were among the few places in the city that queer women into alternative art and punk rock could find friends and lovers.

Many New York riot grrrls had also attended meetings and protests organized by the city's other radical activist groups: ACT UP, Queer Nation, Women's Action Coalition (WAC), and Women's Health Action and Mobilization (WHAM!). To those who stayed with Riot Grrrl, though, the other groups didn't feel like home. ACT UP was massive and intimidating and predominantly male, while WAC and WHAM! felt geared toward an older crowd. "It seemed like Riot Grrrl was the only perfect combination of all the things I was interested in at the time," Diana Morrow, a photographer who was active in the group, said. "Music, art, feminism: It was all right there."

RG NYC functioned less as a personal discussion group than as a network of female artists. "There was a rejection of the trauma-centered focus, and more of a creativity and productivity focus," Claudia said. In addition to making zines, the chapter organized exhibitions of members' artwork and put on rock shows at local venues ABC

NO RIO and Brownies, including several festivals they called Pussy Stock. Members regularly played music with one another: Jill Reiter, a member whose band, Double Zero, played at many of these RG NYC shows, often recruited bandmates at meetings. "I always wanted to play music," Jill said, "but I had very little luck finding people to play with until Riot Grrrl." The cast and crew for her film projects, too, she pulled from the Riot Grrrl network; Abby Moser, an anthropology grad student who was shooting a documentary on the group, did the same. "The common denominator was just people making their way in creative fields in New York City," said Elena Humphreys, who was working on opening up an art space on Thirteenth Street called Womb Gallery. "I think that a lot of people had for a while been the creative one in their little group and had no one to bounce ideas off of, working in their little bubble, and then suddenly it was like, oh my God, here's fifty girls I can be in contact with!"

In the summer of 1993, Ann Carroll and Andee Davis drove from Omaha to the small town of Piqua, Ohio, where some girls they traded zines with were organizing a festival—a sort of mini–Riot Grrrl convention, supposedly. En route, they drove several hours out of their way to pick up Jessica Hopper in Minneapolis. Ann and Andee were psyched. They had read in zines and newspaper articles about the legendary convention of 1992, where over a hundred girls had gathered, but they still hadn't met any riot grrrls except Jessica. By this point, they had read the *Seventeen* magazine article about Jessica's drama, but they didn't much care; they didn't feel particularly loyal to the first-generation riot grrrls who had ostracized her. Andee had once written a letter to the Olympia group, right after reading the *Seattle Weekly* article, and she hadn't heard back for months. Finally, a little while after the *Seventeen* article came out, Andee received her response—an envelope with a few little zines and a brief note somebody had dashed off: *Here are the zines you asked for, I don't have a lot of time, sorry it took me so long. Oh, and please don't talk about Riot Grrrl to the media.* Between these curt, elusive, faraway girls and dynamic, spitfire Jessica, it was a no-brainer.

As the Ohio girl fest got rolling, it became clear that nobody else was coming from out of town; the whole gathering was just a dozen hippie-ish pals from Piqua plus Ann, Andee, and Jessica. There weren't really any activities planned. The girls went to a park, swam in a stream, and ate at a Bob Evans diner, which had no decent vegetarian food for Ann and Andee. The day ended with a slumber party, and one of the hosts insisted on playing the Indigo Girls anthem "Closer to Fine" on repeat all night long—"because that way it's in my dreams," she explained.

Ann and Andee remained polite, but Jessica was having none of it. "If I hear that goddamn 'I went to the fountain' song one more time," she announced, "I'm gonna kill people." She already stood way out, wearing a slip and huge sunglasses and carrying a little fake gun. She was sarcastic and arrogant, talking about Kurt and Courtney, making sure everybody knew she was too cool for this small-town scene.

At the sleepover, the Piqua girls started a game called Snaps, one of those irritating diversions where experienced players trade secret information while the newcomers try to figure out the trick. "Give us a name of a celebrity, and then one of us will guess it," the Piqua girls were saying. The guesser had left the room so the others could choose a name. "We can do any name, just try us." Jessica spoke up smugly: "Deng Xiaopeng." The Piqua girls had no idea how to spell the name of the Chinese leader, and the game broke down.

Ann was mortified. They were these girls' guests! And Jessica was being so rude. The three of them left Piqua before the weekend was through. On the way back to Minneapolis, Jessica ate all the baked tofu Ann had bought in Madison and expressly asked her not to eat. When Ann confronted her, she just laughed.

The trip to Piqua killed Ann and Andee's friendship with
Jessica—"It wasn't a falling out, necessarily," Andee said, "we just
never wanted to speak to her again"—but it gave life to a bigger idea.
It was beginning to look like the only way they were ever going to
meet other riot grrrls would be if they put on a convention themselves. Well, why not? Both of them were perfectionists and devoted planners; they knew they could put together an incredible
event. And Ann was about to come into a modest settlement from a
long-ago car accident, so she'd be able to fund the gathering.

They picked a weekend—July 8–10, 1994—giving themselves
nearly a year to plan and publicize the convention. They drew up
little flyers and sent them out to every zine they knew, dozens of
which printed the announcement:

```
Hey Girlfriends
    Us girls in Riot Grrrl Omaha are trying
to get a girl power convention together here
in Omaha for next summer. A get together
for girls to share ideas and empowerment.
So far our ideas are to have workshops,
discussions, camping, a girl rock extrav-
aganza and basically an amazing weekend
with amazing girls.
```

In January, Ann and Andee went on a monthlong pilgrimage
to the Pacific Northwest, partly to meet people, partly to drum up
enthusiasm about the convention. They were especially excited to go
to Olympia and hang out with Erika Reinstein, who had been writing
them thought-provoking letters about class politics. Erika had come
to identify as working class; she wrote in her zine that her bossi-
ness and loudness and willingness to pick fights were markers of her
working-class background, and that people in Olympia were "polite"

and "genteel": middle-class behaviors, she concluded, meaning that her alienation there was political. But Olympia was not a rich town; its scene was anchored by Evergreen, a cheap state school, and some of the riot grrrls weren't going to college at all. A difference in manners may have existed, but it didn't map neatly onto class. Still, Erika had hit upon a new framework for understanding the world and her place in it, and she set about elaborating on that system.

This notion, that one could draw strength from one's underprivileged background, came as a welcome revelation for Ann and Andee. They had both grown up living in trailer parks—Ann used to wilt with embarrassment at having to use food stamps to buy her family groceries—but they'd never had a political way to think about this; it had just been a matter of secrecy and shame. That having been poor could instead be a badge of honor—"it was amazing," Ann said. "It was important to feel empowered by these things that had disempowered you for so long."

Ever since the Omaha girls had received that first care package of articles and flyers, Olympia had seemed like the Riot Grrrl mecca. But by the time they got to town in early 1994, no meetings had taken place there in half a year. Identifying publicly as a riot grrrl had become a liability: "Why are you still holding on to Riot Grrrl," a guy Michelle Noel knew had asked her once, "when all the people who had the original idea"—he meant the members of Bikini Kill and Bratmobile—"don't even believe in it anymore?" The Olympia chapter had disaggregated back into its component social groups, with Michelle and her Bremerton friends over here, Nomy Lamm and her high school friends over there, and Erika still out in front, trying to keep the idea of the movement alive.

Ann and Andee knew from the mail they received that girls across America were making zines and writing on their hands and proudly calling themselves riot grrrls; new chapters were still forming, in Toronto and rural New York and the outskirts of Dallas; but the movement's cohesion—its momentum *as a movement*—seemed to be flagging. "Riot Grrrl, where are you?" one girl wrote in a new zine Riot Grrrl DC had just made. "I feel like the spirit is being lost but I can't admit it." They needed something to reunite them, renew their purpose, get them moving forward again. Maybe the Omaha convention would do the trick.

THIRTEEN

A CRUEL REVOLUTION

Nineteen ninety-three was a good year for feminist punk music. In May, Kill Rock Stars released Heavens to Betsy's first record, the superb four-song 7" "These Monsters Are Real," and a month later the label put out Bratmobile's debut album, *Pottymouth*. Bikini Kill's "New Radio" 7", the one Joan Jett had produced, came out in September, followed by the full-length *Pussy Whipped* in October. Even as old-school riot grrrls worried that their movement was losing its soul, girls everywhere were being galvanized by these records—and by the zines they ordered from Riot Grrrl Press. Zine-making, too, was having a good year. The number of titles was on the rise overall, thanks to the increasing ubiquity of personal computers and desktop publishing software: A Canadian newspaper article estimated that forty thousand zines were actively publishing in North America. With more zines than ever to sift through, young feminists subscribed to *Action Girl Newsletter*, which listed girl zines, and to *Queer Zine Explosion*, which did the same for work by queer zinesters of all genders. And they ordered from Riot Grrrl Press, which, at a time when so many teenagers wanted to be part of Riot Grrrl and so many people in their twenties had grown out of it already, was the easiest and perhaps the only way for a girl in Alabama or Wyoming or Kansas to connect directly to this movement she'd been hearing about. It was certainly an Oklahoma high school sophomore's only shot at reading *Bikini Kill* #2 or *Jigsaw* #5— highly influential zines that had long been out of print.

In late 1993, Mary Fondriest and Seanna Tully were running Riot Grrrl Press out of the Beehive, a new punk activist community center where they also both lived, along with two or three other members of the Beehive collective. The group occupied a three-story row house in Northwest DC's down-at-the-heels Shaw neighborhood, and the collective's members saw the building as a revolutionary space, a temporary autonomous zone where anticapitalist ventures could coalesce and thrive. When Mary and Seanna were living there, though, it was essentially a poorly stocked record shop swathed in radical rhetoric. The girls' lives at the Beehive were marked by chaos. On the ground floor, the slapped-together store offered records and zines, a lending library, and a box of free clothes that people had discarded. Interminable meetings and ear-slaughtering punk shows took place several nights a week; a never-ending supply of houseguests filled the ratty couches and floor space; donated vegetables stank and rotted in the third-floor kitchen, unused by the Food Not Bombs group; and if somebody came knocking on the window in the middle of the afternoon, wanting to buy records, whoever was home had to go let them in.

At least Riot Grrrl Press was doing well. *Too* well, in fact. Orders poured in faster than Mary and Seanna could fill them, and the girls grew to hate seeing their undone work piled in the second-floor living room, staring up at them in silent reproach.

Mary, Seanna, and a handful of other riot grrrls, including Erika, had been actively involved in the Beehive when it began that summer, but by midwinter relations had deteriorated between them and some other members of the collective—especially with Brad Sigal, one of the group's main strategists. An erstwhile Positive Forcenik, Brad had marched against the Gulf War, organized in support of campus cafeteria workers at George Washington University, and traveled to El Salvador to meet with the Marxist guerrillas of the FMLN. All the while, he delved into political theory and revolutionary history, trying to divine the best way to transform the world.

Mary and Seanna saw Brad as an overly rational, macho elitist. The Beehive meetings, full of intricately structured discussions and consensus processes, felt alienating to them, and when Brad tried to explain that these protocols were designed to give everybody an equal voice, he just infuriated them more. How could any process put people on equal footing, the girls argued, without acknowledging that some people started out behind?

Mary and Seanna moved out of the Beehive that winter. Mary was so fed up with the collective that she couldn't bring herself to attend meetings anymore. But Riot Grrrl Press still needed a home, and the girls didn't want to take everything with them. They were sick of living under the same roof with the only centralized collection of the movement's artifacts: the file cabinet stuffed with zines; the black plastic file trays atop it; the continually growing mound of unanswered mail. Mary typed the Beehive a letter proposing that Riot Grrrl Press move from the living room into a second-floor bedroom and pay reduced rent, and she sent the letter to a meeting in her stead. She explained that Riot Grrrl Press needed a door the girls could close. This, she wrote, "would make having to come here feel a lot safer for myself and other women especially."

Safety had been a key concept in feminist circles since the '70s. All-female events or groups were commonly described as "safe spaces"—insulated from any hint of male violence. *Safe* could be a slippery word, though, sometimes used to mean less "free of danger" than "comfortable" or "unchallenged"—with the added intimation that anyone who dared to disagree was not just a dissenter but an attacker. Anything that wasn't to one's liking, if it could be framed as a political issue, could be described as a threat to one's safety, and Mary was learning how useful this could be. "I saw how power was gained by talking about being a victim," she said. "And I got really good at developing that for myself." The empty room at the Beehive normally rented for $185, but Mary persuaded the collective to let Riot Grrrl Press have it for $50.

Seanna, now living with Mary in an apartment in Northeast DC, stayed involved with the Beehive, and at the March 1 collective meeting, the conversation took an uneasy turn. There had been some kidding about how the Beehive, which constantly struggled to pay its bills, needed a "sugar daddy." To generalized laughter, one male collective member affected a girlish voice and said, "Hey, there's a Beehive meeting tonight, you wanna *come*?" Seanna, who had been working as a stripper at the Royal Palace for several months, wrote to them:

```
    i do not know if anything was disscussed about
totally FUCKED UP nature of this "joke" after
i left the meeting. i felt at the time at this
inciddent, it was not my personal responsibility
to be the sex trade police.  as you well know,
i make my living taking money from sugar daddys
and i PAY MY RENT with it. got the connection?


and what, does the beehive plan to do about this?
buy more books??? you have yet another situation
where one who is "other" is leaving the group,
never to returnx because he/she felt frustrated,
offended, ABUSEd by the other members of the
group (usually the ones with privilege.)

xyxxhaxnxyyxfxxk  fxxkxxxnx, FUCK YOU.
```

Seanna had started stripping the previous summer, when another riot grrrl had announced she was going to audition and Seanna went with her. She had a crush on this girl; plus, she could use a new job, and it would be nice to put her ballet training to some use. Although Seanna had been earning a slow trickle of money by working part-time in her mom's office, she was falling behind on her car payments and not saving anything up for college. She knew one other stripper personally, another riot grrrl who lived at Positive Force House, and that—in addition to the example of Kathleen Hanna, who had herself danced at the Royal Palace—was enough to demystify the gig, even to make it seem appealing. By the end of the summer of 1993, at least half a dozen riot grrrls were dancing at the club. "It seemed like in the blink of an eye everybody was working there," said Angela Seguel, who felt she wasn't skinny enough to get a job dancing and was a little bitter about it. Stripping had become the Riot Grrrl DC job of choice.

Situated across the street from a Hilton hotel just north of Dupont Circle, the Royal Palace was a large carpeted room with a stage at its center, poles for pole dancing, and brass railings on either side of the stage for dancers to prop their legs on. The dancers performed most of each shift entirely nude except for spike heels and a garter worn midthigh to hold men's dollar bills; the patrons, mostly businessman types who were staying at the Hilton plus a handful of regulars, sat with their drinks at tables that were arranged in two tiers encircling the stage. Soon Seanna was pulling in as much as six hundred dollars for dancing three shifts per week, leaving most of her time free to work on Riot Grrrl Press and hang out with her friends.

That was the biggest appeal of stripping: the money. Men stare at and harass and objectify women every day for free, went the common explanation; at least this way women get to profit from it. "I felt angry at men and I felt like I was getting back at them, just by taking their money," Seanna said. "It made me feel like I was smarter than they were." In addition to the one hundred to three hundred dollars of tips each dancer got per shift, the club also paid a minimum wage paycheck, which was unusual for a strip bar. There was no other job where a young woman without a college degree who wasn't a computer programming prodigy or a runway model could earn anything close to what she could get for taking her clothes off. And subsidizing a feminist revolution with the money of leering men felt like the greatest scam of all time—on par with funding an anticapitalist rebellion by robbing banks.

The riot grrrls who worked at the Royal Palace knew, too, that by dancing there, they were signaling a break with a major strain of second-wave feminism. They had been in elementary school during the interfeminist sex wars of 1980s, when antiporn activists clashed fiercely with self-described pro-sex feminists on everything from whether porn ought to be illegal to whether it was acceptable for a feminist to be into sadomasochism. Seanna and her feminist co-workers were inheriting the fractured movement those battles had left behind, and picking their way through the fraught landscape that remained. That men went to strip clubs made the girls furious; they never would've wanted to be friends with any guy who would patronize such an establishment in earnest. Yet conventional feminism's blanket opposition to the sex trade felt too absolutist to them, just like all the other "rules" they'd once learned that feminism imposed, dictatorlike, on its adherents. Any perceived attempt to legislate *anything* for them sparked a fuse of punk-rock defiance: One of the riot grrrls who worked with Seanna used to cue up a Rage Against the Machine song that went "Fuck you, I won't do what you tell me" when she got onstage to dance. Plus, going into these spaces defused them somewhat. The strip club wasn't a chaotic realm of evil that destroyed any woman who set foot onstage; it was a big, dingy room that stank of booze and cigarettes, and the patrons seemed more pathetic than scary.

After nine months of working at the Royal Palace, though, the job was starting to set Seanna on edge. Yeah, maybe stripping was a sophisticated project of feminist *détournement*, with the dancers acting out the most extreme and taboo expressions of femininity in order to blow out the whole system, the way playing a a stereo too loud overloads the speakers and turns all music into a burbling, slushy mess. The men who went to the club, though, were just there for a piece of ass, and the riot grrrls who wanted stripping to be a semiotic blow against the patriarchal leviathan found themselves in the belly of the beast. At the club, they couldn't walk away from lewd comments or make obscene retorts; they had to open their legs for the men, talk sweetly to them, make the patrons feel good about themselves. Taking the men's money had once seemed to shuffle the power balance, but after a while the harassment was just harassment.

One night that winter, a boy from the punk scene, a schoolteacher who had recently moved to Mount Pleasant, showed up at the Royal Palace while Seanna was dancing. She saw him from the stage and her stomach plummeted. "I panicked," she said, "but my dance training kept me from jumping off the stage, and I pasted a smile on my face and kept on dancing." Friends of hers came into the club occasionally, but only if they had checked it out with her first; people didn't just drop by without warning her. Everybody knew that. But this boy, Abram, was new to DC. Seanna had invited Abram's female housemate to come see her dance sometime, and the housemate had told Abram about the club, not understanding that the invitation was only for her.

Abram had no idea Seanna would be working that day. He went because he had a friend visiting who was writing a term paper on the sex trade, and also because he was curious about strip clubs. Okay, to be absolutely frank about it, he enjoyed looking at women. But the moment he realized that he recognized one of the naked girls in five-inch heels onstage, he knew he had done something horrifically wrong. He wanted to leave right away, but he and his friend had ordered their mandatory one beer apiece, which they felt compelled to polish off before leaving. Unsure of how to hold his face or where to look, Abram stared miserably at a hockey game on TV. The Capitals were ahead, or they were behind; he didn't care. He hated hockey.

A few days later, at a punk show, Seanna handed Abram's housemate a long letter about the incident. *I refuse to let people in our community look at me like I'm a piece of meat*, she had written. *There are certain expectations we have in this community, and I need these to be followed in order for me to feel safe here.*

Abram's housemate felt bemused as she read the letter. She didn't have much patience for the pieties of DC punk, and from the letter, it wasn't entirely clear whether Abram's principal sin was showing up uninvited or not tipping once he got there. Of course it was both. If a man didn't tip, Seanna couldn't feel like she was tricking him. Without tips, she was just taking off her clothes for minimum wage, and the whole rationale broke down.

Abram didn't understand all of this right away, but he had already felt confused and guilty about the incident, and he was grateful to Seanna for trying to explain herself. "She was wading through a lot of stuff women have to deal with," he said, "and she did it in a way I had a lot of admiration for."

Many people in the punk scene kept their distance from him after that, and several women he'd been flirting with cut him off. One of them told him straight out that his Royal Palace visit was the reason she wouldn't see him anymore. The riot grrrls' rigorous feminism had suffused the entire scene, costing Abram romance and friendship, yet he remained in awe of it. His mother was a prominent feminist activist in Mississippi; he had held the banner at the front of a pro-ERA march in Hattiesburg when he was nine. But none of that amounted to a hill of beans if it couldn't teach him how not to make women feel uncomfortable. Riot Grrrl, he believed, could help him figure out what kind of man he wanted to be.

Grrrl zines were the coffee table reading and the fodder for dinner conversation in his house of punk rock schoolteachers—"the main texts of our lives," he said. One of his favorite things about the zines was that the writers weren't pretending to have all the answers; they were making visible a process of figuring things out. Mary and Erika, in particular, constantly included calls for dialogue and feedback. "They claimed the space to be wrong," Abram said, "and I found that to be very powerful intellectually."

Yet that willingness to be wrong was fading from some of the riot grrrls' worldview. By the time Erika returned to DC for the summer of 1994, it would be practically gone from her own work. She wrote in her zines that she was having a hard time emotionally, feeling ever more haunted by the traumas of her childhood. And her personality seemed to be changing: She was growing harder, some said, less forgiving of political imperfections, even in her friends. "If being honest means being mean," she wrote, in response to those who complained about her harshness, "it's gonna be a cruel revolution."

Her writing was becoming progressively more poetic and pained. ("'RAPE' the word scratched in my mind with that razor with your hands the word stabs my ears," she wrote; and "I am your bloody valentine. Now fuck me dead.") It was also growing increasingly confrontational ("Fuck your white boy revolution") and even peppered with violence ("I was in a secret girl gang that beat up rapists cause we knew there was no justice for girls in this world"; and "Here is a list of books that you better fucking read or May & I are gonna *kick your ass!*").

Sometimes the violence became graphic. "I go up to random men on the street (oh I mean white men) and beat them senseless just for cheap kicks," Erika wrote in 1993. "I masturbate while standing over their unconscious bodies." This wasn't a genuine confessional, of course; she was making an argument about how radical feminists get dismissed as man haters.

> If I WAS a MANHATER (gasp!) would that mean my ideas wouldn't be worth listening to even though there is no institutional way for me to express my hatred for men the way women hating is shoved down my throat every fucking day. Please.

Still, the scenario's explicitness was in line with some of the feminist aesthetics and extremist politics of the time. Karen Finley, the performance artist and NEA Four member, had recently published a collection of monologues, *Shock Treatment*, that was rife with similarly graphic imagery. And Joyce Carol Oates's 1993 novel *Foxfire: Confessions of a Girl Gang* centered around a posse like the one Erika imagined, a group of girl outlaws taking revenge on abusers and harassers.

Meanwhile, on the far right, real violence was taking hold. On March 10, 1993, a protester had murdered an abortion doctor in Pensacola, Florida. This was the first time a "pro-lifer" had used deadly force to advance the cause; four more abortion-clinic personnel would be killed before the end of 1994. And in the wake of the spring 1993 standoff in Waco, Texas, that left a doomsday cult's compound in flames, many ultraconservative white men set about forming armed militias. Rather than aiming to influence government, a growing number of Americans were taking politics into their own hands, often violently. Filling an arsenal was very different, of course, from fantasizing in a zine about violence. But a confrontational approach to politics was in the air, and Riot Grrrl was not exempt from the trend.

Erika's longtime best friend, May, had drifted away from Riot Grrrl that year and become engrossed in her studies. She took a course on women writers of Latin America and realized she had found her life's work; it was starting to look like she might end up a professor herself. "I needed to explore other things," she said. "I guess I just felt like I was done." But Erika wasn't done. She had spent nearly three years building this movement, and she recruited new allies to replace the old. Cindy Hales and Akiko Carver, two mixed-race zine writers living in Olympia, dissected racial issues with the same righteous anger the riot grrrls applied to gender, expressing their frustration about the racial stereotypes and exclusions they experienced. One page in Akiko's zine, *Evacuation Day*, listed over a dozen people Cindy and another friend of hers would like to beat up, ending with "random white kid."

Erika was planning to head back to DC for the summer of 1994 to help run Riot Grrrl Press. Aware that the project would soon be bigger than she, Mary, and Seanna could manage, she recruited Cindy to come east with her. Cindy didn't consider herself part of Riot Grrrl; like most of the radical young women of color in Olympia, she saw it as a white girls' thing, which it largely was. Although Riot Grrrl Press struck her as a worthwhile project, she had serious qualms about working with the Beehive, whose very premise offended her: A group of mostly white kids, none of them from the inner city, had plunked themselves down in the middle of a black neighborhood and professed to want to help the community—without ever, as far as Cindy could tell, asking the people in the community what they needed. What were these kids actually doing? Selling records; setting up concerts; spouting a bunch of talk about being revolutionaries. It disgusted her. She agreed to go to DC with Erika, but something would have to be done about the Beehive.

In the spring of 1994, Mary traveled from DC to Olympia to hang out with Erika, Cindy, and Akiko for a month; when she returned home, with Cindy in tow, she had drastically changed. Seanna, living with her, saw the shift right away. "She was ready for a fight," Seanna said. "Erika had found her working-class voice and Mary found her working-class voice and so together, they were a team, and they were gonna start calling all the shots about us middle-class people."

Seanna *was* perhaps more refined than befitted a cadre of ferocious revolutionaries: She had never lost her ballet dancer's bearing, and even now she'd sometimes look down to see her feet had found fourth position of their own accord. Suddenly it seemed she couldn't do anything right. All year she'd played the confrontation game with the best of them, but suddenly she was the enemy too.

While Seanna lay low, Cindy and Mary spent their days at the Beehive and the copy shop, getting Riot Grrrl Press back up to speed. In early May, they went up to New York City to sell zines at a Bratmobile show. Seanna stayed home, relieved.

When the three members of Bratmobile converged in New York City to headline a show at the Thread Waxing Space, a hip SoHo art gallery, they hadn't been in the same town with one another, let alone played together, in months. They had toured the UK and the West Coast the previous summer, but since then, each of them had been concentrating on other things. Molly had been living in the Bay Area for over a year, making short films and playing drums with several projects: the Frumpies, Lois Maffeo, and a new band called the PeeChees. Allison had graduated from Evergreen that winter and moved to DC, trying to figure out whether she wanted to settle there. And Erin was finishing her senior year at the University of Maryland. Bratmobile had always been a relatively low-intensity band, something to do on school breaks. So when the Thread Waxing Space offered to fly Molly out to headline one show, with only a few hours' rehearsal time before the performance, it was kind of like, why not? "It seemed like a cool and rather glamorous thing to do," Molly said. "But I took the red-eye and had to practice and play on no sleep. Truly, it was so dumb."

Allison and Erin rode a Greyhound up from DC the day of the show. Cindy and Mary took the same bus, and Allison spent the ride listening to them; it sounded like they were talking shit about her. Those girls—and there were others, too; it wasn't just the few on the bus—they always seemed to be picking her apart. Pick, pick, pick, just looking for something to seize upon, some point of imperfection, some insufficiency of radicalism.

This criticism burned, because Allison always tried to do the right thing, even when it brought her into conflict with her bandmates. The media issue was the main point of contention: Allison wanted to boycott the press, but Molly and Erin didn't have a problem with giving interviews and doing photo shoots. Erin had always been fascinated by mass media, loved working for *Sassy* and was thrilled every time her zine, *Teenage Gang Debs*, was featured in a newspaper article or on a television talk show. (When the riot grrrls refused to go on *Sally Jessy Raphael*, Erin volunteered for duty, and spoke on the air about *Brady Bunch* trivia.) Molly, too, enjoyed the attention. "I was into people covering our band," she said. "I thought it was really validating, even though they got everything wrong and were really embarrassingly poorly written articles generally. It made my parents understand what I was doing."

That wasn't an issue for Allison, whose feminist-activist mom didn't care whether her daughter was in the *New York Times*. Allison was in it for the struggle. She took the mic only in order to pass it around, to open up the spotlight's tight circle. Back when the whole Riot Grrrl thing began, Bratmobile and Bikini Kill and Heavens to Betsy had been part of the same community as the girls who listened to them, but now they were getting written up in *Rolling Stone* and being flown across the country to play cool rock bonanzas in New York art galleries. The band was separating Allison from her community, and Molly and Erin, who should have been her allies, didn't seem to care. Molly—her best friend!—was so businesslike, setting timetables and schedules and goals for the band. Sometimes she acted more like their manager than their bandmate. She had pushed them to record *The Real Janelle* EP last summer when they had just finished three weeks of touring the UK with Heavenly and Huggy Bear, and they were worn out from the nightly playing and partying, Allison's voice a thin raspy joke on itself. It's audible on the record: Erin's distorted guitar chords trade the piercing clarity of her earlier lines for pure fuzz that nearly obscures pitch, and Molly drums relentlessly, racing a bit ahead of Allison's singing. The exhaustion in Allison's vocal cords is obvious as she sings:

If my guts spilled on the street, would you tell me that you cared?
And if my blood spilled on your sheets, would you really be there?

Allison's hoarseness is poignant, the sound of a girl who has been screaming too loud and for too long without time to take a break, rest up, heal. Well, she had gotten her break; they all had. Now they would see if it had done them any good.

Things started going wrong from the moment they arrived at the Thread Waxing Space. The amps and drums they were supposed to borrow for the show hadn't arrived yet, and by the time all the gear was finally in place, none other than Sonic Youth's Kim Gordon had come in to start hanging her artwork on the walls. The Bratmobile girls weren't really friends with Gordon; deeply in awe was more like it. Rusty from their months off, they were having a hard time practicing their songs with this legend in the room. Plus, Allison was so rattled by whatever she'd overheard on the bus that she could scarcely focus. At one point she just started crying.

Cindy and Mary came early to the show, along with Ananda La Vita, who was still living in New York. They started setting up the Riot Grrrl Press table at the back of the room, laying out stacks of zines and flyers. Then the doors opened; the room filled up; the opening bands (DQE, Scarce, and Blonde Redhead) played. Heat rose in thick clouds from the packed-in bodies. The queue for the one bathroom ran the whole length of the space. It was easy to believe that half the people in that room wouldn't get out alive if the building were to catch fire. There were no bouncers visible, nobody to hold the line if things got any more out of hand.

Finally Bratmobile took the stage, pushing through on determination and adrenaline. During the set, a man approached Cindy at the zine table at the back of the room. He leered at a naked photo of Mary and Erika that graced the cover of *Wrecking Ball* #2; he wrote "I want to suck your cock" on the mailing list. Cindy told him to get lost. He wandered off, but he came back a few minutes later and started climbing up on the zine table. Cindy knocked him to the ground and the two of them went at each other full force: "a cartoonish, fur-flying brawl," Ananda called it. When people came to pull them apart, Cindy was told she would have to leave.

A girl kicked out of a Bratmobile show? Outrageous. But there was still hope: Bratmobile was onstage. They could halt this injustice—and they had better do it. Cindy fought her way to the front and attracted Allison's attention. The singer wasn't too clear on what was going on, but she did know that she would never hear the end of it if she didn't let Cindy have her say. She gave Cindy the mic.

"I had been having personal problems with Allison," Cindy said later. "So I'm like, 'Stop the fuckin' show! Where's the girl power? This guy is attacking me, and you guys aren't doing anything.'"

Allison knew the playbook: The show should stop until the guy had been booted from the venue. Someone who worked at the gallery got onstage. "Okay, okay," he said, "show me the guy and I'll kick him out." But there was no way to find the offender among the sea of bodies, and the audience was getting impatient.

Molly and Erin were losing patience too. Eventually Allison took back the microphone, and the band played a few more songs—

> If I cry, will you hate me
> Because you hate to see me cry?
> If I die, will you love me?
> And will you know the reason why?

—but Allison kept handing the mic to Cindy in between songs so she could continue her tirade.

Joan Jett was at the show, and now she got up onstage. *What are you doing?* she asked Allison, exasperated. *Tell this girl to get off the stage so you can play your set, for chrissakes.*

Allison looked from Joan Jett to her pissed-off bandmates to the girls who would never be satisfied no matter what she did. The audience was howling. The girls were scowling. Her bandmates were waiting.

Allison started to cry.

Molly, at the end of her last nerve, threw down her drumsticks and stood up. "That's it!" she shouted. "I quit!" She shouldered her way out of the room and stomped down to the street. Erin got on the mic and said to Allison, "I'm not gonna play with you anymore."

Someone went outside and convinced Molly to come back. Jett stayed onstage, encouraging everybody to go on playing. She rubbed Erin's shoulders, saying, "Keep going, Erin! You can do it!" Bratmobile stumbled through the remainder of the show, with Allison in tears the whole time. But the band was over.

"I remember we packed up and went our separate ways," Erin

said. "We weren't even staying at the same place. It was very sad. But who gets to go out like that, with Joan Jett giving them a back-rub onstage?"

The following week, Erika and Akiko arrived in DC from Olympia, ready to confront the Beehive. To Erika in particular, the space had become a symbol of all that was wrong with white punk rock revolutionaries who talked about changing the world but remained locked in their insular scene.

Soon after hitting town, Erika called the Beehive and said, "You better put your butt pads on, 'cause I'm gonna kick your asses." She and Akiko, along with Mary and Cindy, went over to the collective, and while Erika was downstairs talking to somebody, the others went upstairs to the Beehive's living quarters and expressed their ire in more physical ways: They tore down a "Kill whitey" poster that Mary had put on a bedroom door months earlier. They ripped a band poster off the wall because one of the band's members had a tattoo that Cindy considered racist. They ripped down a "Fuck gentrification" flyer and annotated its margins: "How fucking condescending/hypocritical can you be? A BLACK community does NOT need a 'public service announcement' brought to them by a bunch of white 'radicals.' . . . SHUT THE FUCK UP!" And Akiko—maybe acting out a subconscious frustration at the white riot grrrls she knew who claimed to care about *all* girls but were insensitive to girls of color, though she says she just did it out of boredom—put the lit end of her cigarette through a flyer for Riot Grrrl DC.

The DC Riot Grrrl chapter had about a dozen members at that point, mostly high school girls who were oblivious to all these conflicts. They came together religiously, Sunday after Sunday, to do what riot grrrls had always done: talk and feel better and get politicized and grow up. Some of them had heard of two legendary figures, Mary and Erika, who made incredible zines and ran Riot Grrrl

Press. Many had heard that it was important to talk about class and race in addition to gender—this had filtered down to them, largely through Mary's and Erika's writings—and they addressed this in different ways. Some checked out bell hooks's books from the public library; some explored whether there were any all-female bands playing go-go, a style of dance music rooted in DC's black community; some researched the condition of women in other countries.

Riot Grrrl as a whole was practically self-perpetuating by now. The rancor and cruelty of a small group of people was no match for the ongoing power of the movement's ideas; it could hardly dilute the collected force and urgency of girls desperate to figure out how to become the human beings they needed to be. Within the Beehive teapot, though, this was a raging tornado. It was fiendishly complicated to challenge two radical women of color and two charismatic leaders who positioned themselves as the voice of female working-class survivors of abuse. Plus, the collective's members agreed that they weren't doing enough to combat gentrification or to work with the neighborhood's longtime residents. It wasn't the substance of the critique that they objected to—it was the tactics.

Mary and Erika had helped set a tone in DC's radical punk community that left many people feeling haunted and edgy, constantly on their guard against saying or doing the wrong thing. "This was a time when you could just turn your head the wrong way and you were a racist or a classist or a sexist or a rapist," one of the collective's founders said. "It stunted our ability to be critical about ideas, for fear of being personally ostracized . . . but we were all totally enthralled and in the middle of it."

But the girls had gone too far this time. At a long, tense collective meeting, Brad Sigal proposed that the Beehive ban Mary, Erika, Cindy, and Akiko from the building. The motion passed, essentially exiling Riot Grrrl Press from the scene that had spawned it.

———

This is what politics had become for them—not for everyone, of course, but for Mary and Erika and their friends and pen pals, and for the people who read their zines and were seduced by the strident, powerful tone that was found there. The pair's status as paradigmatic riot grrrls was only increasing, especially as their extremist rhetoric polarized longtime allies and drove many away. Politics was personal; their revolution had become about a purification of one's individual life, habits, language, relationships. This is the revolutionary program of a moment that has lost the ability to envision large-scale change, or that sees institutions as so flawed at their core that they can never be vehicles of transformation. And the Beehive incident shows how such a program ultimately destroys far more than it builds.

By July 1994, when Omaha's Ann Carroll and Andee Davis hosted the second national Riot Grrrl convention, dozens of articles in newspapers and magazines had introduced Riot Grrrl to the world, and many original adherents had distanced themselves from the movement. Those who maintained their affiliation were less and less tied to organized chapters. Many of these girls had stripped their souls raw to one another at the early meetings. They had formed close relationships, and if they still talked about Riot Grrrl as being important to them, they were usually saying that they couldn't imagine who they would've become without these friendships, how they would've pulled through if it hadn't been for these other girls. They didn't really need to meet anybody new.

Newcomers had no trouble connecting to one another, thanks especially to *Action Girl Newsletter* and Riot Grrrl Press. Riot Grrrl was circling back around to be what it had been at the very beginning: a nationwide network of friends and friends of friends who wrote each other passionate letters and occasionally traveled the country to meet up in person. The difference this time was that whereas the initial group had connected through music, with the gospel spread by touring bands, riot grrrls in 1994 were reaching one another through zines.

For all Bikini Kill's repeated urgings to other girls to pick up an instrument and start a band, playing music remained stubbornly expensive and time-consuming. The Simple Machines label had tried to demystify the technologies of it by publishing the Mechanics Guide, but nobody ever needed to write an introductory guide to making a zine. Everybody knew how to put words on paper, how to make copies and staple them, how to stamp them and drop them in a mailbox. And zines were a far cheaper mode of expression. To have a band, one needed instruments, amps, a practice space, maybe a PA. Eventually, a band would have to pay for recording time, a vehicle to tour in and gas to feed it, the twenty-minute blank cassettes for duplicating a demo tape. In contrast, a thirty-two-page zine (eight sheets of paper, double-sided, folded in half) could be copied for forty-eight cents at Kinko's, and very few people paid even that much. They ran off their zines at parents' offices or their own jobs after hours, or at copy shops where friends who worked behind the counter could print pals' zines on the sly. If all else failed, sometimes they learned ways to cheat the copy machines.

They found ways around the cost of postage, too. In 1994, stamp prices went up 10.3 percent, the first increase since before Riot Grrrl began; an average-size zine now cost fifty-five cents to mail, which meant over fifty dollars for a modest print run of one hundred. But if a sender coated the picture side of a postage stamp with a thin layer from her glue stick, the recipient could later remove the cancellation mark by soaking the stamp in water for a few minutes. After word of the stamp-gluing trick got around, a young publishing guerrilla could distribute her zine almost for free using only recycled stamps floated off pen pals' letters and zines; many zinesters received mail whose two stamps fairly shimmered with a glitter glue stick's sparkly snail-trail. As valiantly as Riot Grrrl had tried to lower punk music's barriers to entry, zine writing had music beat without even trying.

So when Ann and Andee realized that none of the riot grrrls' original favorite bands would be able to play at the Omaha convention, it wasn't a big deal. Ann and Andee had never personally known the first-generation bands in the first place, never felt connected to their members. The music was an inspiration, nothing more. For the convention's opening-night show, they booked a mix of Midwestern girl-inclusive bands and convention participants who had projects to showcase. Nomy Lamm from Olympia would perform some songs she'd been writing. Mary and Erika's new band, Diamonds into Coal, would play, as would a band of high-school girls from Lincoln called XXY, and Sweet Tarts, Ann and Andee's band with their friends Christopher and Brandy.

A month or so before the convention, Andee got a call from a girl asking if her band, Pressure Drop, could join the bill. The band was all boys except for her, the girl admitted, but they *really* wanted to play. Andee had a weird feeling about this. She wasn't in a mood to argue, so she just told the girl, "I'm pretty sure the bill is already full, but if anything changes I'll call you back."

Booking bands was only one part of the convention planning. Ann and Andee loved food and loved feeding people, so they announced that all lunches and dinners would be included in the twenty-five-dollar convention admission cost. They ordered cases of cheap food staples from their cooperative buying club, and they cooked meals to feed everyone for the weekend. They bought cans of fruit spritzer and vegan ice cream sandwiches to sell for 50 cents apiece, just to make back some of the cost of these more expensive extras.

They scheduled nearly every block of time, determined not to replicate the free-form ennui of the failed Piqua fest. Friday night was the time for girls to arrive at the American Legion Hall, watch videos (there was a music video by Cuntz with Attitude, and something about the Guerrilla Girls), and eat dinner. After dinner, the bands would play, and then everyone would help clean up the space before going to Andee's mom's house—a huge old family inheritance where it just might be possible to find space for seventy-five sleeping bags. There they all would sit awake together into the night, trading stories and forging friendships.

By Friday evening, July 8, when the second Riot Grrrl convention got underway, nearly a hundred girls had hit town. Many of them had been present at the first convention in DC, too—Mary and Erika, who had just moved to Chicago after being booted from the Beehive; Ananda La Vita, still living in New York; *Girl Fiend's* Christina Woolner, on summer break from Hampshire College. Other convention-goers had become involved in the movement a bit later—Nomy, for instance, whose *I'm So Fucking Beautiful* zine had become required reading among girl zinesters; and Seanna Tully, who had come out for the weekend even though Mary and Erika were no longer speaking to her, and even though the new issue of Ananda's zine, which was being handed out at the convention, included a vicious letter by Mary attacking Seanna's upper-middle-class white-privileged bullshit.

Ann and Andee had always seen themselves as pretty cool, especially relative to the rest of Omaha. But most of these girls were from the coasts. Their clothes were crazier, their hair was dyed flashier colors and arranged in more daring styles, and their whole attitude just screamed, Are you radical enough to be talking to me? They were also far more interested in catching up with their old friends than in paying any attention to their hapless hostesses. Everyone sat in clumps on the floor of the American Legion Hall with their plates of pasta and hummus. Ann and Andee felt left out, no hipper than the Piqua girls in the eyes of these coastal cliques.

"I think I probably felt like I was kind of cool there," Christina admitted. "My zine had been around a few years, I had been putting on shows like the Frumpies and Huggy Bear, I had been at the first conference and was from the Northeast—and have always been a coast-ist bitch even though I try not to be. I imagine that translated into some sort of cultural capital. But I also felt a little weird. I knew other people there, but no one too well, and it wasn't my turf, so for a socially awkward twenty-year-old virgin, it was kind of a stressful situation."

It was stressful for Ann and Andee, too. The conventioneers, it seemed, only came up to talk to them when they needed something. When Ann tried to bring everyone together to make a welcoming announcement, nobody stopped talking long enough to listen to her. Some girls were raiding the hall's kitchen and taking the expensive treats, and on hearing that the goodies were supposed to go for fifty cents, the girls got mad: "You said twenty-five dollars covered everything."

Nobody paid. All the treats were eaten.

After dinner, while the bands were playing, Andee heard somebody say, "I didn't know there were going to be *boys* in the bands." There was a band from Iowa that had some boys in it, and of course their dear, beloved Christopher was in Sweet Tarts with them. How dare anybody question his right to be there! Her patience was fraying.

Midway through the show, about a dozen people—all boys, except for one six-foot-tall Amazon of a woman—showed up at the hall and started dragging in amps, drums, horns. In just a few minutes they had deposited a pile of gear on the floor.

"Who the hell are you?" Ann asked. But she already knew.

"We're Pressure Drop," a boy answered. "You said we could play."

"I absolutely did not tell you any such thing," Ann said.

"No, just let us play. We'll set up and play and break down in ten minutes, we promise."

Ann was terrified and near tears. All the stress of planning the convention, and the disappointment of being snubbed by the very people she was doing all this work for, had worn her down, and now *this*.

But if any situation could redeem Riot Grrrl for her, here it was. She was at a rock show being intimidated—implicitly threatened, she felt—by a bunch of pushy, entitled boy musicians. This was exactly the sort of situation Riot Grrrl had been created to address, right? Stoking her hope, Ann approached the nearest bunch of girls and asked them for help making the boys leave. But they were too absorbed in their own conversations to help.

Pressure Drop began handing out a flyer with pictures of men and women with mutilated genitals and some slogan like "Without genitals we're all the same." This got through to the girls. When Mary did her spoken-word performance, she talked about how offensive the flyer was and how there was in fact a very distinct difference between men and women, and it was ridiculous to reduce it to genitals. "That doesn't make us equal; that just makes us bloody," she said. But who finally helped Ann expel the interlopers? The boys in the band from Iowa.

The show ended at 11 P.M. and the girls went to Andee's mom's house—all the girls except Ann and Andee, who stayed at the American Legion Hall until 3 A.M., cleaning so they could get their deposit back. When they arrived at the house, they saw all the windows dark; easing open the front door, they heard the watery hush of sleep-breath tiding through all the rooms. Ann and Andee tiptoed through the foyer. Almost every inch of floor space was covered with sleeping girls: the living room, the dining room, the basement, even the kitchen. Ann and Andee hadn't thought to rope themselves off a space, because they'd expected everyone to get back to the house at the same time. They found a vacant patch of floor in the laundry room, wearily shook out their sleeping bags, and dropped into sleep. Maybe the next day would be better.

The next morning, the out-of-town girls were messy and unhelpful, leaving their belongings strewn all around Andee's house. Andee was over it—the whole thing. "We had manners and politeness, and it seemed like no one there did," she said. "They thought they could just throw all that out because they were punk rockers or they were riot grrrls. But they were just a bunch of spoiled brats."

The schedule marched on. Saturday morning a decent-sized slice of the crew got together to escort at local abortion clinics, which meant walking with women who were headed for the clinics so they wouldn't have to face anti-abortion protesters' shouts alone. The girls painted slogans on posters before splitting up to go to two different clinics. Ann and Andee's friend Monica, now four months pregnant and separated from the boyfriend who had thrown a jar at her head, hitched up her shirt and wrote MOTHER FOR CHOICE on her bulging belly.

But Andee had to skip the escorting in order to set up for the afternoon workshops. And Ann couldn't really enjoy herself at the clinic, because she was thinking about all the girls who were ditching the escorting to go out for breakfast together, and the girls who were just sleeping through it. "I didn't understand why people were there if it wasn't to do these things together," Ann said.

But whose motivations for political action are ever pure? People join political cultures or subcultures for a combination of reasons: to feel righteous, to feel less helpless, to distance ourselves from a dominant culture that repels us, to feel like we have a purpose, to make friends, to find love or sex, to relive the way you felt once when a certain song swept through you at a rally or coffeehouse or club or basement and aligned all the molecules in your body.

The best political leaders know how to build something out of whatever gets people in the door, are able to take the varied gifts people carry and the drives that propel them and to envision a focused, directed whole. But leaders with that ability are exceedingly rare. Riot Grrrl had propagandists but no master strategists; it had prophets but no organizers. If an organizer had emerged, the movement probably would have torn her down, because between its radical-feminist inspiration and its anarchist-punk provenance, Riot Grrrl had never tolerated anything that smelled remotely like a hierarchy. Girls had turned against Allison Wolfe, hounding her to tears at a show; they had turned against Kathleen, saying she had "microphone privilege" and "pretty privilege." The closest thing Riot Grrrl had to leaders, as of 1994, was Mary and Erika.

Mary and Erika had actually been nicer to their Omaha hostesses than almost anyone else. Erika had happened to walk into the bathroom on Friday night while Ann was in there crying with frustration over the Pressure Drop confrontation, and she had been sympathetic and comforting. And Mary had apologized for calling Ann and Andee "rich girls" a few months earlier, once they explained they were working-class too. She'd been a real sweetheart after that. Mary and Erika were scheduled to lead a workshop on class issues after lunch on Saturday, and Ann and Andee were happy when that time finally came. Surely Mary and Erika would put all the spoiled brats in their place.

"I had never talked to other people who were raised on welfare, and it's so exciting," Ann said. "But it's almost immediately cut off by people raising their hands and talking about how they shouldn't feel bad if their dad wants to buy them a car."

"We get twenty seconds into the workshop," Andee said, "and this stupid girl from Kansas City started whining about how she doesn't want to be part of a workshop if all we're going to do is bash kids for coming from rich homes. Everybody starts coddling her because she's almost in tears. We thought, Mary and Erika are going to show them, but they jump in on the coddling. It was the weakest moment we'd ever seen."

Other participants remembered the class workshop as important and eye-opening, despite the disruptions. But for Ann and Andee, it was just one more thing in a string of disappointments that wasn't finished yet.

The plan for the evening was for everyone to sleep out at a nearby campground. But there was a parking fee, five or ten dollars per car, and a few girls complained about the car fee: the same ones who had just spent an hour talking about how they didn't want to feel guilty for having money. *These girls* were saying that Ann and Andee should cover the fee since all costs were supposed to be included in the twenty-five dollars they had already paid.

"Finally we're like, Fuck it! Just go home!" Andee said. "Pay for the car or go home. Everyone can leave at this point, we don't care."

Nobody went home, much to Andee's disappointment, and the thoughtlessness continued. "We set up a tent, people moved in. We set up another tent, people moved in. Eventually there were no tents for us. Maybe we threw a fit and someone let us in a tent, maybe we slept in my car, I don't remember. By that point we felt like it was a lost cause."

"I hated everyone," Ann said.

That was the end of the convention. The next day, everybody packed up and a bunch of cars, including Ann and Andee's, drove to Olympia for Yoyo a Gogo, a five-day music festival Pat Maley had organized. He was trying to rekindle the spirit of 1991's IPU, to bring back that magical era before all the hype and the hoopla, secessions and suicides, back when things had just been fun. Yoyo a Gogo *was* fun—but it wasn't the same as it had been back then.

When Ann got back to Nebraska the next week, she had over a hundred letters waiting for her from girls who had wanted to come to the convention but hadn't been able to make it. Ann had intended to make a zine about the weekend to send to everyone, the participants and the people who couldn't come. It would have photos, articles, and a blow-by-blow report on the convention's activities.

Not now, though. "I thought, well, if I don't have anything nice to say about this, then I don't want to say anything to them," she said. "I don't want them to be disillusioned like I am." She held on to the pile of letters for a while, thinking that the passage of time might mellow her perceptions or give her a new way to think about the fiasco that was the Omaha Riot Grrrl Convention. But months came and went, and her feelings didn't change. She and Andee left Omaha a few months after the convention, moved to Lincoln, got jobs, and just hung out.

"We were tired," Andee said. "We were tired of trying to constantly organize things and make these differences and gather people together and create these communities that were fairly resistant to it. So what's the next best thing? Do the fun parts of things. Be friends with the bands. Drink and go to shows and still have the same style and aesthetic appreciation, but just do the fun parts and not the hard parts."

Nobody in Lincoln tried to be a prophet and nobody raised any high hopes they couldn't deliver on. Ann threw away all the letters from the girls who had wanted to hear about the convention. She had nothing to say to them any more.

EPILOGUE: THE FEMINIST FUTURE

By the mid-'90s, it was common knowledge among punks and indie rockers that Riot Grrrl had been dead for at least two years, if not longer. The media attention had killed it, people said. Or grunge had killed it, or Courtney Love had killed it, or maybe it had never existed in the first place except as a mirage dreamed up by the press.

None of this was true, of course. Yes, most chapters had stopped holding regular meetings, though the New York and DC groups managed to hold on until 1996. Yes, out of the three bands that had sparked the whole thing, Bratmobile and Heavens to Betsy had broken up, and Bikini Kill was on unofficial hiatus, having just released its final album, *Reject All American*, and completed what would be its last US tour. (The band would play its final show in Tokyo in April 1997.)

Yet signs of life abounded. Some girls who'd been involved since the early days had started up a Riot Grrrl e-mail list—the first sign within the movement of what would soon be a massive shift in communication from pen and typewriter to the Internet. The list members discussed politics and strategy, race and class, and sometimes lit into various girls who weren't owning up to their privilege. There was no way to find the list unless you already knew somebody on it, but the Internet's democratic potential was more visible in the Riot Grrrl message board of America Online, where young women promoted their bands and zines, musicians sent out requests for shows, and everybody—everybody on the privileged side of the digital divide, that is—traded information about what they were reading and listening to.

Fed in part by these online forums, conventions briefly multiplied. In 1995 a Riot Grrrl convention took place in Los Angeles, and a similar event, Midwest Girlfest, happened that same summer in Chicago. The following year saw an explosion of gatherings, in Santa Barbara, Seattle, Portland, Philadelphia, and New York. They included political workshops, with discussions of race and class privilege featuring prominently. These were the last Riot Grrrl conventions on record, but the model continued to live on in gatherings like the Ladyfest art festivals that have happened in cities worldwide since 2000, the queer-art Homo A Gogo festivals that pop up every few years on the West Coast, and the Southern Girls Conventions that took place annually from 1999 to 2008 (tagline for the inaugural event: "Opening up a can of whup-ass on the patriarchy").

If Riot Grrrl meetings had largely petered out by 1996, it wasn't for lack of political evils to oppose. The national political landscape then was in fact far more troublesome for feminists than it had been four years earlier, when a half million people had rallied on the

National Mall to support abortion rights, looking forward to a new Democrat in the White House and a Year of the Woman in Congress. In 1994, two years into Bill Clinton's presidency, the Christian Coalition helped "family values" Republicans win commanding majorities on Capitol Hill, and Newt Gingrich's ultraconservative Contract with America eclipsed national health care as the defining agenda. In addition, voters in Colorado and Cincinnati had passed measures explicitly legalizing discrimination against gays, lesbians, and bisexuals; and Rush Limbaugh, eternally inveighing against "feminazis," was the most popular political commentator in the country. Self-examination and even self-expression weren't enough to counter all this; they could only be a starting point.

Statements of female anger weren't looking quite as revolutionary anymore either, now that major record labels were feeding it to the masses in the "angry women in pop" personas of such sirens as Fiona Apple, Meredith Brooks, and Alanis Morissette. Even "girl power," a phrase that had probably debuted on the cover of the second *Bikini Kill* zine, transmogrified into a cheerleader's refrain when the Spice Girls' first record came out in late 1996—these girls were so empowered, apparently, they didn't even need to have real names or play instruments. Some wondered, Was *this* the twenty-first-century rebirth of feminism the riot grrrls had wrought? But it wasn't.

Top-Forty artists aren't cultural movements; they're ultra-homogenized and über-marketed holographic projections, aspects of culture that get blown up to Jumbotron size and burrow a pic line to the id. Mass culture *always* contains cleaned-up, camera-ready variations on the underground, incorporating just enough of what's "edgy" to maintain its own relevance. Sometimes—if we're lucky—these transformations result in mass culture that's more interesting than usual, that entertains in a way that feels surprising, and that perhaps even helps spread progressive values. But if a political idea is showing up in mass culture, that's because it's happening some-where else in a more concentrated, grassroots way. Today, you can find twenty-first-century feminism online, of course, on blogs and social networking sites where teens speak their minds and connect with friends, and on the women's-issues sites of the major news-and-opinion Web magazines, where feminists of various stripes continue the all-important activities of media and political critique. You can find it at the many girls' rock camps, where kids form bands on a Monday and perform their songs to a screaming crowd on a Saturday, and at the affiliated "ladies' rock camps" that give women a chance to learn the instruments they always wanted to play. You can find it in the powerful female and queer musicians who popu-late the newly expanded middle ground between subculture and mass culture—musicians like Beth Ditto, the lesbian feminist singer of Gossip, who designed a line of clothes for TopShop's plus-size store but will still halt a concert to scold a guy who's mistreating girls in the front row. Most important, twenty-first-century femi-nism is alive in everyone who made it through the horror show of adolescence with the help of Riot Grrrl's ideas about empowerment and DIY, however they came to us. It's in what we've made of our lives, whether we're decades away from our teenage years or still living through them.

"Riot Grrrl brought out the things I liked about myself; it made me feel stronger," Andee Davis of Omaha said. "Suddenly it made it seem cool to be who we were, which was empowering. It made me feel like I could be forming my own ideas. Feeling that you had a community, and that there were other people out there like you, was a big deal."

"It's a process," Ann Carroll said. "It was good that I went through it. But you can't stop there."

People grew out of Riot Grrrl, but that doesn't diminish the movement's value, any more than trigonometry diminishes the value of algebra. Adolescence will always be an angry time. And as long as the well-documented contradictions inherent in What a Woman (or Man) Must Be still exist, they're going to feed into young women's (and young men's) feelings of conflict and frustration. Riot Grrrl, by encouraging girls to turn their anger outward, taught a crucial lesson: Always ask, Is there something wrong not with me but with the world at large? It also forced us to confront a second question: Once we've found our rage, where do we go from there?

I reconnected with my own rage while writing this book. Every day brought new offenses: Women were outnumbered six to one in most magazines' lists of the past decade's best musicians. *Publishers Weekly* came out with a list of the ten best books of 2009, without so much as a single title by a female author. Michelle Obama went on *The View* and nattered about panty hose so she would be less threatening to voters. (And, after the election, our new president scornfully informed Barbara Walters that he would not be getting "a girly dog.") A pop star beat up his girlfriend and his career barely missed a step. It sickened me how often I read about men murdering their girlfriends, shooting their ex-wives, molesting their daughters and stepdaughters and nieces. Weren't we supposed to have gotten over this? I fumed. Why was this still happening? I don't have an answer; I only know that I can't ignore it.

I've raged, too, against the unfortunate parts of the Riot Grrrl story—the parts I didn't expect to find, the parts I would have preferred never to write. Having set out to pay homage to the movement that saved my sanity in high school, I feared betraying it in some way. I worried: Was I overemphasizing the conflicts? Was I succumbing to the boring old media game of Find the Catfight? But I don't think so. In the end, I had to tell the truth as I saw it.

I hope with all my heart that readers will tell their own stories. Tell what I left out. Do it in paint, in plaster, with drums and harp, with words and dance. Start your own scene with your friends, rooted in the particulars of your own lives and what gets you riled up. Craft a mythology around it. Be grandiose; be overblown; do it all the way and then keep going. Maybe right now you're in the van on your first cross-country tour, or you're in a bookstore while you're waiting to perform on a spoken-word night, or you're sitting up late in a silent house, reading and rocking until your baby falls back asleep. Or maybe you're escaping lunch again by hiding in your school library, wedged between the books on feminism and the emergency exit, trying to get through the day, desperate for something that will save you, or help you save yourself. Whatever the case, I know you can do it. This very moment contains all you need. Everything you're hearing right now, where you are—the van backfiring, the bookstore crowd murmuring, the baby breathing slowly, the bell ringing for fifth period—this is the sound of a revolution.

POSTSCRIPT

Becca Albee is an artist and professor living in New York.

Mark Andersen is coauthor of *Dance of Days: Two Decades of Punk in the Nation's Capital* and author of *All the Power: Revolution Without Illusion*. He does outreach and advocacy with inner-city seniors through We Are Family, and he lives in Washington, DC, with his beloved Tulin Ozdeger, their son Soren, and their two cats.

Elizabeth Anthony is your typical radical librarian who plays in a few bands and has cat-eye glasses.

After seventeen years on KAOS, **Diana Arens** ended her radio show, *Free Things Are Cool*, in 2008. She now sometimes DJs around Olympia as DJ Disco Nap, does occasional audio engineering, and recently worked on music for a documentary about the band KARP.

Joanna Burgess is a digital collections librarian at a small liberal arts college in Portland, Oregon, where she lives at the base of an extinct volcano with a marmalade cat named Wilbur.

Ann Carroll is a pastry chef and an undergrad, studying classic through Renaissance literature and politics.

Akiko Carver lives in Seattle, goes to school for neuroscience, and works at a guitar store.

Susan (Sin) Davies has continued her activism around diverse issues of social justice in Minneapolis, Barcelona, and currently Amsterdam. She has a master's degree in gender studies and presently works for an organization that promotes sexual and reproductive health education and abortion rights internationally.

Andrea (Andee) Davis is raising her twelve-year-old daughter and working on becoming a goat farmer and cheesemaker.

Mary Margaret Fondriest composes, performs, teaches composition, and studies systems with the School for Designing a Society in Urbana, Illinois. She works on projects that attempt to bring about social change, including teaching nutritional self-defense to low-income elementary school students in Tacoma, Washington, and providing care and counsel to elder and dying humans.

Cindy Hales is an instructor at Seattle Gracie Barra, teaching kids and adults Brazilian Jiu-Jitsu. She is also a professional Mixed Martial Arts fighter and Brazilian Jiu-Jitsu competitor.

Kathleen Hanna is a New York–based artist/musician best known as a member of the bands Bikini Kill, Le Tigre, and Julie Ruin. She started an archival blog for Bikini Kill at http://bikinikillarchive.wordpress.com.

Jessica Hopper is a music and cultural critic based in Chicago. Her first book, a how-to book titled *A Girl's Guide to Rocking*, was published in 2009. She put out *Hit It or Quit It* #19, the Men in Rock issue, in 2005.

Nomy Lamm is a musician and writer living in San Francisco. She plays with nomy lamm & the Whole Wide World, writes an advice column for *Make/Shift* magazine, performs with Sins Invalid, and is working on her first novel, *The Best Part Comes After the End*.

Ananda La Vita is a multi-issue activist who sees abuse as a root problem. She currently lives and works in Seattle as a print graphic designer.

Ian MacKaye continues his work with Dischord Records and plays music with Amy Farina in the Evens.

Molly Neuman runs a personal chef and catering business in New York City, Simple Social Kitchen, and is training to be a natural health counselor. She's still obsessed with music and girls and punks and opportunity and her friends.

Billie Rain (Erika Reinstein) is a disabled writer, activist, and filmmaker. Years of chronic illness and a rare tumor condition have given hir an amazing sense of groundedness, connection, and self-advocacy that fuel hir passion to bring truth, in all its pain and glory, to audiences everywhere.

Tracy Sawyer lives in Oakland, California, with her family.

Angela Seguel lives in Bellingham, Washington, with her husband Alex, her son Maximilian, and their two cats. She currently works as a technical writer and spends most of her free time enjoying family and friends.

After working as promotion director of Lookout! Records in Berkeley, California, for five years, **Erin Smith** returned to DC, where she works for a nonprofit music performance rights organization. She is an active supporter of Girls Rock! DC, a summer camp for girls ages eight to eighteen.

Jen Smith is an artist living in Los Angeles, where she is making objects and pickling and fermenting vegetables like crazy.

May Summer Farnsworth is an assistant professor of Spanish and Latin American literature at Hobart and William Smith Colleges. Her research interests include feminist performance and women writers in Argentina and Mexico.

Sash Sunday lives near Olympia, where she works for UPS, grows vegetables, and runs a small artisanal fermented-food business called OlyKraut.

Kristin Thomson is education and research director of the nonprofit Future of Music Coalition, which advocates for musicians on the issues at the intersection of music, law, technology, and policy. She lives near Philadelphia with her husband, Bryan Dilworth, a concert promoter, and their son; she also plays guitar in the lady-powered band Ken.

Corin Tucker lives in Portland with her husband and their two children. Her most recent band, Sleater-Kinney, is on indefinite hiatus; her debut solo album comes out in 2010 from Kill Rock Stars.

Seanna Tully spends a lot of time thinking about medicinal herbs and how to better help people with them. She now hires and manages punks at WholeHealth Chicago Natural Apothecary. She also fervently practices zazen at the Chicago Zen Center.

Tobi Vail lives in Olympia, where she continues to write and play music. Her fanzine is now online at jigsawunderground.blogspot.com.

Claudia von Vacano is studying educational policy at the University of California, Berkeley, and is writing a book on the knowledge teachers need to have in order to serve Latinos. She owns and operates a women's commune in Oakland, California.

Allison Wolfe plays in a three-girl band called Partyline and teaches ESL. She is beginning work on a Riot Grrrl oral history project.

Cookie (Christina) Woolner's proudest accomplishments since the end of the 1990s include playing drums in the band Subtonix and performing in the burlesque troupes the Original Fat-Bottom Revue/Big Burlesque and the Chainsaw Chubbettes. She is currently a PhD candidate in the History/Women's Studies joint program at the University of Michigan.

Molly Zuckerman-Hartung is a painter who lives and works in Chicago. She co-runs the gallery Julius Caesar, makes paintings and writings, and teaches part time at The School of the Art Institute of Chicago and Northwestern University.

ACKNOWLEDGMENTS

This book is in large part about the importance of creative communities. It makes sense, then, that it has come about thanks to the support and encouragement of many, many people.

I'm so fortunate to work with the visionary, effervescent Charlotte Sheedy and the all-knowing Meredith Kaffel. And it's been a profound pleasure working with Allison Lorentzen at Harper Perennial, as well as the rest of the Perennial team: Amy Baker, Erica Barmash, Michael Barrs, Trina Hunn, Aline C. Pace, Vanessa Hope Schneider, Chérie Turner, and Amy Vreeland.

My two residencies at the MacDowell Colony changed my life and my work fundamentally and irrevocably. To the colony and everyone who works there, I owe more than I can possibly express. Others who helped me leave Brooklyn for months at a time include Victoria Kereszi and Andrew Lynn, who gave me an upstate haven; Julianna Bright, Seth Lorinczi, and Sarah Shapiro, who did the same in Portland, Oregon; and the Virginia Center for the Creative Arts. My roommates in Brooklyn were unfathomably understanding about the clutter of papers and notebooks that accrued when I was in town.

Funds from the David Berg Foundation, the Susan Hertog Fellowship, the Oberlin Alumni Fellowship, and a Research Support Grant from the Arthur and Elizabeth Schlesinger Library on the History of Women in America, part of the Radcliffe Institute for Advanced Study in Cambridge, Massachusetts, provided crucial support. Many thanks to Nancy Cott and everyone on staff at the Schlesinger, as well as to those who helped me locate materials at the Experience Music Project in Seattle, the Fales Library & Special Collections at New York University, the National Organization for Women in Washington, DC, the New York Public Library, the Smithsonian Institution Archives of American Art in Washington, DC, the Evergreen State College Archives in Olympia, the Timberland Regional Library in Olympia, and the Washington State Library in Olympia. My teachers, mentors, and classmates in the nonfiction MFA writing program at Columbia University's School of the Arts added their expertise and care to this project at a pivotal early moment. I'm particularly grateful to Patty O'Toole and Richard Locke for their wise guidance.

I've been blessed with a number of dedicated and thoughtful readers. Sara Jaffe, Maureen McLane, and Elizabeth Schambelan read the entire manuscript and made it much, much better. So did Stephen Burt, who in addition to being a brilliant and tireless reader has been an extremely dear friend and indispensable cheerleader for over a decade. Adam Cohen, Stacey Cook, Lauren Cornell, Meehan Crist, Dan Fishback, Tupelo Hassman, Erica Kaufman, Nicole Lanctot, Penny Lane, Emily Nepon, and Miranda Weiss all gave valuable input along the way. My uncle Lawrence Harmon was the first to really throw down the gauntlet. Brooke Berman, Aubree Bernier-Clarke, Claudia Gonson, Vivian Gornick, Greil Marcus, Hugh McElroy, Ida Pearle, and Matthew Stadler furnished vital connections. Mark Andersen, Amy Oden, Corin Tucker, and Allison Wolfe hooked me up with video footage. Scores of people allowed me to interview them and photocopy their collections, gave me places to stay, and got me in touch with other people to talk to. Jess Arndt, Carolyn Berk, Adam Frelin, Will Hermes, Khaela Maricich, Brian Selznick, David Serlin, Lauryn Siegel, Susannah Sirkin, Cat Tyc, Mike Wolf, and Douglas Wolk held my hand, pushed me forward, and talked me through tough spots. Anita, Rich, Jeremy, and Mia Marcus loved me unconditionally and didn't ask too often when I would be done already; my young nephew, Nathan, gave me the pleasure of having a family member who didn't ask at all. The denizens of the girls' rock camps in Portland and New York inspired and challenged me. Message to all rock campers: It's your turn now.

There would be no Riot Grrrl history if not for the courageous, audacious, creative people who lived it. Their willingness to share their personal recollections has humbled and awed me countless times over the past five years, and I dearly hope that they feel their trust and candor were not misplaced. One of this book's themes is the impossibility of adequately representing anyone else's life; thus at times during this process I feared I had undertaken a fool's errand. A thousand different books on Riot Grrrl could be written. This is my humble contribution. To all the people whose names appear in these pages, I offer my boundless gratitude. This book is for you.

BIBLIOGRAPHY

DOCUMENTS AND MANUSCRIPTS

Alix Dobkin papers, Arthur and Elizabeth Schlesinger Library on the History of Women in America, Radcliffe Institute for Advanced Study, Cambridge, Massachusetts.

Experience Music Project permanent collection, Seattle, Washington.

Experience Music Project Riot Grrrl Retrospective transcripts and video, 1999.

Moser, Abby. "Riot Grrrl New York City" (rough cut). VHS. 1998.

National Organization for Women. *We Won't Go Back!* VHS. 1992.

National Organization for Women papers, Arthur and Elizabeth Schlesinger Library on the History of Women in America, Radcliffe Institute for Advanced Study, Cambridge, Massachusetts.

Riot Grrrl Radio. Radio show originally broadcast on KAOS-FM. Compact disc. n.d.

Sarah Jacobson Papers, Fales Library & Special Collections, New York University, New York.

Thane, Lucy. *It Changed My Life: Bikini Kill in the U.K.* Quicktime file. 1993.

Thread Waxing Space records, Smithsonian Institution Archives of American Art, Washington, DC.

The Evergreen State College Archives, Olympia, Washington.

Tucker, Corin. Interview with Bikini Kill (unreleased). MiniDV. 1991.

Weinstein, David. *Wake Up! A Profile of Positive Force*. VHS. 1991.

INTERVIEWS AND CORRESPONDENCE

Throughout the book, any quotes not specifically cited as coming from other sources are from interviews conducted by the author between 2005 and 2010.

Abram, Becca Albee, Mark Andersen, Elizabeth Anthony, Diana Arens, Miriam Basilio, Danielle Bastian, Stephanie Boehmer, Hollie Brown, Joanna Burgess, Rachel Caidor, Ann Carroll, Akiko Carver, Dana Younkins Castro, Jessica Catron, Farai Chideya, Irene Chien, Ana da Silva, Morgan Daniels, Susan Davies, Andrea Davis, Amber Dawn, Jen Denitto, Tammy Denitto, Sarah Dougher, May Summer Farnsworth, Kim Fey, Mary Margaret Fondriest, Jessie Frances, Kirsten Frickle, Karin Fulford, Ingrid Gerberick, Zan Gibbs, Dara Greenwald, Cindy Hales, Kathleen Hanna, Angelique Hart, Molly Zuckerman-Hartung, Jessica Hopper, Elena Humphreys, Ana Jae, Joan Jett, Tonie Joy, Melissa Jura, Christina Kelly, Trish Kelly, Sarah Kennedy, Melissa Klein, Ananda La Vita, Kenny Laguna, Nomy Lamm, Julie Lary, Michelle Luellen, Heather Lynn, Ian MacKaye, Josh MacPhee, Lois Maffeo, Pat Maley, Nikki McClure, Keyan Meymand, Jessica Miller, Lili Kotlyarov Montoya, Slim Moon, Diana Morrow, Abby Moser, Molly Neuman, Michelle Noel, Katy Otto, Rebecca Parker, Candice Pedersen, Ann Powers, Jill Reiter, Andy Roberts, Iraya Robles, Tracy Sawyer, Jamie Schweser, Angela Seguel, Evelyn Sempos, Danni Sharkey, Bonfire Madigan Shive, Brad Sigal, Retu Singla, Jon Slade, Erin Smith, Jen Smith, Elizabeth Snead, Lauren Spencer, Sarah Stolfa, Sash Sunday, Astria Suparak, Ne Tantillo, Lucy Thane, Kristin Thomson, Tinúviel, Everett True, Corin Tucker, Seanna Tully, Tobi Vail, Suki Valentine, Claudia von Vacano, Gary Walker, Alice Wheeler, Emily White, Donna Wipf, Allison Wolfe, Jen Wood, Sarah Wood, Cookie Woolner, Melissa York, Tae Won Yu

ZINES

Action Girl Newsletter
Angela's Room
Bikini Kill
Chainsaw
Channel Seven
Cherub

Discharge
Evacuation Day
Fantastic Fanzine
Fix Me
Gift Idea
Girl Fiend
Girl Germs
Goddess Juice
Gunk
Hit It or Quit It
Jaded
Jigsaw
Marika
Queer Zine Explosion
R.A.G.E.
Riot Grrrl D.C.
Riot Grrrl Huh?
Riot Grrrl NYC
Riot Grrrl Richmond
Riot Grrrl Vancouver
Smart like Eve
Smile for Me
Snarla
Star
Teenage Bullet
Ulysses Speaks
What Is Riot Grrrl, Anyway?
White Girls, We Need to Talk
Wrecking Ball

NEWSPAPERS AND PERIODICALS

Boston Globe
Boston Review
Daily Olympian
Evergreen Free-Press
i-D
LA Weekly
Los Angeles Times
Melody Maker
National NOW Times
New York Times
Newsweek

NME
off our backs
Option
Rolling Stone
San Francisco Weekly
Sassy
Seattle Times
Seattle Weekly
Signs
Spin
Time
USA Today
Village Voice
Washington City Paper
Washington Post

BOOKS

Acker, Kathy. *Blood and Guts in High School*. New York: Grove, 1978.

American Association of University Women. *How Schools Shortchange Girls: The AAUW Report*. New York: Marlowe, 1992.

Andersen, Mark, and Mark Jenkins. *Dance of Days: Two Decades of Punk in the Nation's Capital*. New York: Soft Skull, 2001.

Azerrad, Michael. *Our Band Could Be Your Life: Scenes from the American Indie Underground 1981–1991*. New York: Little, Brown, 2001.

Bolton, Richard, ed. *Culture Wars: Documents from the Recent Controversies in the Arts*. New York: New Press, 1992.

Brown, Lyn Mikel, and Carol Gilligan. *Meeting at the Crossroads: Women's Psychology and Girls' Development*. Cambridge, MA: Harvard University Press, 1992.

Brownmiller, Susan. *In Our Time: Memoir of a Revolution*. New York: Dial, 1999.

Cross, Charles. *Heavier Than Heaven: A Biography of Kurt Cobain*. New York: Hyperion, 2001.

Echols, Alice. *Daring to Be Bad: Radical Feminism in America, 1967–1975*. Minneapolis: University of Minnesota Press, 1989.

Evans, Sara. *Personal Politics: The Roots of Women's Liberation in the Civil Rights Movement & the New Left*. New York: Vintage, 1979.

Faludi, Susan. *Backlash: The Undeclared War Against American Women*. New York: Crown, 1991.

Gaar, Gillian G. *She's a Rebel: The History of Women in Rock & Roll. Expanded Second Edition*. New York: Seal, 2002.

Gelles, Richard J., Murray A. Strauss, and Suzanne K. Steinmetz. *Behind*

Closed Doors: Violence in the American Family. Garden City, NY: Anchor, 1980.

Juno, Andrea, ed. *Angry Women in Rock, Vol. One*. New York: Juno Books, 1996.

Juno, Andrea, and V. Vale, eds. *Angry Women*. San Francisco: Re/Search Publications, 1991.

Oakes, Kaya. *Slanted and Enchanted: The Evolution of Indie Culture*. New York: St. Martin's, 2009.

Raphael, Amy. *Grrrls: Viva Rock Divas*, New York: St. Martin's Griffin, 1995.

Reynolds, Simon, and Joy Press. *The Sex Revolts: Gender, Rebellion, and Rock 'n' Roll*. Cambridge, MA: Harvard University Press, 1995.

Roiphe, Katie. *The Morning After: Sex, Fear, and Feminism*. New York: Little, Brown, 1993.

Steinem, Gloria. *Revolution from Within: A Book of Self-Esteem*. Boston: Little, Brown, 1992.

True, Everett. *Nirvana: The Biography*. Cambridge, MA: Da Capo, 2007.

Woodward, Bob. *The Agenda: Inside the Clinton White House*. New York: Simon & Schuster, 1995.

WACK! Art and the Feminist Revolution. Los Angeles: Museum of Contemporary Art, 2007.

ARTICLES, REPORTS, AND THESES

Brasile, Monica. "From Riot Grrrl to Mamagirl in Omaha, NE." In "Young Women: Feminists, Activists, Grrrls," *Canadian Woman Studies/Les Cahiers de la Femme* 20/21, no. 4/1 (Winter/Spring 2001): 63-68.

"Crime in the United States: Uniform Crime Reports." Washington, DC: Federal Bureau of Investigation, 1986, 1987.

"Hostile Hallways: Bullying, Teasing, and Sexual Harassment in School." Washington, DC: American Association of University Women Educational Foundation, 2001.

Lippard, Lucy R. "Too Political? Forget It." In *Art Matters: How the Culture Wars Changed America*, Brian Wallis, Marianne Weems, and Philip Yenawine, eds., New York: New York University Press, 1999, 38–61.

Moser, Abby. "'Oh Bondage Up Yours!' Riot Grrrl, Feminism and Punk Rock" (master's thesis, New York University, 1996).

"Rape in America: A Report to the Nation." Arlington, VA: National Victim Center, 1992.

Schilt, Kristen. "'A Little Too Ironic': The Appropriation and Packaging of Riot Grrrl Politics by Mainstream Female Musicians," *Popular Music and Society* 26, no. 1 (2003): 5–16.

Shaviro, Steven. "Questioning Limits," *Reflex*, July/August 1989.

Tinúviel. "Remembering Bikini Kill's First Tour," *Boston Phoenix*, July 27, 1998: accessed at http://weeklywire.com/ww/07-27-98/boston_music_3.html.

Wald, Gayle, and Joanne Gottlieb. "Smells like Teen Spirit: Riot Grrrls, Revolution, and Women in Independent Rock." In *Microphone Fiends: Youth Music and Youth Culture*, Andrew Ross and Tricia Rose, eds., New York: Routledge, 1994, 250–74.

NOTES

Abbreviations

AWiR: *Angry Women in Rock*
DoD: *Dance of Days*
EMP: Experience Music Project Riot Grrrl Retrospective, 1999
NYT: *New York Times*
WP: *Washington Post*

9   Even feminist books: The encyclopedic *She's a Rebel: The History of Women in Rock & Roll*, by Gillian G. Gaar, tells the story of the movement solely through the stories of Bikini Kill and Bratmobile, while Simon Reynolds and Joy Press's erudite *The Sex Revolts: Gender, Rebellion and Rock 'n' Roll*, which thoughtfully reads some of Riot Grrrl's ideas and images, barely acknowledges the movement's significant grassroots component.

19   The largest women's rights demonstration: To reconstruct the march, I drew on interviews with riot grrrls who were present; *We Won't Go Back!*, a video produced for the National Organization for Women documenting the day's events; internal NOW records and communications collected at the Arthur and Elizabeth Schlesinger Library on the History of Women in America; articles in the *National NOW Times*; and newspaper and magazine articles including Christine Spolar, "Thousands Expected for Abortion-Rights Rally," *WP*, April 2, 1992, C1; Karen De Witt, "Huge Crowd Backs Right to Abortion in Capital March," *NYT*, April 6, 1992, A1; Christine Spolar, "Abortion-Rights Rally Draws Half a Million Marchers," *WP*, April 6, 1992, A1; Karlyn Barker, "Stars Turn Out to Take a Walk for Their Cause," *WP*, April 6, 1992, D3; Elizabeth Neuffer, "500,000 March for Choice," *Boston Globe*, April 6, 1992, 1; and Kevin Sullivan, "All-America Day Has Something for Everyone," *WP*, April 6, 1992, D1.

20   "I'm going to the Supreme Court": Mimi Hall, "A 'Defining Moment': Abortion Rights Marchers Target Politicians," *USA Today*, April 6, 1992, 1A.

22   a 1989 *Time* magazine article: Claudia Wallis, "Women Face the '90s," *Time*, December 4, 1989, 81.

23   *Washington Post* columnist: Judy Mann, "Echoes of Vietnam," *WP*, April 10, 1992, E3.

24   "The Senate has done more": Maralee Schwartz, "Feminists Vow to Seek Political Changes," *WP*, October 17, 1991, A7.

31   To tell the story of Bikini Kill's origins, I relied mainly on interviews I conducted with Kathleen Hanna and Tobi Vail in 2006 and 2009–10; on an interview Andrea Juno conducted with Kathleen Hanna in the mid-'90s, published in *Angry Women in Rock* (hereafter *AWiR*); and on two videos shot by Corin Tucker in early 1991: an interview with Bikini Kill, and a video of a show the band played on February 14, 1991, at the North Shore Surf Club in Olympia. Throughout the book, any quotes not specifically cited as coming from other sources are from interviews I conducted.

31   small-scale heavy metal and reggae concerts: Oakes, *Slanted and Enchanted*, 127.

32   Acker's visit to Seattle was written about in Steven Shaviro, "Questioning Limits," *Reflex*, July/August 1989.

32   We don't hate: Acker, *Blood and Guts in High School*, 34.

36   "A great thing": Juno, *AWiR*, 124.

37   Nikki McClure: Author interview, January 2006.

38   "I did everything": Juno, *AWiR*, 89.

39   "Essentially": Andersen and Jenkins, *Dance of Days* (hereafter *DoD*), 310.

39   Kathleen knew the facts: Arriving at statistics on rape and abuse is necessarily a complicated business. Rather than get into unresolved questions of accuracy and research methods, I've chosen to focus on the statistics that were commonly cited in the time, the metrics that formed the backdrop to activists' concern in the late '80s and early '90s. The figures in this paragraph are derived from Richard J. Gelles, Murray A. Strauss, and Suzanne K. Steinmetz, *Behind Closed Doors: Violence in the American Family*, Garden City, NY: Anchor Press, 1980; "Crime in the United States: Uniform Crime Reports," Washington, DC: Federal Bureau of Investigation, 1986, 1987; and a 1987 study on rape conducted by psychologist Mary Koss for *Ms.* magazine.

40   Montreal massacre: Howlett, Debbie, and Bruce Frankel: " 'Just like Rambo': Feminists Decry 'Vengeful' Killings, Say 'Society Has to Change,' " *USA Today*, December 8, 1989, 10A.

41   Dworkin's response: Juno, *AWiR*, 93, 95.

42   With distressing frequency: Juno, *AWiR*, 97.

42   when they had to open: *Bikini Kill* #1, Kathleen Hanna interview with Jean Smith.

44 unusual encouragement: One friend from her high school days whom Tobi particularly looked up to was Donna Dresch, three years older than Tobi and a bass and guitar juggernaut in the making. In the late '80s, Donna moved to San Francisco, where she got hooked up with a scene of gay punks and queer zines like G. B. Jones's (of the Canadian all-girl punk band Fifth Column), *J.D.'s*, and the movement-defining *Homocore*. Tobi stayed in touch with Donna, who started her own zine, *Chainsaw*, around the same time that Tobi started *Jigsaw*.

45 People talked trash about Tobi: Some of these comments make an appearance in Charles Cross's *Heavier Than Heaven*.

45 Kathleen was doing: Juno, *AWiR*, 97.

46 "I was like": Unreleased video interview conducted by Corin Tucker, 1991.

46 Lois had done: Juno, *AWiR*, 129.

49 Turning on MTV: "We hit a real low spot in the mid- to late '80s, when there appeared to be a preponderance of videos where the women were basically relegated to the background," Judy McGrath, MTV's executive vice president and creative director, admitted in 1993. "It was kind of 'I'm with the band,' I guess you would call it." Craig Marks, "Girls on Film," *Spin*, July 1993, 41.

49 "Let's go out": Cross, *Heavier Than Heaven*, 167.

50 Charles Cross, in *Heavier Than Heaven*, reads Tobi into several of *Nevermind*'s songs, but Cobain once wrote in an unsent letter to Tobi that he'd only written one song about her, "Lounge Act" (164, 313).

53 the band's zine: The *Ulysses Speaks* zines are archived at http://ulyssesspeaks .blogspot.com/.

64 Eugene's rallies: Riot Grrrl discussion, EMP.

64 President Bush: Richard Morin, "War Boosts President's Popularity," *WP*, January 29, 1991, A1.

66 her pre-Bratmobile existence: Interview with Erin Smith, EMP.

72 On May 5: My account of the Cinco de Mayo riots is drawn from coverage in the *Washington Post*, including Nancy Lewis and James Rupert, "D.C. Neighborhood Erupts After Officer Shoots Suspect," May 6, 1991, A1; Ruben Castenada and Nell Henderson, "Simmering Tensions Between Police, Hispanics Fed Clash," May 6, 1991, A1; Carlos Sanchez and Rene Sanchez, "Mayor Dixon Imposes Curfew on Mt. Pleasant Area as Police, Youths Clash for a Second Night," May 7, 1991, A1; William Raspberry, "Grim Reruns of the '60s, May 8, 1991, A31; Rene Sanchez, "3rd Night of Curfew Quiet but Uneasy in Mt. Pleasant Area," May 9, 1991: A1; Paul Farhi, "Mt. Pleasant: A Melting Pot Feels the Heat," May 9, 1991, C1; Skip Kaltenheuser, "How to Kill a Neighborhood," May 12, 1991, C4; Richard Morin and Nell Henderson, "Miles Apart in Mount Pleasant," May 19, 1991, A1. Also helpful were B. Drummond Ayres, Jr., "Violence Follows Police Shooting," *NYT*, May 6, 1991, A10; and Pamela Constable, "After Two Days of Strife, D.C. Resentments Fester," *Boston Globe*, May 8, 1991, 3.

76 Kathleen was thrown: Mark Andersen interview with Kathleen Hanna, Molly Neuman, and Allison Wolfe, July 31, 1991.

79 Sharon Cheslow: Interview with Sharon Cheslow, EMP.

82 "I think it's important": from the Mark Andersen interview of July 31, 1991.

86 "That's one of the critiques": Ibid.

86 "It was like, 'God' ": Juno, *AWiR*, 99.

86 For more on Positive Force, see Andersen and Jenkins, *DoD*.

89 that day's *Washington Post*: Mary Jordan, "3 Women in Affidavits Accuse Smith of Sex Attacks: Statements Describe Alleged Assaults in Graphic Detail: 'Ferocious . . . Almost Animal-like,' " *WP*, July 24, 1991, A5; Howard Kurtz, "New York Rape Story, 2nd Edition: New Account Denies People Just Gawked," *WP*, July 24, 1991, D1; Spencer Rich, "HHS Cancels Teen Sex Survey After Conservatives Complain," *WP*, July 24, 1991, A2.

93 "It was really about": For this and many other details about the IPU, I am indebted to Chris Nelson's article "The Day the Music Didn't Die," *Seattle Weekly*, August 8, 2001; http://www.seattleweekly.com/2001–08–08/ music/the-day-the-music-didn-t-die.php.

99 "an audacious idea": "The Day the Music Didn't Die."

99 Moon sold: Ibid.

99 "It was the first time": Azerrad, *Our Band Could Be Your Life*, 489.

101 According to one account: True, *Nirvana*, 291. To reconstruct this moment in Nirvana's career, I relied largely on True, *Nirvana*, and Cross, *Heavier Than Heaven*.

101 the Halloween show: True, *Nirvana*, 314.

102 "agreed it wouldn't be appropriate": True, *Nirvana*, 292.

102 major-label representatives: "The Day the Music Didn't Die."

102 "You don't get it": Gaar, *She's a Rebel*, 383.

103 This infuriated the label: True, *Nirvana*, 314.

113 girls' problems: *Rape In America: A Report to the Nation*, Arlington, VA: National Victim Center, 1992; Katie Roiphe, "Date Rape Hysteria," *NYT*, November 20, 1991, A27; "Unsettling Report on an Epidemic of Rape," *Time*, May 4, 1992; "Rape Cited as 'Tragedy of Youth in America,' " *Seattle Post-Intelligencer*, April 24, 1992, A3; Mary Jordan, "Wide Gender Gap Found in Schools," *WP*, February 12, 1992, A1; Lyn Mikel Brown and Carol Gilligan, *Meeting at the Crossroads: Women's Psychology and Girls' Development*, Cambridge, MA: Harvard University Press, 1992.

117 Only a last-minute: Jarrett Murphy, "Roe Almost Overturned in '92," CBS News, March 4, 2004; http://www.cbsnews.com/stories/2004/03/04/supremecourt/main603944.shtml.

146 feminist art history: cf. Yoko Ono, inviting audience members to cut her clothes off her; Ana Mendieta, who cast herself as the victim in a simulated aftermath of a brutal sexual attack; Carolee Schneemann, daubing her torso with pigment and unfurling a scroll from within her vagina; Janine Antoni, using her hair as a brush to paint a gallery floor; and Marina Abramović, brushing her hair violently till her scalp bled. To read more about these and other gestures, check out the excellent *WACK! Art and the Feminist Revolution*.

147 Soon the audiences: Juno, *AWiR*, 100.

152 Close to a thousand: Andersen and Jenkins, *DoD*, 334.

153 "Hey! Get on with the show!": Tinúviel, "Remembering Bikini Kill's First Tour," *Boston Phoenix*, July 27, 1998; http://weeklywire.com/ww/07–27–98/boston_music_3.html.

154 Cartier: James Ragland, "D.C. Woman is Fatally Shot in Boston by Ex-Boy-friend," *WP*, June 1, 1992, D1; George Lardner, Jr., "The Stalking of Kristin," *WP*, Nov. 22, 1992, C1; and Rose Ryan, "How I Remember Him," *Boston Review*, February/March 1996; http://www.bostonreview.net/BR21.1/ryan.html.

157 a tampon she was finished with: Tampon-throwing was in the air that summer; L7's Donita Sparks famously hurled hers at the crowd at the Reading Festival in England a month later.

158 Bush would come under fire: Andrew Rosenthal, "Bush, Asked in Personal Context, Takes a Softer Stand on Abortion," *NYT*, August 11, 1992, A1; Ruth Marcus, "Bush: Choice on Abortion Would Be Granddaughter's," *WP*, August 12, 1992, A12; Howard Kurtz, "Limelight Sours for President as Family Issues Intrude on Statecraft," *WP*, August 14, 1992, A19.

159 Robertson's attack on Clinton: As of 2010, the full text of Pat Robertson's convention speech was available at patrobertson.com.

164 bluntly titled "Rape": Melissa Klein wrote a report on the convention for *off our backs* (Riot Grrrls," *off our backs* 23, no. 2 [February 1993]: 6) that described the "Rape" workshop:

> *Two facilitators began the workshop, one by reading a piece she had written, and the other with a short performance about attempted date rape where she switched back and forth from male to female narration of the incident. Many girls recounted their experiences with sexual abuse, speaking in voices filled with emotion and determination. Several women stressed the importance of opening up about sexual abuse before the trauma implodes within. One spoke about the experience of confronting her rapist. It was also emphasized that many situations other than clinically defined rape constitute sexual abuse. Feelings of sexual abuse can be brought on by a variety of behaviors involving psychological, emotional, or social as well as simple physical coercion. Women spoke of older "cooler" boyfriends who never hesitated to utilize unequal power dynamics to their advantage, or male "friends" who abused trust in situations such as drinking with a girl until she passed out and then taking off her clothes.*

166 an amateur documentary filmmaker: Lisa Rose Apramian was making a film about women and rock titled *Not Bad for a Girl*, and she thought some convention footage would fit in well with her concert footage of L7, Hole, Babes in Toyland, and Lunachicks.

167 "Female journalists": "She'd been asked not to use any quotes from anyone, and she did." Angela Johnson, "Start a Fucking Riot: Riot Grrrrrl D.C.," *off our backs* 23, no. 5 (May 1993): 6.

169 *USA Today* published: Elizabeth Snead, "Feminist Riot Grrrls Don't Just Wanna Have Fun," *USA Today*, August 7, 1992, 5D.

185 young women's sexuality: "Teenage Girls Found to Be Increasingly Sexually Active," *WP*, January 5, 1991, A10; Barbara Kantrowitz, "Teenagers and AIDS," *Newsweek*, August 3, 1992, 44; "Teenagers and AIDS: The Risk Worsens," *NYT*, April 14, 1992, C3.

186 Christian Coalition: Michael Isikoff, "Christian Coalition Steps Boldly Into Politics; Tax Exempt Robertson Group Has Raised $13 Million, Eyes GOP Takeover," *WP*, September 10, 1992, A1 ("'We want . . . as soon as possible to see a working majority of the Republican Party in the hands of pro-family Christians by 1996,' Robertson told delegates to the conference").

186 George Bush was addressing: David Von Drehle and Michael Isikoff, "Bush Focuses on Economy in Talk to Fundamentalists," *WP*, September 12, 1992, A10; Colman McCarthy, "Pandering to Pat Robertson," *WP*, September 19, 1992, A21; Maralee Schwartz and Kenneth J. Cooper, "Equal Rights Initiative in Iowa Attacked," *WP*, August 23, 1992, A15.

187 "If you had to choose": Peter Applebome, "Religious Right Intensifies Campaign for Bush," *NYT*, October 31, 1992, A1.

189 Xers: Gwen Ifill, "Youth Vote: Clinton Goes Eye to Eye with MTV Generation," *NYT*, June 17, 1992, A22.

190 Choose or Lose: Judith Miller, "But Can You Dance to It?: MTV Turns to News," *NYT*, October. 11, 1992, F31.

191 "Hanna, however": Daisy Von Furth, "For Girls About to Rock," *Spin*, April 1992, 26.

191 the verdict: Celia Farber, "The Trial," Salon.com, June 9, 1997; Constance L. Hayes, "Spin Employee Was Harassed, Jury Says," *NYT*, April 11, 1997, B9.

193 Dana Nasrallah, "Teenage Riot," *Spin*, November 1992, 78–81.

193 "Something was very passive": Angela Johnson, "Start a Fucking Riot: Riot Grrrrrl D.C.," *off our backs* 23, no. 5 (May 1993): 6.

209 Grunge was already: Elizabeth Snead, "Finding Riches in Rags: Fashion Designers Rummage Up Grunge Chic," *USA Today*, November 5, 1992, 1D; Rick Marin, "Grunge: A Success Story," *NYT*, November 15, 1992, section 9, page 1.

211 Farai Chideya, "Revolution, Girl Style," *Newsweek*, November 23, 1992, 84.

213 Amanda Taylor is a pseudonym.

223 COINTELPRO: See Ward Churchill and Jim Vander Wall, *The COINTEL-PRO Papers: Documents from the FBI's Secret Wars Against Dissent in the United States*. Cambridge, MA: South End Press, 2002.

223 Fred Hampton's assassination: John Kifner, "F.B.I., Before Raid, Gave Police Plan of Chicago Panther's Flat," *NYT*, May 25, 1974, 14; Kifner, "F.B.I. Files Say Informer Got Data for Panther Raid," *NYT*, May 7, 1976, 14.

223 cultivated personal growth: See Suzanne Snider, "est, Werner Erhard, and the Corporatization of Self-Help," *The Believer*, May 2003, available at http://www.believermag.com/issues/200305/?read=article_snider.

235 *Los Angeles Times* et al: Steve Hochman, "Mean, Mad and Defiantly Underground," *Los Angeles Times*, November 8, 1992, 59; Linda Keene, "Feminist Fury: 'Burn Down the Walls that Say You Can't,'" *Seattle Times*, March 21, 1993, online at http://community.seattletimes.nwsource.com/archive/?date=19930321&slug=1691577; Louise Continelli, "In-Your-Face Feminism," *Buffalo News*, June 6, 1993, Lifestyles, 1; Lauren Spencer, "From the Youngest, Toughest Daughters of Feminism—Self-respect You Can Rock To," *WP*, January 3, 1993, C1.

235 *Cosmopolitan*: Louise Bernikow, "The New Activists: Fearless, Funny, Fighting Mad," *Cosmopolitan*, April 1993, 162–65, 212.

235 *Seventeen*: Nina Malkin, "It's a Grrrl Thing," *Seventeen*, May 1993, 80–82.

238 *off our backs*: Angela Johnson, "Start a Fucking Riot: Riot Grrrrrl D.C.," *off our backs* 23, no. 5 (May 1993): 6.

240 "girls are starting": Joe Brown, "Banding Together," *WP*, September 11, 1992, N9.

245 a *Washington Post* article: Joel Achenbach, "Another Failed Presidency Already?" *WP*, May 27, 1993, D1.

253 the elder statesmen: Robert Christgau, "Consumer Guide: *Bikini Kill* by Bikini Kill," *Village Voice*, January 26, 1993, 76; Greil Marcus, "Top Ten," *Artforum*, February 1993, 10; Chuck Eddy, "Bikini Kill," *Rolling Stone*, February 4, 1993, 68.

258 To tell the story of Huggy Bear, I drew on interviews I conducted with Jon Slade, a guitarist in the band; Gary Walker, whose label, Wiiija, released Huggy Bear's records; Lucy Thane, who filmed Bikini Kill's UK tour; and Andy Roberts and Tammy and Jen Denitto, of the British band Linus. I also consulted online writings by Everett True about the era (available at http://everetttrue2.blogspot.com), the Huggy Bear chapter (written entirely by the band) in Amy Raphael, *Grrrls: Viva Rock Divas*; and on many, many articles and letters—some with bylines, some not—about Huggy Bear and Riot Grrrl published in *Melody Maker* in 1992 and 1993. These include Sally Margaret Joy (SMJ), "Huggy Bear," June 27, 1992; SMJ, "Trouble Bruin," July 11, 1992, 6; "Grrrls! Grrrls! Grrrls!," September 26, 1992, 26–27; SMJ, "Revolution

Grrrl Style Now!," October 10, 1992, 30–32; Everett True, "Starsky in Their Eyes," November 14, 1992, 17; "Fur Powered," October 3, 1992, 10–11; "Revolution Grrrl Style Now!," December 19/26, 1992, 53; "Grizzly Be-arrrs!," February 27, 1993, 5; SMJ, "The Revolution Will Not Be Televised," February 27, 1993, 35–37; "Rebel Grrrls," March 6, 1993, 30; Sarah Kestle, "Swimsuit Issue," March 13, 1993; SMJ, "The Rebel Girls and Bender Boys Tour," March 20, 1993, 6–7; and "Reading the Riot Act!," March 27, 1993, 3. *NME* coverage included Steve Lamacq, "Pooh, What a Scorcher!," September 19, 1992; "EP of the Week," December 5, 1992; Dele Fadele, "Single of the Week," February 13, 1993; Liz Evans, "Borrrn in the (Med)USA," March 13, 1993, 16–17; and Gina Morris, "Grrrls Just Wanna Bait Scum . . . ," March 20, 1993, 11. I am also indebted to Mark Andersen for screening the band's entire appearance on *The Word* for me.

263 over a million: Channel 4 doesn't have audience figures for the first three seasons of *The Word* (Huggy Bear's appearance was part of the third season), but the average audience the following season was 1.5 million, and the season after that was 1.7 million. .

265 Nils Bernstein: Seventeen years later, Slim Moon and Nils Bernstein discussed the incident (and Bernstein apologized) at http://everetttrue2.blogspot.com/2010/02/why-girls-cant-rock.html#more.

266 "The Runaways had *nobody*": author interview, February 20, 2010.

269 Rock for Choice show: Lorraine Ali, "Charismatic Set from Bikini Kill," *Los Angeles Times*, May 3, 1993, 5.

284 "I even stopped": Monica Brasile, "From Riot Grrrl to Mamagirl in Omaha, NE," in "Young Women: Feminists, Activists, Grrrls," *Canadian Woman Studies/Les Cahiers de la Femme* 20/21, no. 4/1 (Winter/Spring 2001): 63-68.

301 interfeminist sex wars: For more on these conflicts, which are necessarily given short shrift here, see the autumn 1984 (vol. 10, no. 1) issue of the feminist journal Signs, which devoted a whole section to the debates, and Lisa Duggan and Nan D. Hunter, *Sex Wars: Sexual Dissent and Popular Culture*, New York: Routledge, 1995.

308 "I was into": interview with Molly Neuman, EMP.

327 Rush Limbaugh: John Tierney, "How Talk Radio Gets at What's Real," *NYT*, April 30, 1995, section 4, p. 1.

INDEX